The Journey of
Navajo Oshley

An Autobiography and Life History

Edited by

Robert S. McPherson

Foreword by

Barre Toelken

UTAH STATE UNIVERSITY PRESS
Logan, Utah

Utah State University Press
Logan, Utah

Typography by WolfPack
Cover design by Michelle Sellers

Library of Congress Cataloging-in-Publication Data
Oshley, Navajo.
   The journey of Navajo Oshley : an autobiography and life history /
edited by Robert S. McPherson.
      p. cm.
Includes bibliographical references and index.
   ISBN 0-87421-291-X (pbk.) — ISBN 0-87421-290-1 (hardcover)
   1. Oshley, Navajo. 2. Navajo Indians—Biography. 3. Navajo
Indians—History. I. McPherson, Robert S., 1947- II. Title.
   E99.N3 O766 2000
   979.1'004972'0092—dc21

                                                              00-008147

The Journey of
Navajo Oshley

Navajo Oshley in his later years sitting outside of his "half-a-house." (Photo courtesy of Francell Blickenstaff)

Contents

Illustrations

Acknowledgments

WRITING ACKNOWLEDGMENTS FOR THE BEGINNING of a book at the end of the process is enjoyable for three reasons. First, it is an opportunity to go back to the inception of the work and retrace the various steps that led to its completion. In this case, approximately ten years elapsed from start to finish. Perhaps that is entirely too long, but I hope it will prove worth the wait.

Second are the people involved. There were many over the years who proved essential in recreating the events and feelings of Navajo Oshley's life. The most obvious is Winston B. Hurst, who not only helped tape-record Oshley's story, preserved it at the Utah State Historical Society, and provided a companion study of the growth of the Westwater community on the outskirts of Blanding but also encouraged the entire process of translating the tapes and writing the manuscript. His heart is buried deep in the people and places of southeastern Utah, and I admire him for that. Right beside Hurst stand Joanne Oshley Holiday and Marilyn Oshley, two daughters, who provided information, pictures, and memories of their dad. Amidst the laughter and the tears, they were able to paint a very human picture of what he was like as a father, grandfather, and friend.

There were others who assisted in providing a closer view of the man. For instance, John Holiday, an eighty-year-old medicine man and relative of Oshley, was extremely influential in clarifying places, people, and events that otherwise would have been lost to the historic record. His perspective and intimate knowledge give a clarity to the past that will serve future generations well. There were also members of the Anglo community such as Ray Hunt, now deceased, who worked in trading posts and with Oshley for years: William Riley Hurst, store owner; Norman Nielson, livestock-man and Oshley's foreman; and Bill Redd, store owner and friend—all of whom contributed to a better understanding of him as an individual. Each of these men held Oshley in high esteem.

Other people provided the "nuts and bolts" of the project. For instance, Janet Wilcox and LaVerne Tate, through the Blue Mountain

Shadows Organization, secured funding for the translation of the taped interviews from Bruce Loutham, archaeologist for the Bureau of Land Management. Bertha Parrish translated the interview from tape to text and from Navajo to English, while Marilyn Holiday read the rough draft and advised on content, assisting in maintaining accuracy and the proper "voice." Without their guidance, much could have been lost. Garth Wilson, an excellent teacher of the Navajo language, spent hours helping with the orthography in the text. Appreciation is also expressed to Charlotte J. Frisbie, John Farella, Joyce Griffin, and Barre Toelken for their reading of the manuscript, with an extra thanks to Barre for his excellent foreword. A final thanks is given to John Alley, editor of Utah State University Press and enthusiast for the project. He has made the latter part of this work both fun and rewarding.

The third and final reason that writing this acknowledgment is enjoyable is that it prefaces a hope. Most authors think that their work is important and helpful, and I suppose I am no different. What I would like, more than anything else, is to have the people of southeastern Utah appreciate the life of this one man and realize that there are many other men and women in all of our shared cultures that have lived honorably under trying circumstances. If people grasp this one point, then Oshley's life will have made us all better.

Foreword

Barre Toelken

THE FORCE OF THIS BOOK LIES IN ITS INSIDER'S PORTRAYAL of everyday Navajo life in one of the West's most culturally dynamic areas: the so-called "Four Corners," where Utah, Colorado, Arizona, and New Mexico meet. While that distinctive spot—the only place in the United States where four states intersect—is clearly visible on today's maps, the fascinating cultural forces that shaped the surrounding area's human identities are not so well recognized. Not only did the Anasazi culture leave a material legacy of abandoned cities and cliff dwellings, pottery, irrigation systems, and petroglyphs, but more recent arrivals over the past five to seven hundred years—Navajos from the far north, Utes and Southern Paiutes from the west, Spaniards and later Mexicans from the southeast—added their active presence to the ancient tenure of the Pueblo peoples.

In this vast desert area, people once traveled by foot or horseback, and virtually every large stone, hillock, arroyo, and water seep had a name used for direction, comfort, protection, and survival. For the Navajo, the fading of a minutely articulated landscape probably started with the advent of cars, pickup trucks, and a more formal road system. Many of the old names and places have become obsolete, having been replaced by the names of gas stations, trading posts, schools, missions, and mines. To be sure, some old names are still there, many of them because they represent water sources: Oljato (Moon Water), Chilchinbeto (Sumac Springs), Mexican Water, Sweetwater. Navajo Oshley lived intimately in the older, intensely familiar Navajo world in which places like Teec Nos Pos (Cottonwoods in a Circle, or Whirling Cottonwoods) were common, not quaint puzzlements on a tourist's map. He lived during a period many would consider the zenith of that cultural era, between the trauma of Navajo internment at Fort Sumner in the 1860s and the bureaucratization of the Navajo tribe in the 1950s. Make no mistake: the Navajo tribe did not vanish conveniently during that time, as many Americans supposed it would; rather, the people grew from an estimated twenty thousand to about fifty thousand by the 1950s and over two hundred thousand today. The Navajos are very much still there, inhabiting a reservation about the size of Belgium, the possessors of a complex political system, the speakers of a language so esoteric it was used as an unbreakable code during World War II. But the rich cultural world of hogans, horse herds, singers ("medicine men" as glossed in English), and thrilling exploits out in desert country among the Utes, the whites, the Mexicans—that world has been eroding so rapidly that only the recollections of elderly people who experienced it can bring it back into focus for us.

Navajo Oshley's account, along with the helpful comments and perspectives of family, friends, and neighbors, provides a colorful and moving view of an everyday Navajo man who lived traditionally in a rapidly changing world. Unlike the Native American subjects of similar studies, he was not a powerful or famous singer, nor a tribal leader, nor a mysterious philosopher. He was instead a traveler in an everyday world in which he was simultaneously part of an extended Navajo family system, with its obligations and expectations, and a livestock worker, farmhand, and early settler in Blanding (just north of the Navajo Reservation). That predominantly Mormon village later became a prominent location in the 1950s uranium rush and, more recently, the site of an army missile station and the home of a uranium mill.

His age alone would recommend him to our attention as an exceptional character, for the mortality rate among Navajos of his generation was extremely high, the average life expectancy for a man being about forty. Thus, in Navajo Oshley's recollections we have a view that extends from the 1880s almost to our own moment and displays a striking command of detail rarely encountered in vernacular biographies. Oshley does not simply provide what a modern historian might call reliable data: he gives insight into the interactions between the Navajos and the Mormons; he holds forth on the love/hate relationships between the Navajos and Utes and the Navajos and Mexicans; he describes in great detail the family networks of the Navajo and recalls the complex logic by which personal and family problems were resolved. In ethnographic terms, his account is a treasure: avoiding the severe focus on the individual that has become the fashion in ethnographic writing today, his cultural narrative, given from the inside, uses himself as a reflection of, and a critique on, the intersection of cultures he experienced. And he does not gloss over his frustrations—shared with most Navajos of his day—about family frictions, drudgery, grinding poverty, and the plainness of everyday life.

When I visited Blanding in the mid-1950s as a young uranium prospector, I usually stayed with Navajo friends who lived in Westwater, a small cluster of Navajo and Ute hogans, tents, and brush shelters situated across a small canyon to the west of town. As I recall, most Indians who came to Blanding lived at Westwater; some eventually moved into town, but the strained relations between Natives and whites, between Mormons and non-Mormons, made many of my friends nervous. Navajo Oshley, to the contrary, though he had lived earlier at Westwater, had already moved right to the center of town, lived in a frame house, had joined the Mormon church, and enjoyed cordial relations with everyone. He was considered a remarkable man, not only for his talents at diagnosing illnesses (he was a "hand-trembler" diagnostician and remained one for most of his life, seeing no discrepancy between that role and his new religion), but also because he was a cultural bridge, a living intersection between people, a promoter of cordiality and harmony. In short, he is one of those local monuments to humanity who exert a considerable impact on their neighbors but seldom come to our attention because they are not rich, powerful, or influential—or because they belong to a culture that is thought of as only marginally important. We are indebted to Robert McPherson for bringing Navajo Oshley's account forward, for it is a genuine and compelling interpretation of cultural history that turns up the volume on the sort of Native voice seldom heard, often overlooked, and usually misunderstood.

Navajo Oshley's voice speaks to us of a vibrant landscape full of personal and cultural richness, of an exciting time that has nearly vanished, of a traditional way of life that has changed immensely for better and for worse, of a geographic arena that has entertained everything from ancient petroglyphs to the atomic bomb. His voice may sound mundane on one level, but on another, we hear a rare articulation of the human conditions that have formed the living matrix of Indian everyday life in the American Southwest.

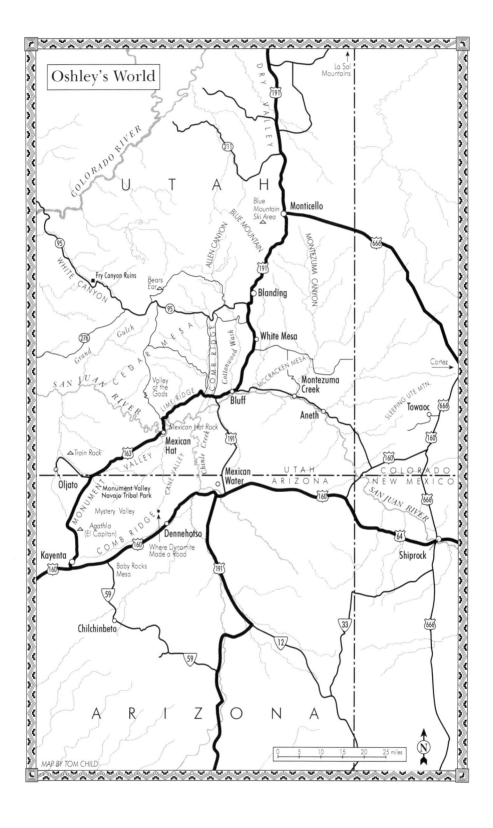

Oshley's World

La Sal
Mountains

DRY VALLEY

COLORADO RIVER

UTAH

191

211

95

Blue
Mountain
Ski Area

Monticello

666

WHITE CANYON

Fry Canyon Ruins

Bears
Ear

BLUE MOUNTAIN

ALLEN CANYON

191

Blanding

MONTEZUMA CANYON

276

95

Gulch

Grand

CEDAR MESA

COMB RIDGE

White Mesa

Cottonwood Wash

Cortez

SAN JUAN RIVER

Valley
of the
Gods

LIME RIDGE

MCCRACKEN MESA

Montezuma
Creek

SLEEPING UTE MTN.

Towaoc

666

Bluff

Aneth

Train Rock

163

Mexican Hat Rock

Mexican
Hat

Chinle Creek

191

160

160

666

Oljato

MONUMENT VALLEY

Monument Valley
Navajo Tribal Park

CANE VALLEY

Mexican
Water

UTAH
ARIZONA

COLORADO
NEW MEXICO

160

SAN JUAN RIVER

Mystery Valley

Agathla
(El Capitan)

COMB RIDGE

Dennehotso

64

Shiprock

Kayenta

160

Where Dynamite
Made a Road

160

191

33

666

Baby Rocks
Mesa

59

Chilchinbeto

12

59

A R I Z O N A

0   5   10   15   20   25 miles

N

MAP BY TOM CHILD

Introduction

Oshley in his black hat and self-beaded hat band was a common sight in Blanding. (Photo courtesy of the Oshley family)

Genesis of the Project

SETTING THE STAGE

NOT TOO LONG AGO IN THE CENTER OF BLANDING, UTAH, there stood the "half-a-house." Located just east of the post office, the wooden frame structure, covered with a veneer of gray stucco cement, sat as the only Navajo home in the midst of a white community. A woodpile next to the east-facing door, a few windows that peered out on manicured lawns to the north and the backside of businesses to the south, and a high-pitched roof far more pointed than those surrounding it all seemed out of place. However, the home's most distinctive feature, setting it far apart from others, was its west side. Straight and uncompromising, this wall looked as if a giant cleaver had severed half of what had once been whole and carried it off to a distant site. The abrupt partition had been healed with a coat of cement to match the more conventional walls that remained. As for the other "half" of the house, located a block south, it had been destroyed long before (1955) to make room for "progress" in the form of business development.

As strange as this structure appeared, it was home to another well-known symbol in Blanding—an elderly man named Navajo Oshley. He, like the home he lived in, was only partly visible to the white community. His sharp features; slim, tall frame bent with age; large black hat, and steady gait were part of a personality familiar to generations of young and old raised in the town. Indeed, he was so familiar and accepted that few people ever really got to know his other side, the less obvious one he had experienced as a Navajo. At this point in his life (the 1970s), he was an interesting eighty-to-ninety-year-old oddity who had superficially accepted the outer trappings of the white man's world. The rest, to most of the townsfolk, was history not worth considering.

Yet of all the hundreds of Navajo people who came up from the reservation twenty-five miles to the south, or who lived on the outskirts of town in the Navajo Westwater community, Oshley stood as an example of the best from the Indians' world in the white man's eyes. He was a friendly man who enjoyed communicating his daily experiences in broken English and fluent pantomime, but anything more complex had to be

handled in his native tongue. Still, he was respected, some of his white
neighbors referring to him as Grandpa Oshley.

Navajo Oshley or Ak'é nídzin, as he was known to his people, was a
far more complex character than many realized. He had lived a colorful
life, participating in significant events in Navajo and Anglo history in the
Four Corners area. Some of these experiences included camping in the
spot where Blanding would one day stand, watching the advent of the
Native American Church in southeastern Utah, working in the Civilian
Conservation Corps during the New Deal, encountering the devastating
effects of the livestock reduction of the 1930s, and witnessing the impact
of technology and the settlement it brought to the region.

Before going further in the personal narrative, it will be helpful to get
a clearer understanding of the context within which Oshley's life was lived.
In many respects, his experiences are typical of what many others in his
tribe encountered during these years. Historically, the Navajos have been a
mobile and expansive people. Their economy, based on livestock and horti-
culture, justified a search for grazing and agricultural lands that pushed the
population outward from its ancestral home sitting astride the New
Mexico/Arizona border. Following the release of approximately half of the
tribe held captive at Bosque Redondo (Fort Sumner, New Mexico) in
1868, the Navajos returned to their territory and started to expand at a
rapid rate. Those who had not been incarcerated joined those returning
and began to apply increasing pressure on lands peripheral to the core of
Navajo settlement.

While expansion took place in all directions, the southern and eastern borders of the reservation generally had greater Anglo and Hispanic
populations, leading to more resistance against the Navajos. Land deals
followed that created "checkerboard" ownership, as towns, railroads,
mines, ranches, and farms developed within the Anglo community. The
Navajos adjusted, took what was available, and cast about for other parcels
of real estate or, as an alternative to ownership, trade and temporary
employment in the white communities.

To the north and west, where populations were far smaller, Navajo
expansion appeared more promising. True, the Utes—inveterate enemies
of the Navajos during the Fort Sumner period—were still a threat in the
north, but as time passed, animosities cooled. Between 1870 and 1905,
three phases outline the general growth in the northern area, straddling
the San Juan River in the Utah portion of the reservation. The first,
roughly between 1870 and 1884, was characterized by government officials who recognized the value of the San Juan area. Because of turmoil in

the northern part of the reservation, however, decisive action remained more of a hope than a reality. Coupled with a high turnover rate in agents, a huge geographical area to be supervised, and a multiplicity of problems, this left any development in the north tentative at best.

The second phase began in 1884 when a presidential executive order added the Utah Strip to the Navajo Reservation. During the next ten years, white settlements such as Bluff, trading posts at Aneth and Montezuma Creek, and boomtowns like Mexican Hat dotted the public lands considered by the white communities to be under their control. Rangelands on both sides of the San Juan River, the official boundary between Navajo and Anglo holdings, came under dispute. A gold rush in 1892–93 forced part of the Utah reservation lands west of 110 degrees longitude (an area called the Paiute Strip) back into the public domain, only to have them bounce into, then out of, then into Native American control again during the first quarter of the twentieth century. All this time, the Navajo population was growing.

Between 1895 and 1933, the third phase, Navajos increasingly controlled territory on both sides of the river. The government finally added the Paiute Strip, the Aneth and Montezuma Creek area, and a final piece called the Aneth Extension to the reservation during this time. In return, the Navajos agreed to relinquish their right to establish individual home-steads in the lands north of this new tribal boundary. At the same time that the Utah Navajos were receiving major concessions from the government in the form of additional land, the second-most traumatic incident in the history of the tribe commenced in 1933—livestock reduction.[1] Navajo herds across the reservation had grown astronomically, creating a series of problems that included overgrazing, soil erosion, poor quality of animals, tension over range rights, and an imbalance of wealth and power. This was also the era of the Great Depression, when sales were at rock bottom, government intervention in the economy was expected, and solutions were sought through action as much as careful consideration. The Soil Conservation Service assumed the responsibility for reducing herds of sheep, goats, horses, and cattle—sometimes by as much as 50 percent.

Besides dealing a fatal blow to the traditional livestock economy, this program also challenged cultural values that served as a foundation for Navajo social organization. Many men and some women had no choice

---

1. For a more complete explanation of the effects of this action, see Robert S. McPherson, "Navajo Livestock Reduction in Southeastern Utah, 1933–1946: History Repeats Itself," *American Indian Quarterly* (Winter/Spring 1998).

The Civilian Conservation Corps (CCC) in the 1930s provided various types of employment for Navajos, including range improvement, road construction, and other public works. (Photo by Milton "Jack" Snow, courtesy of the Navajo Nation Museum, Window Rock, Ariz., #NG10-10)

but to leave the reservation and seek employment in white communities. These itinerant workers took jobs wherever they could find them—laying track for the railroad, harvesting seasonal crops, clearing lands, performing odd jobs, or managing livestock for Anglo owners. The Civilian Conservation Corps also offered employment to Navajos both on and off the reservation. Improvement of roads, ranges, and facilities on government and tribal lands helped strengthen the economy and put cash into the pockets of laborers. Indeed, some Navajos thought that this program was part of the agreement to justify their loss of sheep. Regardless of the particulars, the Navajos were now part of the struggling wage-force economy.

This is the larger backdrop against which Navajo Oshley's life is counterpointed. There is, however, a smaller, more local picture that also should be drawn. As will be discussed later, the Oshley taped interviews were obtained during a study investigating the migration of Navajo and Ute people into the Blanding area.[2] From this research comes a valuable

---

2. Winston B. Hurst, "The Blanding Navajos: A Case Study of Off-Reservation Navajo Migration and Settlement," master's thesis, Eastern New Mexico University, 1981.

understanding of the economic and cultural forces that coaxed, pushed, and prodded individuals to leave their reservation homes for the foreign environment of a white community. Oshley, as one of many, becomes an Everyman, representing the life of a migrant worker who eventually settles down. Unless otherwise indicated, the following portrayal of these people is drawn from this larger study conducted by anthropologist Winston Hurst.

By the late 1890s, many Navajos were living along the San Juan, utilizing resources on both sides of the river. Trading posts and other purveyors of white culture brought benefits that enticed Native Americans to the boundaries of Anglo civilization, introduced them to new economic opportunities, then presented the question of how to fulfill these desires. No doubt the barter system, combined with an endless need for labor in these relatively new communities ("frontier" is an apt description), encouraged Navajos to work for the goods they desired. For instance, in 1901, as many as fifty Navajo and "Mexican" sheep shearers worked for one of the prominent livestock families in Bluff. At the same time, friction was growing between the two cultures over range rights and the first major land acquisition (Montezuma Creek-Aneth area) north of the river in 1905. This push/pull, attraction/repulsion characterized relations into the 1960s as white and Indian communities increased their contact.

Twenty-five years after Mormon settlers established Bluff (1880), the town of Blanding arose from the sage, pinyon, and juniper of White Mesa twenty-five miles to the north.[3] Many of its first inhabitants were related to the early settlers of Bluff and Monticello (founded in 1887). Eking a bare existence from a stingy land, the town's founders struggled to obtain sufficient water, clear enough land for crops, and create roads to support shipping efforts. Nine years after the first canvas tent proclaimed the city's establishment, Blanding boasted a population of 500 people; five years later, in 1919, there were 1,100.[4]

The town now served as a magnet to draw Indian people farther north and into the proximity of white communities. By the mid-to-late 1930s, Blanding had become the center for a small labor-export industry. Several times a year, trucks from the area between Monticello, Utah, and Cortez, Colorado, picked up Navajos either to plant or harvest crops of

---

3. The history of the settlement of southeastern Utah is found in Robert S. McPherson, *A History of San Juan County—In the Palm of Time* (Salt Lake City: Utah State Historical Society, 1995).

4. "Grayson, Utah," *Montezuma Journal*, January 22, 1914, p. 1; "San Juan County, Utah," 1920, Special Collections, Brigham Young University Library, Provo, Utah.

Unidentified Navajos in Blanding, ca. 1930s. Many Navajos came in search of employment opportunities and decided to remain. (Photo courtesy of the San Juan Historical
Commission)

beans in this dry-farm region. Hurst wrote, "It is said that the bean fields
looked like antebellum southern cotton fields in those days with long lines
of Navajo ladies dressed in their colorful calico and sateen clothing, bent
over at the waist and all moving in unison."[5] Although the work was temporary, the pay was relatively good, compared to what was available during
other times of the year.

The first trickle of Navajos to live in the vicinity of Blanding began
around 1915. While records of this time are sketchy at best, dependent
primarily on oral-history interviews, these earliest inhabitants came from
two areas on or near the reservation—Dennehotso and Bluff. This is particularly important, since people from these two locations comprised the
highest percentage (56 percent) of those who settled in the Navajo community called Westwater today. Indeed, Hurst's study points out that
many who came to this area not only knew each other previously but were
often related. "Over half of the migrants on whom data are available had
kin in the area prior to their arrival, 65 percent were preceded by either

5. Hurst, 86.

kin or previous acquaintances, and an impressive 86 percent were known to have been either preceded or followed by kin or acquaintance."[6]

When those coming from the Oljato-Monument Valley area are added to this total, it appears that 81 percent of the new population came from locales within a hundred-mile radius of Blanding during the period from 1910–1960. Oshley was typical of these migrants, having relatives from all three locations. He also belonged to the second most prominent clan—Tódích'íí'nii (Bitter Water People), the largest being Táchii'nii (Red Running into the Water People), three times larger.

Westwater and its environs were ideally suited to accept this growing population while maintaining a distinct Navajo lifestyle. Located across a canyon that offered a number of seeps and springs, this area supplied sufficient water, wood, and grazing to support the people. It was also accessible enough to town to buy and sell goods and labor. An additional advantage was the growing number of roads that tentacled out from the community to facilitate the procurement of wood—for fuel, fences, and construction. At the same time, while the Anglos were anxious to avail themselves of a constant supply of labor, there was little desire to open up the closely knit white community to this outside Navajo element. The canyon that separated the two settlements was as much cultural as physical.

A few anecdotes illustrate the sometimes intentional and sometimes unintentional gap existing between these two worlds. A subtle and sometimes not-so-subtle interplay remained between the Navajo and the white man, who did not understand one another but wanted to take advantage of what each had to offer. For example, one time there was a group of white men in a store who decided to have some fun. When a Navajo man approached, they put a silver dollar on the counter, hid, and waited for him to pick it up. Coming from a world of poverty, the man yielded to temptation and pocketed the money, only to be surrounded by a scornful group of righteous law-enforcers. He was shaken down, then escorted out of town at the end of a pointed stick. Hurst, who was born and raised and still lives in Blanding, characterized this type of behavior and local sentiments by comparing the Native American experience to that of blacks in the South. Describing this general attitude, he said, "To most white folks, Indians were just quaint relics of something not worth saving."[7]

---

6. Ibid., 141.
7. Winston Hurst, interview by author, tape recording, April 24, 1996, tape in possession of author.

"Bob-e-Kiss's [*bob bik'is*, "his or their friend"], a.k.a. Bob Keith's, wife and chil-dren at the Grant Bayles home (1930s)." The Keiths, like the Oshleys, typify the Navajos who moved off the reservation to find employment. (Photo courtesy of Carol Bayles Hurst)

There were, however, many families who worked well with Indian friends and associates, helped with economic necessities, extended love and friendship, and were scrupulously honest in their dealings. Even in many of these situations, however, there were underlying sentiments of paternal-ism and a desire to "improve" and "progress" the Indian into the benefits of white culture. The Mormon religion, the predominant belief in Blanding, added encouragement with the view that the Lamanites (Indian ancestors, based upon a scriptural account in the Book of Mormon) should become a "white and delightsome people." Thus, economically, socially, and reli-giously, Native Americans were continuously on the receiving—rarely the sending—end of cultural exchange.

In summarizing the growth of the Westwater community and Navajo population between 1915 and 1960, Hurst sees three phases, paralleling quite closely the experience of Navajo Oshley. The first phase featured pri-marily young men who came for a short period—perhaps a few weeks—and worked in the town. This was a time to become familiar with and explore the area and its potential. If homes were built, they were shared or aban-doned and left for future migrants. The second phase began in the 1920s, when entire families, many from the Bluff-Dennehotso area, took up more permanent residence. The final phase was characterized by relatively short moves and the creation of a more tightly grouped community. Hurst writes,

Bob Keith's abandoned hogan at Westwater in 1977. This home was in use up to the early 1960s. (Photo courtesy of Winston Hurst)

> Starting during the 1930s, settlement shifting was more and more a micro-phenomenon, observable as movements of a few meters, or a rearrangement of outbuildings. By the late 1940s . . . sites were becoming increasingly complex, with structural remains frequently superimposed as new structures were erected from time to time over old building sites.[8]

Thus, whether looking at settlement patterns, family relations, or work experience, Oshley's life reflects what many Navajo people encountered. Both as migrant workers and settlers, the Navajos were edging closer to white culture and a different way of life. For this time and place, the epithet of Everyman for Oshley seems totally appropriate.

Another aspect of this life history that appears typical is the network of personal daily experiences that reflect Navajo culture and its slow but inexorable move into the changing twentieth century. Throughout Oshley's narrative, there are continuous references to family relations. Indeed, with all of his travel and varied experience, the single-most-important element that held his life together and brought him back home

8. Hurst, 151.

was the desire to maintain strong ties with both his nuclear and extended family. Navajo society reigned supreme as an adhesive in social relations, a point of focus in economic practices, a means to support religious beliefs, and a type of informal government. Time and again, Oshley depends upon as well as serves the members of his family, emphasizing the power of kinship ties. To members of the dominant white society, where individuality and competition are emphasized over the group and cooperation, this way of life may seem restrictive. But to the Navajo, strong family bonds were (and are) the glue that held life together. To miss that point is to misread this autobiography.

Another important theme that runs throughout the narrative is the importance of Oshley's religious worldview. From his earliest recollections to the moment when the tape recorder switched off, his narrative is threaded with experiences and thoughts about spirituality. Oshley participated in ceremonies—both as a recipient and an assistant—but his most important power was his ability to divine what was wrong with a patient. He received this gift of divination called hand trembling when he was young, but as he explains, the power actually selected him. Between occurrences surrounding the ceremonies and the positive effects of hand trembling, there is a sense of the power that resides in a religious worldview.

There is also a sense of the power that comes from the dark side. Oshley discusses quite openly his experiences with witchcraft, where people actively worked against him and his family. His narrative contributes interesting information on this practice, since many Navajos are reticent to mention experiences of this type, though many of the old people have witnessed witchcraft's power. Oshley's honesty, a virtue he practiced throughout his life, is unquestionable. What he saw and experienced was the reality of his world.

THE PROJECT

To summarize the town's feelings about Oshley, Winston Hurst used the term "beloved," reflecting that "He was like the sagebrush and cedar [juniper] trees, he was always there." With this type of visibility and acceptance in the white community, it was not surprising that Hurst, then a graduate student working on a master's degree in anthropology from Eastern New Mexico University, decided to visit Oshley during the winter of 1978.

His research topic focused on the evolution of the Navajo and Ute community on the western fringe of Blanding near Westwater Canyon.

Navajo Oshley and son Wesley as they appeared a few years after the interview. (Photo courtesy of the Utah Navajo Development Council)

Hogan rings dating back to around the 1920s provided evidence of the first historic Navajo occupancy, but local literature was silent on the details. Ethnographic interviews provided some information, filling part of the vacuum that lay beyond the physical remains.

Hurst had gone to school with Wesley Oshley, one of Navajo's sons, and so after signing him on as interpreter, both agreed that interviewing the old man would be a good project. Tapes, a tape recorder furnished by the Utah State Historical Society, and a list of questions fleshed out what was going to be a fairly simple inquiry. Since Hurst spoke no Navajo, he outlined a general direction to Wesley, arranged for the initial interview on January 5, 1978, and arrived at the small tar-papered house where Wesley lived, just east of the half-house.

Navajo Oshley was there, dressed in a red plaid shirt and Levi's with a red bandanna around his neck. A brow creased with wrinkles sat above owl-like eyes and a distinctively shaped nose.[9] Without his hat, the old

---

9. John Holiday, a friend and relative, (see note 12), recalls how Oshley received the distinctive shape of his nose. "One time Oshley brought five horses home after working somewhere. These horses were huge, with long hair around their hooves

man's short, silver gray hair bristled in every direction. One of his children or grandchildren had taken the time to ink in a peace sign, a popular symbol in those post–Vietnam War days, on the circular patch of his high-top Converse sneaker.

Although the room was dimly lit, there was nothing somber about the occasion. Once the preliminaries ended and the interview started, the session became animated. Navajo, "calm, relaxed, with constant humor," took charge, setting his own agenda. Hurst recalled, "Everyone was laughing, even me, though I didn't understand what was being said. . . . He was a fascinating person to watch, completely free of any self-consciousness, totally at ease with himself, and obviously not hung up on any ego thing."[10]

The tape recorder was a novelty to Navajo. He was unsure how to relate to it and talked and gestured as if it could see. Sometimes sitting too close, other times pointing with his lips in the Navajo way, his memory unfolded events from the past as if a large, full-color movie was playing before his eyes. His detailed reminiscences were specific and factual, almost uncanny. Later, as the interview progressed, Wesley and Navajo took out a deck of cards. They kept the flow of monologue going but punctuated their gaming success with the slap of cards and frequent guffaws. It became obvious that this would be the first of many sessions.

As one interview led to another, a familiar pattern emerged. Hurst, realizing that father and son were saying much more than he had anticipated, wisely decided to let the recording assume a life of its own. Occasionally, Wesley interrupted the process to give a thirty-second synopsis of what had been said, but as time went on, even that faded. After a few sessions, Hurst left the tape recorder and tapes with the two men with the understanding that they should just continue, and he would pick up the interviews when they were finished. Though he never knew more than perhaps 10 percent of the information on the tapes, he understood they had immense value.

As with many scholars focused on a specific goal, Hurst never had the time to investigate what he deemed peripheral to his search—the complete contents of the fourteen taped interviews. Site visits to the Westwater community with Oshley and other informants occupied much

---

and black manes. One of these horses ruined Oshley's nose while he was trying to tame it. The horse bumped him and broke his nose. This happened in a corral at a place called Sitting in the Water, behind Baby Rocks on the way to Dennehotso."

10.   Hurst, interview.

Fannie and Max Billsie's hogan in use at Westwater in 1977. (Photo courtesy of Winston Hurst)

of his time, so he eventually sent the tapes to the Utah State Historical Society for storage. There they sat, untranslated, for the next ten years.

In the winter of 1988, the tapes returned to San Juan County long enough to have copies made. I had learned of their existence from Hurst, who encouraged me to obtain them and get them translated to make public their contents. The next summer, the Bureau of Land Management and a private donor provided funds through a local history organization named Blue Mountain Shadows to pay for a translator and typist. Bertha Parrish, a middle-aged Navajo woman, fluent in both English and Navajo, set to work uncovering a missing piece of county and Navajo history. Ironically, within a month or two of the completed translation, Navajo Oshley died at a local rest home, never aware of what was taking place.

Bertha Parrish worked long and conscientiously to interpret the tapes accurately. She spent three months listening to and recording information from a man she had never met. Armed with Robert W. Young's and William Morgan's *The Navajo Language,* she sought clarification of things that are difficult to express when moving between two languages, two

Bertha Parrish, translator and transcriber of the Oshley interviews, in 1999. (Photo by author)

perceptions. She often listened to a section of tape two or three times to ensure that her understanding and translation were correct before committing them to paper. Each sentence was mentally tested to make sure it accurately portrayed both the literal and connotative meaning Oshley intended.

Ten years after her work on the manuscript, she still recalled how difficult it had been to find the exact words or phrase that communicated facts and feelings properly. Bertha had done well. Long after this process had been completed, a member of the family listened to some of the tape with its accompanying translation and declared it was accurate. Even later, this person read the entire manuscript, and on behalf of the family, pronounced it satisfactory.

Following a period of grieving after Oshley's death, the family concurred that his life history should be made available to the public. A formal agreement signed by all family members, Winston Hurst, and me set events in motion, resulting in this book. Now the second phase of translation and work commenced.

Readers familiar with the genre of Native American autobiography are aware of the increasing ethnographic and literary commentary concerning the way these materials should be processed. The problem of moving an oral narrative with accompanying gestures and a specific physical setting onto a written page raises the issue of losing much in the translation. Also the word choice of the translator, especially when providing a gloss that catches the feelings and connotation of a word, sentence, or paragraph, is extremely important. I believe Bertha Parrish faithfully and accurately carried out that part of the process. Still, one needs to recognize that in this type of exercise, there is no such thing as an exact translation in its purest sense. As one reader noted, "People operate on the premise that a native autobiography is the person's words; it isn't anymore than the [translation of the] King James Bible is God speaking English."[11]

The next stage—to mold the manuscript into a form palatable to readers—was my responsibility. My goal was to rearrange as few words, sentences, paragraphs, and sections as possible. In many parts of Oshley's narrative, I was successful. In others, I was not, and for good reason. The first and most obvious problem was that the tapes were not initially designed to be read as a complete history. Although it is a story about a man's life, told to his son, it flowed onto the tape in large unrefined chunks. Rarely was clarification sought. No opportunity was taken to link Navajo place names to specific geographical locations; both Navajo and Anglo people slip in and out of the narrative with Navajo nicknames that are difficult to pin to a particular individual; and some of the personal experiences may be referring to a number of different recorded historical events. Pronouns were also at times unclear in their reference. This became particularly problematic when there were several people in the narrative, and suddenly the "he," "she," or "they" took off on a tangent leading to a murky dead end.

Most frustrating of all were the chronology problems. During the interviews, Oshley remembered things discussed some time before and added supplemental information, then continued with the topic at hand. How these floating bits of information were to be connected was left to the translator and reader. Fortunately, there were a few well-documented chronological signposts that provided general guidance as to where the more personal, unrecorded events fit in, but to be truthful, a number of instances were best-guess scenarios.

Where these problems occurred, older Navajo or Anglo people have provided some help. For instance, Ray Hunt, who traded with part of Oshley's family when they lived in Monument Valley, clarified some of the travel routes and place names between that location and Dennehotso.

---

11. John Farella, letter to author, July 27, 1998.

Ray Hunt and unidentified girl as he appeared in the 1930s. (Photo courtesy of Grace Hunt)

Having ridden the trails and observed the landmarks, Hunt was able to give accurate estimates of distances and places. At the same time, he clarified certain family relationships and grazing areas. A Navajo friend, Marilyn Holiday, from Monument Valley, also read the manuscript. She is very knowledgeable in traditional practices, fluent in the language, and familiar with some of the people and places mentioned by Oshley. Her father, who has lived in Monument Valley all his life, also helped clarify place names and answered questions. When Marilyn completed her reading and comments, she said that she could "hear Oshley's voice"—the pattern that older Navajo people use in speaking of the past. This is an important observation, indicating that the editing process did not disturb the fabric of the interview.

John Holiday, an eighty-year-old medicine man and relative of Oshley's, proved to be a priceless resource in supplying other chunks of missing information. For four hours in June 1999, Marilyn Holiday, a clan relative of John's, uncovered a past that had been buried two generations deep from most of the Navajos in Monument Valley.[12] Oshley's interview

---

12. John Holiday, interview by author and Marilyn Holiday, tape recording, June 8, 1999, transcript in possession of author. Further citations from this interview will be referenced by quotation marks and J. H.

is filled with names of forgotten people and places. With a few exceptions, the people whom he talked about have died; the geographical region and topographical features that were so well known and named by the Navajos have been replaced by the nameless, silent landscape of a younger generation. Indeed, as one reads Oshley's words, it seems as if every rock, hill, and watering hole had a name, like a familiar friend. John Holiday knew this and was able to recall most of the places and individuals—an impressive feat in itself. He also shared stories about the way many of these sites received their names and short anecdotes about individuals. His contribution to this manuscript is so important, especially for the Navajo people of southeastern Utah, that I have quoted from him extensively in the footnotes. A "J. H." follows the quotations so his "voice" can also be clearly heard. I will be forever indebted to him for what he has been able to add about this lost period of history.

All of this was part of the problem-solving and refining procedure. To overcome other problems, I had to play more of an editor than I would have liked. Certain sections of the interview had to be moved into appropriate places to help Oshley tell his story coherently to the reading audience. To be truthful, there were a few instances where a particular comment did not appear to fit anywhere and was omitted. These were few and far between, but in this age of textual critics, it is important to acknowledge this fact. Such were the problems and challenges of working with a taped interview from a person who could no longer clarify what had been recorded. As the editor of the manuscript, I take responsibility for these few emendations and any errors that have crept into the text.

At the same time, as little editing as possible has been done to maintain the speaker's voice and thought. In some instances, events are repetitious. Herding sheep, constant travel, the emphasis on kinship responsibility, and work in white settlements filled Oshley's existence. These elements were the fabric of Navajo culture and provide a feeling for what life was like around the turn of the century. Textual patterns have been faithfully retained, though the incidents are redundant. What the reader will notice immediately, however, is the tremendous amount of vivid details Oshley recalled about his daily life.

For the reader expecting the dramatic, there is some of that. Encounters with witchcraft, confrontations between man and beast, the introduction of the Native American Church into southeastern Utah, and the healing power of traditional ceremonies have a place here. But just as important is the feeling that is evoked. Oshley, holding true to his reputation for honesty, tells of problems he faced. Marital conflict, grinding poverty, family disagreements, sickness, death, theft, and the sheer drudgery of daily survival in a marginal livestock economy paint a picture of a difficult life in a harsh land. There is nothing terribly grand or glorious in his life, other than the fact that he worked long and hard under trying circumstances.

On the other hand, Oshley's personal philosophy and traditional background served him well. Even in the most difficult times, the reader rarely hears him complain or curse his luck. Indeed, when he does break with the narrative and philosophizes, he speaks of a spiritual world based on order and faith. When things are wrong, it is the fault of man, who has upset the design of life as created by the holy beings, whose presence is manifested everywhere. Humble to the end, Oshley had a sure knowledge of his place in the divine scheme of life and, as Winston Hurst said earlier, was "completely free of any self-consciousness" and "totally at ease with himself." That fact alone makes reading about this man's life worthwhile. It speaks to the human experience of us all.

Thus, the strength of the manuscript is that it truly reflects Oshley's views. In one respect, its emphasis on seemingly unimportant, day-to-day events is its greatest contribution. Because the recordings evolved as more of a monologue than a treatise sculpted by an ethnographer, Oshley spoke of the things that were important to him. Much of his detailed account might have been lost if a closer interview focus had been maintained. This was his life as he saw it, and both white and Navajo people have expressed interest in learning about a man whose experiences spanned the history of a town. But Oshley provides not only breadth but also depth in understanding the Navajo world—that other half of his life that appeared, like the half-house, to have been severed and moved to the distant past.

When the taping sessions ended, Oshley unwittingly created another problem. He had not reached a particularly good time to end; for some reason—whether he ran out of tapes, time, or energy—is not known, but the interviews came to an abrupt halt. Ten years later, when renewed interest in the project took a different form, I was faced with the problem of reconstructing approximately fifty years of the man's life to bring the story to some kind of closure for the reader. Chapters appended at the end of Oshley's narrative tell the rest of the story in broad brush strokes. Family members and acquaintances helped in the reconstruction, and their assistance is greatly appreciated. Still, the heart of this book is Oshley's voice, speaking of his life.

A final word needs to be said on the place of this book in the growing literature of Native American autobiography, in general, and Navajo autobiography, in particular. There is extensive interest in this genre and a growing ethnographic and literary criticism to accompany it. The autobiography form has provided the grist for a good deal of scholarship that attempts to recreate an inside perspective of historical and cultural events. The Navajo are no stranger to this phenomenon.

Some Navajo autobiographies that come closest to the Oshley narrative are those recorded by Walter Dyk.[13] *Left Handed, Son of Old Man Hat* and its accompanying *Left Handed: A Navajo Autobiography* are two of his best-known works and focus on the same individual.[14] Dyk's *A Navaho Autobiography* about a man named Old Mexican living in southeastern Utah during the early twentieth century is not as well known but just as poignant.[15] All three depict the daily life and culture of Navajos and their struggles to survive amidst change. This is particularly true of the last book as Old Mexican becomes increasingly involved with farming in Aneth at the government station and social and political events connected with the newly established Shiprock Agency. The candor in all three narratives helps capture the unvarnished truth of this lifestyle. In many respects, this is true of Oshley's story also, although the sexual side of life, prevalent with Dyk's informants, is conspicuously absent. The detailed endnotes in Old Mexican's life history also help solve the problem in this narrative, i.e., filling in the background information necessary to connect the story clearly to time, place, and people.

Another autobiography that is more skillful and sophisticated in providing an understanding of Navajo culture and history is Charlotte J. Frisbie's and David P. McAllester's *Navajo Blessingway Singer: The Autobiography of Frank J. Mitchell, 1881–1967.*[16] As the title suggests,

---

13. Other autobiographies that the reader may want to look at that are similar to Dyk's work include Alexander H. Leighton and Dorothea C. Leighton, *Gregorio the Hand-Trembler: A Psychobiological Personality Study of a Navaho Indian*, Papers of the Peabody Museum of American Archaeology and Ethnology, vol. 40 (Cambridge: Harvard University Press, 1949); Irene Stewart, *A Voice in Her Tribe: A Navajo Woman's Own Story* (Socorro, N. Mex.: Ballena Press, 1980); and Joyce Griffen, ed., *Lucky the Navajo Singer*, recorded by Alexander H. Leighton and Dorothea C. Leighton (Albuquerque: University of New Mexico Press, 1992).

14. Walter Dyk, *Left Handed, Son of Old Man Hat* (1938; reprint, Lincoln: University of Nebraska Press, 1995); Walter and Ruth Dyk, *Left Handed: A Navajo Autobiography* (New York: Columbia University Press, 1980).

15. Walter Dyk, *A Navaho Autobiography* (New York: Viking Fund, Inc., 1947).

16. Charlotte J. Frisbie and David P. McAllester, *Navajo Blessingway Singer: The Autobiography of Frank J. Mitchell, 1881–1967* (Tucson: University of Arizona Press, 1978).

Mitchell, as a practicing medicine man, lived in a much more ceremonial world than Oshley. Frisbie, as a trained anthropologist, had the opportunity to go back on various occasions and polish the manuscript by seeking clarification of topics and events, eliminating repetition, editing out parts that seemed irrelevant, and arranging the taped interviews in chronological order.[17] The result is a highly readable and fully developed account of a man's life, accompanied by a wealth of information in the endnotes. Mitchell's life history, therefore, is significantly different from that of Oshley. He played a prominent role in many major events, had a deep knowledge of Navajo religion, and was generally a far more sophisticated individual. Mitchell's autobiography hardly reflects the more typical workaday world of the majority of Navajo people, though the time span in his and Oshley's story is comparable.

Kay Bennett, the Navajo woman who wrote *Kaibah—Recollection of a Navajo Girlhood*, offered an interesting account of her early life, but the book is less scholarly than these other works.[18] The text reads like a novel, replete with dialogue, description painted in poetic prose, and use of the third-person voice even though it is based on Bennett's and her family's experience. Although it claims to portray everyday life, the events and description are highly selective and miss much of the daily drudgery and hardship in other narratives.

Another autobiography written in similar fashion is *Miracle Hill—The Story of a Navaho Boy* by Emerson Blackhorse Mitchell and T. D. Allen.[19] The dust jacket claims that Mitchell "is intelligent and aware but not yet trained to analyze and dehumanize his account. Even his handling of the English language is unique. The words are sometimes puzzling, but his prose is beautifully rhythmic. . . ." Mitchell, a graduate of the University of New Mexico and a writer and teacher, along with Terry Allen, a teacher of creative writing, have purposely left grammar problems in the text to give a quaint feeling of authenticity. Like *Kaibah*, *Miracle Hill* has dialogue that reads like a novel, descriptive and interpretive passages, and a third-person voice. Both books have had their material heavily worked for a reading audience.

An example of the final move of the reader away from the original voice of an autobiography is a biography based on interviews. *Hosteen*

17. Ibid., 8.
18. Kay Bennett, *Kaibah—Recollections of a Navajo Girlhood* (n.p.: the author, 1975).
19. Emerson Blackhorse Mitchell and T. D. Allen, *Miracle Hill—The Story of a Navaho Boy* (Norman: University of Oklahoma Press, 1967).

Klah—Navaho Medicine Man and Sand Painter by Franc Johnson
Newcomb is this kind of book.[20] It spans the history of four generations,
culminating in Klah's life. Newcomb describes the way she sat around the
winter campfire, listening to the stories but only occasionally jotting down
what was said. The reader can totally agree with the author when she
admits, "I certainly wish I had written much more."[21] Without a tape
recorder and with only sporadic notes, a person wonders how much was
lost, what things were intentionally left out and why, and how much of
what he supposedly said would be accepted by Klah, especially since his
words originally came through an interpreter. Newcomb also uses historical records to buttress her account, but the information is woven into the
narrative and not documented in endnotes. Thus, this story offers the
reader an interesting and informative portrayal of a man's life, but in form
and feeling, it is far removed from either the works of Walter Dyk or
Navajo Oshley's narrative.

BACKGROUND

In piecing together Navajo Oshley's life, I learned there were a number of
other times that he had been formally interviewed. In each instance, additional information supplemented his oral history and gave a broader picture of the man. The first interview took place in 1961 during the Navajo
land-claims cases.[22] The purpose of the interview was to survey older
Navajos throughout the Four Corners area, both on and off the reservation, to determine aboriginal land claims. The government attempted to
define the earliest use and residence on tribal lands among different
Native American groups to ascertain who should get what.

Oshley was a natural choice for an interview since he had spent his
entire life in northwestern New Mexico, northeastern Arizona, southwestern Colorado, and southeastern Utah. At the time of the interview,
his birthdate was listed as 1882, yet in other places, it says he was born in
1879, 1885, or 1893. Whatever the case, he was at least in his seventies
and had experienced a lot.

20. Franc Johnson Newcomb, *Hosteen Klah—Navaho Medicine Man and Sand Painter*
    (Norman: University of Oklahoma Press, 1964).
21. Ibid., xxii.
22. Haakeh Nezin "Ashley Navajo" [sic], interview by Aubrey Williams and Maxwell
    Yazzie, January 27, 1961, Doris Duke #735, Special Collections, University of
    Utah, Salt Lake City.

Oshley was interviewed often because of his historical knowledge. Here, a camera crew from KSL Television film him in 1985 at Montezuma Creek. (Photo courtesy of the Utah Navajo Development Council)

The survey followed an established format, asking about the geographical area the individual was most familiar with, relatives on both the mother's and father's side of the family, knowledge of material remains such as hogan sites and pottery making (pottery pieces are almost indestructible once they've been fired), and resource and other general use areas. Informants, generally, were held to these strict categories.

Oshley stated that he belonged to the Tódích'íi'nii clan; was born and lived in Dennehotso, Arizona, for thirty-five years; moved to Monument Valley (Dove Spring in Cain Valley), where he remained for fifteen years, and then to Blanding, where he had lived for thirty years. The areas he felt he knew the best were bounded by Blue Mountain to the north, Recapture Wash to the east, Montezuma Creek to the south, and Allen Canyon and the Bears Ears to the west. Much of this familiarity was due to his herding activities in this region.

His father belonged to the Bit'ahnii clan, was born and raised in the area of Mexican Water on Chinle Wash, and lived with his mother, Wide

Tooth, for some time. Other than that, Oshley knew nothing about his father.[23] However, he had a greater understanding of his mother's side of the family, the most important half in Navajo genealogy. His maternal relatives hailed from the area of Star Butte at the head of Canyon de Chelly. The Utes captured his grandmother, Woman with the Four Horns, during the "fearing time" of the late 1850s or early 1860s, when the United States government employed the Utes as military auxiliaries to conduct operations against the Navajos.[24] Woman with the Four Horns, therefore, never went to Fort Sumner, as many other Navajos did, but returned to the Star Butte area following the conflict. After a number of moves within the Four Corners region, she eventually died close to where she had been born.

During a second interview in 1968, Oshley shared some of the teachings of Woman with the Four Horns.[25] Before she died, she told Oshley what to expect from the white man, who in the early days was not called *bilagáana* (unknown derivation) but "narrow shoes." She warned, "There is the white man up on the hill. He has his God somewhere past the 'wide water' [ocean] and that is where his religion is."[26]

Besides Woman with the Four Horns, the only other relative fleshed out in some detail in these interviews is an uncle named Hastiin Béésh bizis—"Mr. Knife Sheath." Around the time of the Long Walk by captured Navajos to Fort Sumner (early 1860s), this uncle played a prominent role in protecting family members from marauding Ute war parties. Knife Sheath was a great runner and warrior, "giving competition to the enemy." When the enemy approached, he gathered the women and moved them to remote areas, then sat at the entrance of the hiding place with bow and arrow in hand. "Night after night he would sit and sleep like that, always alert . . . and so he saved the women and he did not go to Fort Sumner."[27]

Oshley remembered hearing his uncle's stories of this period. As with many Navajo families, these events became almost legends and an

---

23. Oshley's father, according to J. H., was One Who Never Sleeps or One Who Sings Ceremonies and came from Green Vegetation Along the Rock Ridge.
24. There is a discrepancy here because John Holiday says she was captured by an enemy, most likely a Comanche, who took her and her husband to Texas. See Chapter 2, note 4.
25. Navajo Oshley, interview by Gary Shumway and Clyde Benally, August 13, 1968, Doris Duke #526, Special Collections, University of Utah, Salt Lake City, pp. 1–15.
26. Ibid., 5.
27. Ibid., 13.

important part of family heritage at a time that was, by any other measure, a period of defeat and degradation. One incident occurred in the vicinity of the Carrizo Mountains, when Utes attacked a group of Navajos. Both were armed with bows and arrows and muzzle-loading rifles. As each side skirmished for position, Knife Sheath placed his bow on the soles of his feet and launched an arrow that landed in the midst of the enemy, then shot another behind them, causing them to disperse. On a different occasion, a mounted Ute charged a small band of Navajos backed against a rock wall. Knife Sheath shot an arrow that went completely through the horse, toppling animal and rider. He then helped his group to escape. Oshley ended the story by emphasizing that his family members remained free because "this kinfolk of mine was dangerous," and the Utes feared the "great warrior."[28]

Oshley obviously took pride in his heritage. When he described his own life, there was little boasting. He came from humble circumstances which he matter-of-factly tells the reader he did not enjoy. Poverty was a constant companion that never seemed to leave, even up to that winter day in 1978 when the interview process began. But underneath the exterior of plain clothes and old age, there rested a certain nobility of character that the white and Navajo communities recognized for what it was—honesty, hard work, and the desire to keep his reputation clean. Indeed, the Navajo name by which he was known in the 1961 interview—Ak'é nídzin (the One Who Greets with Deep Respect)—describes the way others viewed him.[29] This trait of understanding kinship relationships and extending his feelings of brotherhood characterized his entire life.

As Oshley sat by the woodstove, relating his experiences to the crackle and snap of the burning juniper logs, he recalled times that were not always pleasant. In straightforward prose, he started his account at Dennehotso, the place of his birth. These were painful memories of a difficult life, but they were accepted, as were many other trials he had encountered. His story begins . . .

---

28. Ibid., 12–15.
29. "He got that name when he was a small boy. Unlike some children, Oshley was not shy. As a child he would shake hands, sometimes more than once, with anyone who came to visit his home. The people thought of him as being friendly and respectful by shaking their hands and so they started calling him that name." J. H.

The Autobiography

This earliest known photograph of Oshley was
taken in the 1930s. (Photo courtesy of the San
Juan Historical Commission)

The Life of Navajo Oshley

EARLIEST MEMORIES

I WAS BORN AT DENNEHOTSO,[1] NEAR A RED, ROUND ROCK.[2] The winter was over, and it was the beginning of summer. My father was of the Bit'ahnii [the Within His Cover People] clan, but I never knew him and do not know his name because he passed away when I was very small.[3] As time went on, my maternal grandmother, 'Asdzą́ą́ déé' díí' [Woman with the Four Horns];[4] my mother, 'Asdzą́ą́ hasbídí [Mourning Dove

1. Translated as Yellow Meadow Extending Up, Dennehotso (spelled in Navajo *Dennihootso*) is located approximately twenty-five miles east of Kayenta on Highway 160. Laguna Creek provides sufficient water for irrigation agriculture during the spring and summer. "The community came into being when a trading post was built in 1920. Before then, people lived mostly at the Comb Ridge area raising livestock and moved to the farming area in the summer time only. After harvesting, people moved back to the ridge." (Larry Rodgers, *Chapter Images: 1992 Edition* [Window Rock, Ariz.: Navajo Nation, 1993], 50.) This description fits exactly the pattern that Oshley's family followed during these early years.

2. "Sitting Red Rock is near a place called Volcanic Ash Rock that is located between Baby Rocks, Arizona, and Comb Ridge—about ten miles north of Baby Rocks. It is also called Calm Water. Lady Mourning Dove used to live there." J. H.

3. The mother's clan provides the primary fabric of social relationships for an individual, although both maternal and paternal clans hold certain social and economic identity within traditional Navajo society. A person's ancestry may theoretically be traced back to the time of the myths when clans first formed. This heritage may determine who a person can marry and affect the place he or she may live, as well as certain financial obligations to kin. Oshley's maternal or primary clan was Tódích'íi'nii (The Bitter Water People). For a complete explanation of the importance of these social bonds and responsibilities, see Gary Witherspoon, *Navajo Kinship and Marriage* (Chicago: University of Chicago Press, 1975).

4. "They say that long ago her [Woman with the Four Horns] family used to have a cornfield near the San Juan River. They lived in the Page-Navajo Mountain area. During the time of local conflicts [Fort Sumner], her husband wanted to join in and fight. One day he got ready and left on his horse, but his young wife decided to go with him. They were newlyweds, and she was a little girl. She got dressed in all her turquoise jewelry and ran after her husband. After she caught up to him, they both got on the same horse and traveled as far as Baby Rocks when the enemy captured

Woman];[5] and the rest of the family roamed the Dennehotso area.[6] My mother used to live near Comb Ridge, and there was a small box canyon that had a spring and a lot of mourning doves.[7] That is how this place got the name Dove Springs [or Spring with Mourning Doves]. My mother had another name, but I forgot it. She was known to people as Mourning Dove Woman. When she died, her youngest son went to that spring often so the people called him Hasbídí yázhí [Little (or young, junior) Mourning Dove]. We did not have many sheep, but we did have a lot of goats, and many of the rams had four big horns. This is how my grandmother got the name Woman with the Four Horns.

When I was a boy, I was called Ashkii nééziì [Taller Boy]. Our names were awful back then.[8] Eventually, my mother had six children, but my first sister died, making me the oldest one in the family. A younger brother also died. As I remember, I did not have any shoes, and my pants were a horror to see. They had holes and were too short. The fabric in my shirt was from a flour sack, but where my relatives got it, I do not know. I did not have a hat so I used a piece of rope or cloth tied together. This is how I grew up.

---

them. They took her and her husband to Texas. During this time, her family back home held special ceremonies and sings for her return. With that she escaped and walked to Fort Sumner, where other Navajos were being held captive. Somehow my great grandmother managed to survive and return home to Baby Rocks near Dennehotso. She owned nothing but four horned sheep when she was released from Fort Sumner." J. H.

5. "I only knew her [Mourning Dove Woman] to be a farmer. She had a big cornfield in the valley [Cane] where she would plant melons and squash, then dig storage pits in the sand dunes and store all her produce after wrapping it in tree bark. She did not have very many sheep and did not do much weaving." J. H.

6. "Woman with the Four Horns was my very distant grandmother. Her daughter, Lady of Streak Running Red Grass, was my mother's mother, so there were three ladies of three generations. Lady of Streak Running Red Grass's little sister was a mother to Mr. Oshley. Woman Who Owns the House had a son named Adika'í. Oshley and Adika'í were cousin brothers. Woman Who Owns the House was Little Mourning Dove's sister." J. H.

7. Comb Ridge or Tsékaan [Rocks Standing Up] is a large sandstone monocline of the Monument Upwarp that extends for over a hundred miles from Blue Mountain in Utah to Kayenta, Arizona.

8. Naming was a private affair that occurred after a child was born. There has been much discussion about bestowing so-called war names. These were titles of power recognized by the holy beings during ceremonies and were considered sacred. Not all Navajos adhered to this or any other particular naming scheme. Names for everyday use were tied to kinship; they clearly identified a person based on who they were related to. This system reduced any confusion when there were a number of

A typical Navajo camp in the austere lands of southeastern Utah. Left to right, Frank, Clyde, and Sadie Benally (milking the goat), with Fatty Yellowhair astride horse. (Photo courtesy of Baxter Benally)

The trading post was very far away.[9] My mother and grandmother would take the burros there, but it was time consuming and very tedious. They brought back flour, coffee, and sugar. It took three to four days before they returned. The children would wonder when grandmother and mother would come back, so one of us would run to the hill and look for them. When grandmother returned with the food, we would get milk from the goats, then butcher a sheep. Everything was used.[10] Even the

people with the same name. Kinship relationships provided clarification, making it important to know a person's social context. There were also nicknames based on a personality trait, incident, or some prominent physical characteristic. These names were the ones that Oshley is probably calling "awful back then." They often referred to something that could be an embarrassment. For further information, see Gladys Reichard, "Names and Naming," in *Social Life of the Navajo Indians* (New York: AMS Press, 1928): 96–107.

9. Oshley is not referring to the Dennehotso Trading Post built in 1920 since that is far in the future.

10. "Back then we were fed like dogs. After they [family members] butchered a sheep, they would partially cook a portion of liver and throw it to us to eat and then have us go after the sheep. This is the kind of lifestyle that Oshley experienced when he was growing up." J. H.

blood and intestines were fixed, and the wool removed from the hide. After cleaning the skin thoroughly, it was cut into strips, then curled around a piece of fat.[11] We ate it like that.

Life was a very hard, long struggle. Sometimes there was little food so we would have just a few mouthfuls to eat before we went to sleep. In the morning, we would drink milk and then go without food the rest of the day. We had a cornfield which we planted when it rained. If there was no moisture, we would go hungry during the summer and into the winter. Life was hard when I was growing up.

When I was a child, sheep were the main source of food for survival.[12] The sheep were separated from their lambs and the goats from their kids. They grazed while the lambs and kids stayed in the corral. One time around sundown, the sheep came home and took their lambs. I went after them, bringing along a can with a spoon. After awhile my family missed me. Mother looked for my tracks and saw that I had followed the sheep far away. As she got closer, she saw me standing face to face with a coyote. I was shaking the can in my hand, causing the coyote to hesitate to charge, but it did not prevent me from wetting my pants. My mother saved me, but my aunt scolded her for letting me wander off. When my sister came home from herding sheep and found out what had happened, she picked me up and cried, saying that I had almost been eaten by a coyote.

During that time, the place called Where Dynamite Made a Road was not yet made, and the roads were terrible.[13] When we went to Dennehotso to plant or to the trading post, we went by that route. We

---

11. The sheepskin is prepared while it is still fresh. The wool is removed, and the skin is cut into narrow strips, wrapped around a piece of fat, then cooked on the coals. It is both tender and tasty.

12. Oshley's entire life, like that of many Navajos at this time, revolved around livestock. Old people still say "sheep are life" and interpret that in a very literal sense. Social status, personal and family economy, and informal political power were all affected by the number of livestock—sheep, goats, cattle, and horses—as well as the care given to them.

13. This portion of Comb Ridge was later blasted with dynamite to make a narrow path over this slickrock formation between the upper end of the Cane Valley/Monument Valley region and Dennehotso and Mexican Water. John Holiday recalls when Navajo construction crews (probably in the 1930s) improved the road so that wagons could traverse it: "We lived right below at the base of the mesa. We saw and heard them blast with dynamite the rocks to make the road. Navajos used to take their wagons through there. The road was passable until an avalanche occurred halfway up the mesa. That blocked off the road, and rain washed it out, making it impossible to use. It was never repaired."

traveled on the road many times to take care of the cornfield, and in the fall we harvested the crop and stored it in a hole as deep as a man standing up. Burros carried the corn and melons down that awful trail, and if they slipped, they fell off and died.

One time we were asked to move to Dennehotso because the harvest was more plentiful. I packed the burros and drove them up the trail with the sheep following after. One burro slipped and fell, barely making it to the top. We stayed at our usual campsite, and after settling in, I went to the cornfield. I gathered as many melons as I could carry on a horse and took the melons back to our camp. We stayed in that vicinity, using a shelter [made of tree branches in a circle with an opening to the east] for our home. We borrowed an ax and shovel to make a hogan for our winter camp. When I was much older, I helped make hogans.

This is how I used to live; it was not a beautiful life. We even got water from a long distance, a mile away, carrying it in pails by hand. A person needed to get up early in the morning. When we washed, we used the same water the last person used. Since water was very scarce, if one person washed his hair, the next person also used the same water, no matter what it looked like, because that was all we had. There was no soap, either.

We ate rabbits, pack rats, and prairie dogs. They were hard to catch. When winter came, we started hunting rabbits, which we killed with sticks and stones. Sometimes there was nothing to eat. We also had a few horses, cows, and burros. During that time, people butchered horses when they were fat, wasting nothing. Sometimes it was hard to get a meal, and so we stayed hungry throughout the day. Life was not a pleasant time when I was growing up.

During the summer, things got better because we looked for plants like green yucca fruit to eat. There were wild onions and sumac berries. Sometimes these did not grow because they only flourish when it rains. When the water did not come, life was extra hard. That is why when there are heavy snows in the winter, people are happy. My elders were right when they said they would have plenty of food in the summer. When it rains a lot, we have an abundance of all things. For instance, when it really rained in the fall, there would be piñon nuts the following year. Almost the whole family went to pick them.

I picked piñon nuts in my younger days and remember how the tips of my fingers hurt, so I would use my other hand. After we had gathered lots of nuts, we went home and mixed toasted corn with piñon nuts. This food was prepared by roasting the piñon nuts and corn separately, then crushing the shells of the nuts and mixing them together. This is called *haza'aleeh* [literally, "put into mouth"] and is often combined with meat and a sprinkle of salt. We needed any kind of edible thing to eat.

There were other plants such as wolfberry, edible tubers that were dug up, green yucca fruit, and yucca stalks. We would gather these plants when they were ripe, along with small spiny cactus. We also had corn, which was ground with stones and cooked with water. The stones we called *tsédaashjéé'* [metate] and *tsédaashch'íní* [mano], and with them we ground corn to make mush. Leaves from the juniper tree were burnt and the ashes added to water. Mother then filtered this through a brush, added it to the corn, mixed it well, then took the *haza'aleeh* and dipped it into the mush. We thought that this tasted really great.

We moved from one place to another around Where the Red Rock Is Sitting. Then we moved to the rocky part of Comb Ridge, which the people call Where Dynamite Made a Road. We moved from one place to another in that area. My mother had two sisters, 'Asdzáá bikinii [Woman Who Owns the House] and 'Asdzáá bijéékałí [Deaf Woman], and all three sisters lived in the same area. My aunt, Woman Who Owns the House, had a son who was called Adika'í [Gambler]. He was a wealthy man with a lot of sheep, horses, cattle, and jewelry, but I did not get any from him.[14]

I was a slave for my aunt, Woman Who Owns the House.[15] I herded sheep and took care of Gambler's horses, cattle, and burros, which I used to ride. I would sit backward on the burro, pull its tail toward its head, and make it buck. We really laughed about that, but it was crazy. I also tried small bulls, but they do not buck straight and were not as enjoyable as burros. We roped cows and horses and did things to them. I could even lasso a cow from a horse. I think I was really good at

---

14. "Adika'í had a big herd of sheep, cattle, goats, donkeys, and horses. He was also a farmer and had a large field in Dennehotso. He was a hard worker, taking care of his livestock and irrigating his field on a daily basis, but he was not a medicine man. He was always working, but as he got older, he enjoyed going to many social activities like Enemy Way dances and other ceremonies. He raised some horses and would take them to different places to race them. He was also very strong and would always win at a tug-of-war with ropes or in the horse-wrestling contest. His opponents could never throw him off his horse because he was so strong." J. H.

15. The importance of the matrilineal line and the close association between sisters are common themes running throughout this narrative. Much of Oshley's daily efforts focused on providing support and allegiance to these kinship ties. Certainly his use of the word "slave" carries this strong sense of obligation.

Hogan (possibly built by Oshley) located at the foot of the trail known as Where Dynamite Made a Road, running diagonally down Comb Ridge in the background. Nearby is a spring dug by Oshley. (Photo by author)

this. This was what I did for entertainment when I was still a boy. After I grew a little older, I became aware of how dangerous it was for me to do these things, and playing games no longer thrilled me. Now I am decrepit.

When we were living behind Comb Ridge, my cousins and I left our chores and played in the rocks all day long. We took big flat rocks for sleds and slid down the rock slopes, which was a lot of fun. One time we were doing this, and the rock came out from underneath me when I was halfway down. It barely missed sliding over me, but although I was badly scraped and had a nosebleed, we still laughed about it. We must have been really foolish, and now that I think about it, I could have been killed. Once when I was young, it seemed like I was going to die. A sickness got me when my aunt, Woman Who Owns the House, and Gambler came to see me. They said I would have a ceremony performed on me. When a child is sick, a medicine man is notified, and the family talks about what might be the cause of the sickness. The medicine man brings in a rock and plants such as snakeweed, bent grass [*boute loua gracilis*], and rock sage. The illness may be caused by either of the parents mistreating a doll by burning or breaking it while the baby is still in the womb.[16] This affects the unborn child when she/he grows a little older. If this is what is bothering the child, part of the root of a tree is cut. The length of the doll is the distance on one hand from the thumb to the middle finger. It is said the doll will be made whole again. A prayer and chants go with this part of the ritual. I just had some short ones, but other individuals may have long chants that go with hand trembling.

Woman Who Owns the House was a really good hand trembler, who knew what was wrong with a patient. Hand trembling is called *tinílèí* [Gila monster] or *n'dilniihjí* [Moving of the Hand] and is used to diagnose a sick person.[17] After the ceremony, I felt much better, ready to get on with life.

An Early Trip to the Blanding Area

Another memory that I have of my early years is when my brother wanted to know if there were any piñon nuts on Blue [Abajo] Mountain.[18] He saddled the horses because I was not big enough, and we packed some meat and bread. I think we crossed the San Juan River near Comb Ridge; I remember the river was very high, because the water went over his horse's back. On some parts of the trail, rocks were piled up, and there was a spring where we drank water. My brother said this place was called Navajo Springs, but I was surprised that there was no one living there. When I asked why it was called Navajo Springs, he told me the people used to live all around here, but now it was different.

We went along Comb Ridge and came to Allen Canyon, where there was a road in poor condition. My brother said that the Utes lived here and we would go over there. Then he said they were living at

---

16. Oshley is describing a ceremonial practice in which the carved object is placed on the affected part of the patient's body as the medicine man recites prayers and chants. Later the image is placed in an Anasazi ruin. For more information see Franciscan Fathers, *An Ethnologic Dictionary of the Navajo Language* (St. Michael's, Ariz.: St. Michael's Press, 1910), 496.

17. The Gila monster is one of the major beings associated with divination. This creature's supernatural powers were first recognized in the mythological worlds beneath this world, the one that Navajos now live in. Oshley later describes how he received this power and became a proficient hand trembler.

18. While Oshley is not using the term "brother" clearly, he is referring to his cousin (in Anglo terminology), Gambler. The confusion may stem from using this English word to describe a relationship that is handled differently in Navajo. Here the mother's sister's son on the female side is called *hak'is*, translated as brother.

Towaoc.[19] When we got to the canyon, there was no sign of life or that people had once lived there. Then he wanted to see some horses, so after eating by the creek, we made our own trail through trial and error to somehow get across to what is now Blanding. People bought and sold horses there, and my brother wanted to go. But we got stuck on the other side of Westwater Canyon.

We finally made it across and found the place had not been tamed. There was large sagebrush, and so it was called Amidst the Sagebrush, but the whites later named it Blanding.[20] The whole surrounding area was called Hairy [or Furry Mountain—Abajo or Blue Mountain], and there were a lot of horses that once belonged to the Navajos but now had become wild. My brother said the Navajos used to live just a ways from here and had held an Enemy Way ceremony. They left because of the enemy that was coming their way. We went a little further and got stuck again because of high water. We were not getting anywhere finding piñon nuts. There were no Utes living in the area as we traveled to the Bears Ears. I never did see any Utes though I wanted to know what they looked like; my brother said they had braided hair and talked in a strange manner. We spent two days and nights picking nuts, then returned home and told the people where piñon nuts were plentiful. They packed up and left immediately.

At this time, there weren't any white men living in the Blanding area. My grandmother told me we had enemies, and when I asked who, she said the white men. I asked where do these people live, and she replied very far from where we lived at the Mountain that Gropes Around [Carrizo Mountains]. Later, land became an issue with the white man. I wondered why they were taking the land away from the Navajos. It had been our land for a long time.

---

19. Allen Canyon was a favorite planting area of the Utes in the summertime and was officially allotted in individual parcels to them in 1923. Towaoc, located on the eastern base of Sleeping Ute Mountain in southwestern Colorado, became the official agency of the Ute Mountain Utes in 1895. This agency was responsible for administering the government program for the Utes in southeastern Utah.

20. Blanding, first named Grayson, was founded in 1905 when Albert R. Lyman and his family pitched their tent near the present Blanding Elementary School. There were no Navajo or Ute people living there at that time. According to John Holiday, the town received its name—Amidst the Sagebrush—because "Blanding was being cleared of sagebrush so they [Anglos] could build some homes. There was nothing there but two or three shacks and several tents. People were clearing the land by hand; there were no tractors." For a history of this area, see Robert S. McPherson, *A History of San Juan County—In the Palm of Time* (Salt Lake City: Utah State Historical Society, 1995).

All of these mountains around Navajo land are ours. For many generations, all of these things were placed for us to utilize, but now the Anglo has put a stop to this by fencing up the land. Without telling us about anything, they took up residency, and now they say this land belongs to them. Who gave them that right? When we asked them about it, they would answer, "The law." Who had the right to make these [laws]? They were not made in front of us, and if they [Anglos] think so highly of it, they should read it to us. We do not know of these written laws. Maybe I am the only one who thinks this way. This is all.

There are many places named by the Navajos as they live and work in an area.[21] For instance, Blue Mountain is also called Pointed Dark Mountain. Across Westwater Canyon, it is called Across from It; the Navajo people live there. To the south, it is called Teec Nos Pos [Cottonwoods in a Circle]; then a ways from there, The Road That Leads Up then beside that is Horse Canyon. A little ways from there, it is called Slender Rock That Stands Up [possibly Mule Ear diatreme on the San Juan River]. Then there is Bears Ears, which extends to K'aayééłii's [Arrow Quiver] place, which is known as a Ridge That Stops Abruptly [Elk Ridge].[22] This had been Navajo land, this was our land, for a long time. Behind Blue Mountain, there is a spring called Navajo Spring. This was what my grandmother told me. Then there is another mountain called Big Sheep [Hesperus Peak, Colorado], where some Navajos are buried. The Utes use these sites as a place to perform their ceremony against the Navajos.[23] Still, the mountain belongs to us because of the Navajo bones buried there. I think and feel this way.

---

21.   Navajo place names provide a fascinating portrait of relationships to the land. Every spring, canyon, large rock, or prominent geographical feature has a name derived from a characteristic, mythological occurrence, or historic event. Some are widely recognized, but most names are known only locally. Oshley supplies many names that were at one time familiar to Navajos in the Four Corners area but have since fallen into disuse. For more information on Navajo place names and beliefs concerning locations in southeastern Utah, see Robert S. McPherson, *Sacred Land, Sacred View* (Provo: Brigham Young University, Charles Redd Center for Western Studies, 1992).

22.   K'aayééłii was a prominent Navajo leader who lived around the Bears Ears during the 1860s when many other Navajos went on the Long Walk and a four year exile at Bosque Redondo (1864–68). During this time, a Paiute and Ute faction helped him avoid capture by the military and its Indian allies. One of his camps was located at Kigalia Spring on Elk Ridge near the Bears Ears. Today a temporary ranger station is there.

23.   The use of ceremonies "against the Navajos" suggests a form of witchcraft that directs supernatural power toward enemies to weaken or destroy them.

Looking southwest at Bluff City and the San Juan River as they appeared in November 1895. (Photo courtesy of the San Juan Historical Commission)

Our boundary runs from the mountain called Big Sheep to Navajo Spring. The Navajos pointed to mountains as borders of their land. Arrow Quiver made the border over the Bears Ears and this side of Oljato [Moon Water], outside of the San Juan River. My grandmother told me this. We got on top of a small hill, and she said, "My grandson, we are warring now." Near Blue Mountain, the Enemy Way ceremony was just finishing.[24] The Navajos were performing it during the war against the Utes because the Utes were putting bones against us.

One time I went to where Arrow Quiver used to live. It was in the canyon with the San Juan River flowing on one side. There were forked pole hogans on the north side of the river along the canyon wall, but all I could see were the logs, warped and gray. This place is between Head of

---

24.   The Enemy Way ceremony was formerly used to protect warriors from enemy ghosts killed in battle. Today it is used as "a cure for sickness thought to be caused by ghosts of non-Navajos. It is classed with the other Ghost Way (Evil Way) ceremonials" and may last either three or five nights. (From Leland C. Wyman, "Navajo Ceremonial System," *Southwest*, vol. 10 of *Handbook of North American Indians* [Washington, D.C.: Smithsonian Institution, 1983], 541.) The ritual is based upon a myth in which Monster Slayer, a male hero, is cleansed after killing monsters inhabiting the earth. The ceremony is often called a squaw dance in English because of a social feature in the evenings where a girl chooses her partner for a dance.

Earth Woman [Navajo Mountain] and Oljato. How long these homes had been sitting there, I do not know.

On another trip, we traveled through the place now called Bluff, but in those days it was called Tooh [River or San Juan River]. My brother wanted to buy a horse so we went through there, but there was no road between the rocks.[25] We had to walk up on a wagon trail to the top. Once I was walking back from Bluff, and there was a white man carrying firewood on his back just like the Navajos did. As I looked around, I saw another person carrying a log. The buildings in Bluff were built of wood and stones and looked poorly made. During the time when wagons were in use, there were only a few buildings in Bluff. This was what I saw during this time.

RECOLLECTIONS OF UTES

My brother and I later went to Allen Canyon, where he got his big horse. There was an Anglo living at the edge of the canyon under a big cotton-wood tree. He motioned to us, but we did not know what he was saying. A white-haired Ute woman was there, playing cards by herself. She asked my brother what his name was, and my brother told her; her name was Binálí [Benally—paternal grandparent or grandchild]. We asked where her people were living, and she replied that she was the only one there, but when we went to another place, we found another Ute with a crippled walk. The Utes said their land was at Towaoc, but that they had moved to Allen Canyon and did not know if they were to move again.[26]

---

25. Today's road that goes through Cow Canyon to the river plain upon which Bluff stands had not been built. The old road used to snake its way up Recapture Canyon, pass south of Mustang Mesa, then wind through Devil's and South Montezuma canyons to Monticello.

26. John Holiday recalls what he considers the history of the Utes, actually the San Juan Paiutes, who live in this area. While his version varies from what these people say, it offers interesting insights into how the Navajos perceive Paiute migrations. "These Ute people migrated from Wide Prairie of Willows and moved through this territory—from Navajo Mountain to the mountains northeast of Monument Valley. Some decided to remain in certain areas, while the rest went on. Some stayed behind in Navajo Mountain. They moved through lower Oljato and camped in the sand dunes. But while they were there, they became ill from some disease, and many perished. Those who survived moved to Douglas Mesa. The rest moved on to Bluff City and to Allen Canyon, northwest of Blanding, and then back to White Mesa [eleven miles south of Blanding], where they now live. I was old enough in those days and can still remember that." For a detailed history of the San Juan Paiute, see Pamela A. Bunte and Robert J. Franklin, *From the Sands to the Mountains: Change and Persistence in a Southern Paiute Community* (Lincoln: University of Nebraska Press, 1987).

Utes photographed in Bluff in 1915. Oshley visited these people in Allen Canyon and in their camps west of Bluff. (Photo from Special Collections, University of Nevada-Reno)

Their homes were formed by a circle of branches, and their bedding was made of juniper leaves covered with juniper bark on top. They made food for us which my brother ate, but I did not like. I did not see them make any kind of structure for themselves until recently, when one built a hogan in the canyon. Then they started looking at life in a different way and got help with their houses. We left there, and as we were traveling, I asked him if he really liked the food. He just laughed at me. This was the first time I saw the Utes.

After this journey, many trips followed. Suddenly, there were a lot of Utes. Some were in Bluff City; others, I heard, lived on Douglas Mesa and some near where Blanding is today. Their leader was called K'os ádinii [No Neck]. Eventually, they no longer lived in the area of Blanding, as the town grew before my eyes. It seemed like the Utes' favorite pastime was playing cards. Even the women were involved.

There were also things that I heard about the Utes in these early days. I was told they were our enemies. There was a man called Át'íinii [One Who Did It], who started the warfare between the Utes and Navajos. This man was a Paiute. I do not know who he was, but he caused the war and then fled. We [Navajos] did not have anything to do with it. The Utes became hostile and killed some Navajos who had nothing to do with them. In my opinion, they should have killed the person who started it. Several innocent people—men and women—died because of this man. We were living around Tonalea [Where Water Flows and Collects] at a place called Red Grass when we got news that the Utes were warring.[27] This was back when I did not have a wife.

Some of the Utes were living near the wash on this [west] side of Bluff. Often they lived in the crevices of the rocks nearby. They set up a trap for the white people who were oppressive. One of the Utes fled, and another went to the gray-hill area because someone had stolen something. One of the Ute leader's sons was going to be taken to prison, and his father got mad. The father had a log for cover and placed the wood near where he was going to ambush the people that were taking his son. But it did not take place. The people that were taking the son got scared.

In Bluff there is a cemetery. The leader tried to get up the cliff, and he was shot right in the forehead. After this incident, the Utes fled to Comb Ridge, where they hid out. The white people from Blanding arrived there on horseback in the nighttime. They imitated the coyotes as they looked for them. On this particular night, it was raining, and the ground was muddy. I did not see this incident. I was on the reservation, and I was still single then. One white man was killed by the Utes. That is all I heard.

Finally, the most prominent leaders came and gathered somewhere on Comb Ridge. There was a huge crowd. They had everything there. There was food, slaughtered cows hanging there, and people tracking the killers. Some set up ambushes from the brush, and they killed one Ute. Some said two white men were shot. What is the true story, I do not know. Then the leaders left, and one white person was in the middle of the road, yelling. He was yelling to gather the people back up.

Everybody came back to the camp and also to Bluff. It was said that a lot of Utes were in jail in Bluff. The Decrepit Cowboy [Clarence Perkins] was the one rounding up these Utes. His sons were also helping. There were some other cowboys who were mean. Then there was another

27. The following account about the Utes, as Oshley points out, is hearsay and some-what confusing. There was a low-grade conflict between the whites and Utes from the 1880s through 1923, when the last incident occurred. Oshley appears to be mix-ing two different incidents—the fight in Bluff (1915) and the one in Blanding (1923), both of which resulted in compromising Ute survival in San Juan County even further. If these are the two events that he is describing, additional information can be found in *A History of San Juan County*. At the least, this story reflects Oshley's perception of the Utes and Anglos at this time.

Sheep and goats in Monument Valley, a grazing area well known to Oshley. (Photo by author)

white man who was called One Who Cackles [Arthur Spencer]. He really hated the Utes. He was also part of the group that tracked them down. It was said that the Utes would be fenced in. No Hat [James Douglas] was there. He was some sort of leader among the white men and even among the soldiers. I did not get to see him. I was just told this. Then things settled down. This is what I heard. Only one Ute was killed, and he was very aggressive. He was a soldier. I do not quite remember if one or two white men were killed. This is what they did. This is all I know.

AN INTRODUCTION TO WITCHCRAFT

Another thing I learned about as I was growing up is witchcraft. My grandmother told me about it as I became more aware of my surroundings [maturing]. I did not believe her and asked, "How could someone come up with such stories?" This was in the spring when the wind blew hard. Sometimes we would lose sheep in this kind of weather, so it was not surprising when we started to miss some of our castrated rams. We lost three or four of them, yet I still did not believe that anything concerning witchcraft was happening. But when the wind was blowing, and the sheep went to the rocks, I would find coyote tracks. If there was no wind, it did not happen, and we lost no animals.

I counted the sheep. The next day, the wind blew. I gathered the sheep, counted them, and found that one was missing. I thought maybe some had fallen back. I went to where they had been grazing but saw no tracks leading away. Then I found a big dog's track and those of a coyote and wondered if they had killed the sheep. I discovered only a little bit of wool on the rock but no sign of blood.

I told my aunt, Woman Who Owns the House, about it, and she said there was a song that skinwalkers used to make something small so it can be patted into a small package.[28] At the start of this ceremony, the once-living object was a normal size. The skinwalker then sang as it patted the object into a smaller size that could be easily carried. I was told this and did not believe it. But after I could not find the sheep, I started to think of some possible ways to explain what had happened. Woman Who Owns the House was really good with hand trembling, so I told her and my older brother that I kind of believed in what had taken place and asked them when the skinwalker might return. My aunt told me that it would come in two days, but I was still not sure. I wondered how it was possible to know ahead of time when this thing would happen.

The morning of the day that the skinwalker was to return, we put the lambs and kids into the cave that was corralled off on the sunny side of a large rock. The question was brought up as to who would enter the sheep corral. They told me I was a good choice. As night approached, there was a ceremony performed to get the skinwalker. The rifle had a sacred name, one not used every day, which they used in this ceremony. They put something on me called *'atł'izh* [bile].[29] The skinwalker may put something on a person to kill him. This thing was put on me to protect

---

28. The ability to sing songs or say prayers to shrink objects and make them portable first developed in the worlds beneath this one. First Man, a Navajo deity, held powers for good and evil and was the first person to practice witchcraft. The power to shrink and later expand something may be applied to objects as large as a mountain or hogan and as small as an animal or pebble.

29. Gall medicine is one of the most common antidotes to ward off the effects of corpse poison used by skinwalkers. The medicine is frequently made from the gall of eagles, bears, mountain lions, and skunks. Gall medicine is also carried by Navajos when they travel away from home or familiar surroundings because they may encounter a stranger who wants to place a spell on them. Later in Oshley's account, just such an event occurs. For further information on beliefs concerning witchcraft, see Clyde Kluckhohn, *Navajo Witchcraft* (Boston: Beacon Press, 1967).

me. The skinwalker puts *'ánt'ííh* [corpse poison] on people.[30] My grandmother said that the skinwalker makes this corpse poison by pinching off
pieces at the joints of a dead person. I did not see this happen but just
heard of it. This material is made into a fine powder that is very dangerous. When skinwalkers are in the process of getting corpse poison, they
do it behind some sort of curtain, where they take out the dead person's
saliva and many other things.[31]

The potion that counteracts this corpse poison is bile. Nowadays,
people do not use the bile that was used in the old days. I think now they
use bird bile. My aunt had bile that had been given to her and passed
down from generation to generation. This bile was from bobcats, wolves,
and mountain lions. I was taken inside and told that some skinwalkers
were like us: They traveled upright. Others are in an animal form. I still
did not believe it.

After the ceremony was done on me with the bile, I was given a
sheepskin, water, food, and a rifle and told to stay in the corral the whole
day and not leave for even a minute.

Inside, the children asked about me and were told that I went somewhere, but really I was hidden in the corral. I was in a sitting position, but
after awhile my body ached. The sheep were brought back from grazing,
and the lambs and kids were taken out.

There I sat in the night. The moments went by but I sat still. It was
toward morning, when the breeze came, that the sheep became restless.
They made snorting noises while the dogs whimpered, then quieted
down. The moon was shining. I put the bullet in the gun. Then I heard it
coming, and it came with a loud sound—really loud. It sounded like a
horse running. It was in the sheep corral and tried to get the sheep into a
corner. It was as big as the finest large dog. This one had red fur and a
white streak down its face. Its tail was just hanging there and did not look
like it was connected to the body. Maybe it was just sewn on. I think it

---

30. Corpse poison is made of decayed flesh or fluids from dead bodies and is used to
cause fainting, lockjaw, swelling, unconsciousness, and general loss of health and
vitality in a victim. The substance is said to be ground into a fine powder similar to
corn pollen and administered by dropping it down a smoke hole in a hogan, putting
it on someone asleep, or blowing it on a person in a crowd.

31. Some Navajos say that witches meet as groups in a cave or a crack in a rock which
opens up into a large room. Once assembled, they plot, pray, and sing against their
victim; practice cannibalism; and participate in other activities that are the antithe-
sis of acceptable Navajo behavior. Corpse poison is made during this time from
bodies stolen from graves.

was either its tail or its claw that was making a sound like a pack rat. I looked at it very closely and could smell something. As it walked by me, I shot, and it howled like a human.

I didn't want the dogs. I wanted to shoot them all when they took off after it. I stayed behind for awhile, then later started after them. My brother and I spotted the tracks, but they just kept on going up the canyon. One of our horses was very fast so my brother sped after it. He said that quite a ways off, there was a clearing where the skinwalker had sat to clean off the blood with some plants. Farther on was the same thing—blood on some plants and a blood trail leading away. It went past Much Wool [or Fur—El Capitan] and onto the higher plateau.[32] My brother said that by this time, it had gotten dark, so he just turned back and arrived home when it was really dark. He had last seen the tracks at a place we called the Place Where It Vibrates Up and Down.

We next used hand trembling. Woman Who Owns the House said we would know in five days. In five days, a man named Biłįį' dilwo'ii [His Fast Horse], son of Man Who Flies of the Tł'ízí łání [Many Goats] clan and who was from that area, came to visit us. He said a man named [name deleted for confidentiality] of the Dibé łizhiní [Black Sheep] clan shot himself. There are ways for these skinwalkers to weasel out of these messes.[33]

As the visitor's story went on, he said the person that shot himself was getting at a lynx with the butt of his rifle. As a result, the lynx grabbed onto the trigger and shot the man. He died before the next sunset, trying to get home. This man had two wives who buried him right there. He lived above [place name deleted], on top of the mesa. If you were to go there, it would take a day or so. His home was right past a place called Cleared Space Land. So it was really him.

This experience made me realize that there really were skinwalkers. This is real because I shot one, and that is proof enough for me. I just wonder about it and how it could be. I even asked another person how this could be. That person said it is very holy. He said they have grease or

---

32. El Capitan is a large volcanic neck about fifteen miles outside of Kayenta, Arizona. There are a number of stories and powers associated with this prominent feature. For example, it is said to be a support that holds up the sky, a twiner used in processing wool for weaving, and a resting place for Big Snake during the time of the myths. See McPherson, *Sacred Land, Sacred View*, 29–31.

33. This is a common explanation that runs through most stories about skinwalkers who get shot. There is always an accident to explain how a person was wounded or killed, which removes any possibility that he or she was practicing witchcraft at the time. This explanation frees other family members from suspicion.

El Capitan, a volcanic neck found in Monument Valley. This important landmark has many teachings associated with it. (Photo by author)

an ointment of some type used to harm people. When they point this grease toward a person or hold it over them, that person just passes out and dies. This is what it was like, so this was a very powerful potion to use against people. This is when I started believing that the power to do wrong was in the midst of us.

It is very sacred.[34] This was when I was told about how sacred it was. These things were talked about behind closed doors—even though they had only a blanket for a door then. From that day on, I took extra care of myself. I have become more aware, and I observe more. Now I feel I have really matured.

34.　The word *sacred* has a different meaning here than in the Judeo-Christian world. Many traditional Navajo people think of power as merely existing; a person may choose to manipulate it for good or bad. Just as electricity can either cook food and heat a home or electrocute an individual, the power in the universe can be used to help or harm. In either case, appropriate prayers and actions are needed to summon and control the power, by putting one in contact with supernatural forces. The entire role of power—for good or bad—was planned in the underworlds by First Man, First Woman, and other holy beings. Choosing how to use this power is left to the individual.

Another time my grandmother told me that someone had gone hunting and shot a coyote that had run into some bushes. The person looked to see which way the animal would come out, then slowly crept to where the coyote had gone. There sat a woman, a skinwalker, with a coyote skin beside her. The hunter said that he did not mean to shoot her and that he had thought she was a coyote. The woman remained there. The person who shot the coyote cleaned off the hooked thorns from a cactus and put it on the woman's wound. He gave her food and water, and after thirty days, he asked her if she was well again. She said she was so the man told her to be on her way. She tried to put her coyote skin back on. Then she finally said that if someone was watching, the skin would not do it. The person went over the hill. As he glanced back, the coyote was running the other way, going back to where it had come from.

Before leaving, this woman told him to come to her home because she had a lot of sheep and her father was very knowledgeable. Many days passed, however, before the hunter went there. A man asked him where he was from, and he told him. The woman had said she was from a place called Burnt Corn. The hunter told the other man what he had done, and they shook hands. The woman had gone to herd the sheep that day. A message was sent to her, and she came back. He was given forty sheep, a red coral necklace, and told this was for not telling about the woman. He brought the sheep back.

I questioned my grandmother after hearing this story. How could this be true? My grandmother said it was. This witchcraft and skinwalking are very powerful and used to get rain.[35] That is how powerful it is. They also ask for certain things through it, and they get it. Some use it to kill a person, and sometimes it backfires, and the person that knows this [witchcraft] dies.

---

35. This seeming dichotomy—the connection of rain (synonymous with fertility and growth) with witchcraft—is another example of the way good and evil are interconnected and situational. Some Navajos explain that witchcraft has been in this world from its beginning and will not end because "there is a birth every moment." It will only cease to exist when this creation does. The world endures because through witchcraft and skinwalking, rain comes to the earth. Practitioners put *ntł'iz*—a mixture of sacred white shell, turquoise, abalone, and jet—near water seeps so clouds will form and rain can nurture the soil. Just as a person may obtain benefits like livestock and success in hunting by using witchcraft, so this power can summon clouds, rain, and life-producing moisture to make someone richer.

The Power of Hand Trembling

I also learned about hand trembling.[36] My mother had sisters, and one was very good at it. I asked her if I could be her apprentice, but she said no because it was a very powerful thing to have. I said if it is so powerful, why am I not allowed to learn it? So later, when there was a sick man, she started teaching me. This is the only time such learning is permitted. She lightly clapped her hand over mine, urging it to move. Then it happened. My hand went out, and that is how I learned hand trembling. The man was suffering from Evil Way.[37] It felt like feathers were standing, and that has to do with Evil Way. She said, "Yes, that is the one," as the hand trembling signaled the problem that ailed the man. She said, "You will lead your life this way. People will want help from you. My son, this hand trembling is not for you to get rich on. Only a few dollars are the reward for your service. Maybe from one person you might get a sheep in exchange for your service, while another man might give you very little. So, my son, through this you do not get wealthy." I said, "So be it."

When a person's hand begins to tremble, a chant is started for that person, and then another. My hand trembling comes to me when I hold out my hand. It just starts; that is all. Sometimes I hadn't even started the chant when my hand would go at it. I used to get strong signals from hand trembling, but now they do not come in that clearly. Maybe my aging has to do with the decline in receiving the signals; I do not know what is causing it. You have to have good thinking called *hóyéé'* in order to get the signals.[38]

---

36. There are four types of Navajo divination or diagnosing—listening, stargazing, crystal gazing, and hand trembling—all of which are related and serve similar functions. They are used to examine the unknown, find lost people or objects, identify a thief or witch, locate water or other desirable resources, prevent danger or evil, and, most frequently, determine the cause of an illness in order to remedy it.

37. The Evil Way is a classification of ceremonies with rites that last no longer than five nights and that remove the influence of ghosts of foreign enemies. The most prominent ceremonial characteristics are blackening the patient's body with ashes, brushing evil away from a patient with an eagle-feather fan, and cutting yucca fibre tied around parts of the patient's body. All of these are accompanied by songs and prayers. One of the most widespread Evil Way ceremonies is the Enemy Way ritual. For a brief synopsis of various Evil Way and Blessing Way rituals, see Wyman, "Navajo Ceremonial System," 536–57.

38. Something that is *hóyéé'* is very powerful and evokes a deep respect that borders on fear. It may be literally translated as "dreadful" or "terrifying," indicating that thin line between reverence and fear when dealing with holy beings. Knowledge of something that is *hóyéé'* may be burdensome because using it properly requires personal responsibility.

If hand trembling turns against you, it is also called *hóyéé'*. My aunt said if hand trembling turned against you, you would punish yourself by ripping yourself apart. I said I would not allow this to happen to me. I did not believe it at the time, but my aunt said that was how it was. She said that when a person is hand trembling, he might poke himself in the eye or in the nose. I said the person should move his head this way or that way. My aunt asked me in a disappointed voice what I was saying. She wanted me to stop talking in this way. It took a lot of convincing to have her teach me hand trembling. She was trying to tell me that she was giving me something very holy and that it cannot be passed on just for the sake of giving it. It must be held with wisdom and respect. Holiness is sacred and comes with prayers and chants. So the main thing is to make a bridge across from daily life to the sacred to receive the signals and interpret them as *hóyéé'*.

One time I was hand trembling in Dennehotso when the power told me I was an idiot and twisted my nose. The patient was very sick with a swollen stomach due to Evil Way. It was easy to interpret the signal, but I didn't. Therefore, the power told me I was a fool and asked why I had a big nose and looked like an ogre. I tried to dodge it, but it twisted my nose and almost ripped it off. I thought of a burial site, and it told me that was right. If I hadn't gotten the interpretation right, I would probably have no nose now. One person who was watching asked me why I did that, and I replied, "My hand did it." Woman Who Owns the House said, "See what I told you. You almost ripped off your nose."

Songs accompany hand trembling. For me just a few short ones, but other individuals have long chants that go with it. When a person's hand begins to tremble, a chant is started for that person, then another. My hand trembling comes to me when I hold out my hand. It starts; that is all. Sometimes I don't even start the chant, and my hand goes at it.

Conflict and Evil Way

While I was still a young man living in Dennehotso, we would dam the runoff water when the planting season began. This was a lot of work, but there were a lot of people helping each other. When everybody was resting, someone would suggest that we play cards before going home to eat. The next day, we would play cards again during the rest period.

One time I won a braided leather rope that another man wanted. He wanted me to fight for it. I was strong at that time, but now I fall over my

The portion of Cane Valley where Gambler's Camp was located (against the rock formation on left side of photo). Photo taken from midpoint of Where Dynamite Made a Road.
(Photo by author)

own fat.[39] I picked him up, and the other players got out of the way. He
tried to kick me but missed. I was trying to get him on the ground, just
like he was trying to do with me. We both fell on our sides. The people
watching saw dirt fly up as we fell with a loud thump. I was the first one
back up; he was slow. I grabbed him, and that was when the people pulled
us apart. He was told when he got back up that he had said he was strong,
but he had lied to intimidate us. He was silenced by the event. People who
lived around there heard of it. Later I went back to my mother's place.

The man told my mother how strong I was, and he said he would
get stronger. My mother heard this and got after me for wrestling. She
said she had heard that the man I wrestled knew witchcraft and that it
was a bad thing to provoke a person who knew it. I asked if it would be
better to let him do what he wanted to me, since he had started the trouble, and I had fought in self-defense.

---

39. Oshley is using a metaphor that borders on a joke. He was always thin—even
skinny—because of the active life he led.

This fight occurred two days before the people went on a rabbit hunt. My older brother [again, probably Gambler] had beautiful-looking horses, which we saddled for the hunt. As I chased a rabbit on the rocky surface, my horse lost its footing and tumbled over me. I wore moccasins for shoes, and so the horse smashed my foot badly. What I think caused my mishap was the wrestling with that man who fought me. My ankle and leg gradually healed.

After I had gotten well, I roamed. Two of us were climbing a cliff, and as I poked my head above the rim, I heard a loud thump, and there above stood a mountain lion. The cat almost grabbed onto my hair, which was tied up in the traditional knot. We chased the mountain lion, but it was fast and outran us to the upper cliffs. It seemed like I was having bad luck.

Another time during the summer, I had rounded up the horses in a box canyon. I used a short rope to catch a horse, but after lassoing it, the horse ran off, causing me to fall. I held onto the rope as the horse ran and pulled me. The rope tightened around its neck, the horse fell down, then I jumped up and ran after it. To avoid getting dragged over a pointed stick, I jumped to one side, but a little while later, there was a pain in my chest.

My older brother also roped a horse to ride while looking for a cow that was going to have a calf. But I could not join him because of the pain, so I lay down under a tree and rested. When I walked around, the pain felt slightly better. My brother came back very late in the afternoon and told me the cow had had her calf.

The next day, we went after the horses again. I only had ropes and a bridle with me. When I found the horses, I tried to drive them into a box canyon, but they would not go in so I drove them against a cliff. I was going to rope a certain horse but lassoed the wrong one, the one that was not tamed. The horse jumped over a twenty-foot cliff so I let go of the rope. All I heard was a thump; all I could see was dust. The horse was dead. It had belonged to my older brother's wife. I had a very depressing feeling as I removed the rope from the dead horse and watched the other horses run out into the open space.

Again I drove them back into the hills and cliffs of the mesa, where I finally roped the tamed one. After this I drove the horses back home but thought about the one that had just died. I knew my intention was not to harm the animal, so I decided to tell my older brother's wife of the event just the way it had occurred. She did not get mad at me, saying that things happen that we sometimes have no control over. There were no harsh words from her or my older brother, confirming that the best thing to do in this type of situation is to tell the truth. The following day, I went again on foot with only my rope and bridle for the horses. As I climbed to the top of Red Sitting One, I thought of how I should have roped a horse and rode it, but I was in good health, feeling like I could overcome any obstacle. There were two horses there, and I drove them on top of Red Sitting One. The horse I roped was very spirited and had not been really tamed. When I first sat on the horse, it just gave me a little bump, and that was all.

My older brother and I now worked with the cattle. He asked me to ride a two-year-old calf that was a little bigger than most of the other calves. I had ridden horses and burros that bucked, but cows were very different. This one bucked with sharp movements so that I could not get a solid grip with my legs. Soon I was on the ground. My brother said that he thought I had said that I was powerful and mighty, and now he asked what had happened! The calf bucked so hard that neither I nor anyone else could stay on it. Eventually, we marked the calves' ears, and since I had only a few head, my older brother gave me three of these cows, which later had calves; I was very happy about it. We both had the same brand.

My older brother's father joined us for two or three days to perform *asht'eezh*. This is when two people exchange things at the Enemy Way ceremony. A person blackens you for a payment, such as a blanket, cow, or horse. For the rest of one's life, this exchange continues each year or once every two years. This is called *deest'a'* [annual exchange]. This man was given a horse, but I followed him back because I thought he was only borrowing it. I set out on foot for my mother's place and told her about it, but by then I was not feeling well. I felt irritated all over and asked my mother why. When I went after the goats, I felt chills, but they were not from the cold. I built a fire, then felt all right, but it was almost sunset when I got the sheep into the corral. My mother told me that if it was cold, for me to get back to my brother's home at On Top of the Water, where the road was blasted down.

Since I felt better if I moved around, the next day I went to see my older brother, Gambler, and told him I did not feel well. It felt like ants had stung me all over, and I had no desire to eat. I went back to my mother at Dove Springs and told her I could not stand it anymore. My mother said that something called Evil Way was bothering me.

It seemed like everybody that looked at me said I appeared sick. My relatives started talking about what should be done. My brother said that first we needed to get some firewood. I was asked to take the horses to the water to drink. My sister-in-law asked why they were making me do chores when I was sick, but they were hiding from me what they were going to do. My brother told me to take the horses slowly to the water. I said okay and was off.

I was a little ways from the water, which was somewhat hard to get to, when something happened. I got off this tame horse, and that is all I can remember. Suddenly I saw, right out in the middle of nowhere, a lot of people. It was late in the afternoon, and these people were dancing and throwing things in my face. When I opened my eyes, no one was around; I was very weak and could hardly stand up. The horses were still standing there so I let them drink water before I drove them home. By this time, I had to hold onto the saddle to stay on the horse. My aunt and mother came running out. I lay down and started hallucinating, seeing people who were not there. When I opened my eyes, I heard people saying the illness called Evil Way was bothering me. That evening a ceremony was started.

At first my head hurt; then my whole body started to throb. It seemed my hands were the only things that had strength; the rest was weak as if something was subduing me. As soon as I closed my eyes, some people would come and try to overpower me, then I would start to vomit. The medicine man fluttered eagle feathers over me and around the room. When a medicine man is shaking the feathers, he is chasing the spirits away, and so a person should not bother him when he is doing this. My relatives thought they had lost me to the other side of life so my mother and aunt were crying. The ceremony started, and I was blackened with ashes from burned herbs. The next day was the first fire building. Some people were having another ceremony elsewhere and wanted to know if I was still alive. They came constantly to find out if I was dying. At first I did not believe in the ceremonies, but when I was healed, I knew that they were true. They really cured me.

Evil Way and Blessing Way

The origin of Evil Way tells of when a coyote had a skin from the dead.[40] He visited some people and told them that if they were so knowledgeable in sacred ways, that they should prove it to him. He threw the skin of a

---

40.   This is actually another part of the origin story of the Evil Way ceremony. The beginning tells how Monster Slayer and his brother, Born for Water, returned to their mother's (Changing Woman's) home after killing *Yé'iitsoh*, a giant monster who had plagued the Navajo people with his cannibalism. After he had been killed and his body parts tossed around the landscape, *Yé'iitsoh's* ghost still bothered the Twins, causing them to faint and feel weak. Herbs and other ceremonial objects

dead person onto another being, who became ill. It was a really dry skin of a ghost, but what kind I do not know. The being's life was slowly fading away. The coyote acted naughty and laughed at the sick person. The coyote said, "If you are so knowledgeable, heal this being." So the being prepared an arrow as the coyote sat there. The others chanted against the coyote and in the song, the arrow was directed at him, but coyote did not believe the arrow would kill him. As the Evil Way was being sung, the coyote said, "That won't be the case. I am above all that." The performer of the ceremony cried, and as the singing continued, the arrow raised and started moving around the room.

At first the coyote made fun of the ceremony, even though he knew the arrow was being prepared for him. The arrow made a lot of noise as it sailed around the hogan. Then pretty soon, the coyote was trying to get away from the arrow. It took off after coyote, who yelled, "Whoohii," as he ran over the hill. The coyote hid in a rock crevice called Standing Rock, but where this is, I do not know. Now at that place, there is a pine tree, which was the arrow that killed the coyote. This tree has the skin of coyote strung around it. From that time, medicine men acquired the Evil Way ceremony. This is the way the Evil Way originated, showing that the being who tried to harm the other person can become part of the ceremony.

The arrow used to kill a coyote was placed before me. These days medicine men who perform Evil Way do not have the arrow that killed the coyote. This man, who was an in-law by clan, was really good with his ceremony. On the fifth day, I wanted to go outside so I told the people to help me. I sat outside, and they played games. When different people came, they said that I was really near death, and now I was all right, even though I was just skin and bones, a pitiful sight. Now my joints felt strong, and I thought I was well again.

When people have this ceremony performed, the medicine man tells them they are not to eat things such as the head, heart, liver, lungs, windpipe, and the intestines of a sheep, goat, cow, horse, or any other type of animal ordinarily eaten by Navajos. I wondered why anyone would do such things. The next day, after the people departed for their homes, I saw a cooked sheep's head sitting near the fire. I told my relatives, as I picked up the head,

---

were applied while songs and prayers were recited, and the boys were healed, initiating an important ceremony that is widely practiced today.

The story of Coyote, the trickster, shows what happens when the ceremony is not respected. In his usual way, he took the performance of the sacred Evil Way too lightly and was chastised and killed. Thus, powerful things should not be handled carelessly or mocked.

that no one had told me that I should not eat certain things. I wanted to get well and eat well, so I ate the sheep head. This is what happened.

In the past, it was different. My grandmother said that the forbidden food was the tip of the tongue. Most of the things you were not to eat were the tips of things. Nowadays, the medicine men tell you not to eat the whole thing, like the sheep head.

Part of the ceremony done on the last night included cooking the forbidden parts in a Navajo pot that has had pollen added. This was called *ałtąąná' ashbéézh* [literally, "things boiled together"]. The next morning, the appropriate songs were sung, and the people ate the forbidden food after the medicine man sang and gave the first taste to the patient. Throughout this meal, one prays for good things like health.

All the other people eat the stew while praying for their well-being and that of their neighbors. They also pray for better livestock, rain, plants, and water. Also included in the prayers are the sacred mountains, starting with the east and going around to the south, then to the west, and then to the north. Then all of the mountains are prayed to: Navajo Mountain, Henry Mountain, Blue Mountain, and La Sal Mountain. They are prayed for along with the immediate surroundings, like the cornfields. We ask for more corn pollen for the year's crop. On the trail of corn pollen, we travel along on the beauty trail. It is our life, our journey through life, as well as our future.

This ceremony was done on me, and I got well through it. I really believe in the power of healing through this ceremony. During the Blessing Way part of the ceremony, corn pollen is used to put a person on the beauty trail.[41] The medicine man says we hold onto corn pollen, arrowheads, and the Blessing Way pouch containing sacred materials. The ceremony is not a frightening thing. It is there for getting well. The Blessing Way ceremony is for the baby. If the ceremony is not done for the baby, it is said the baby needs to eat corn pollen. The proper way to have the Evil Way ceremony performed is to have it first before you have the Blessing Way. The Evil Way ceremony contains mostly prayers against bad things [such as witchcraft]. After this ceremony, you clear the way for the Blessing Way ceremony.

---

41.   A portion of the Blessing Way ceremony is performed at the end of most ceremonials to mitigate the effect of any mistakes and insure good health and protection for the patient. There are five types of Blessing Way ceremonies, all of which are intended to restore good luck, harmony, peace, and balance as well as provide protection. Traditional Navajos view the Blessing Way as "the backbone of their religion and give it historical precedence over all other ceremonials." Wyman, 540.

In the Blessing Way ceremony, a yucca root is dug up and used for the washing of the hair. Then white [for males] or yellow [for females] cornmeal is used to dry off the patient. After this there is another prayer, then the real ceremony begins. It starts off when it gets dark. The different chants are sung. Nowadays, the people spread fabric [and blankets] for the girls just as the sun sets. A long time ago, the ceremony, fabric and all, did not start until midnight. There were stories to be told between sunset and the time of spreading the fabric and blankets. It used to be said that just as soon as the sun went down, the evil spirits came out, along with the gossipers and the ghosts. That is why the ceremony takes place late at night with all the fabric and blankets spread out for the medicine bundle. The ceremony ends when the dawn is visible. It was good this way.

Now people are doing the ceremony all wrong, partly because this younger generation of men and women is going to school.[42] For this reason, they do not believe in the ceremonies, which have been our life. They [ceremonies] are our well-being and our body. For this reason, our environment is not what it is supposed to be. There is no rain and no snow because of this. If the people really believed in the ceremonies, the rain would be here again. It would be like this, I think. What I am telling you is not folktales but is true, and I have lived it.

A long time ago, there was a giant monster called Yé'iitsoh [Big God, giant], who ate humans. This was when coyotes were like people, and he ate them.[43] The birds were once people, and he ate them, too. This is according to what some say. I do not know this myself.[44] There was this

---

42. This comment is somewhat ironic and reflects Oshley's ambivalence about the mixed blessings of education. In terms of economic prosperity, education is helpful, but it may have a negative effect on traditional beliefs and practices. Navajo Oshley encouraged all of his children to obtain as much education as they could. As will be discussed later, he took an active role in walking them to school, sitting with them in the classroom and freeing them from home responsibilities so they could get an education. His wife, Mary, often did not share his feelings.

43. Oshley is referring to the time of creation, the time of the myths, "the Palm of Time," when animals spoke to humankind just as people communicate today.

44. This is an interesting comment since Monster Slayer, Born for Water, and the killing of the monsters play such a prominent role in traditional Navajo beliefs and ceremonies. This phrasing could also be a storytelling formula, glossed as "That is what they say," meaning that he was not personally present. Oshley is relating a very abbreviated form of the origin of the Enemy Way ceremony. One of its primary uses is to protect against enemies such as the Utes, Comanches, Japanese (in World War II), and the white man.

human named Monster Slayer, but who he was, I do not know, except that he killed the monsters. By doing this, it somehow affected him, and he was dying. He was one of the twins. The other twin [Born for Water] stayed back and took care of the home. Monster Slayer was told that the Enemy Way ceremony would be held for him. Where they got part of the ceremony, it is not known. Some say the need for it arose from the killing of Big God. Part of Big God was brought back. Ashes were put over this object.[45] That is how Monster Slayer was cured.

I had an Enemy Way ceremony done on me, and it really healed me. At first I did not believe in it and went to the clinic, but when I had the ceremony performed, it worked. I really believe that the ceremonies heal you because I got well and am still here. Sometimes I am sick, but no matter what hardship I have, I still get better.

This was the first time a five-day ceremony was done on me. I now believe in the healing powers of Navajo ceremonies. My elders said the same things. The Mormons do not believe in what I believe. They think it is a bunch of nonsense. For this reason, I am not going to tell anyone what they ought to believe, but I believe what I believe. These beliefs made me aware of what I am, a Navajo. My mother is a Navajo, and the people that I associate with are Navajos.

There are medicine pouches which contain the whole ceremony and the tools to perform it. Some of these ceremonies are Blessing Way, arrowheads, Blessing Way pouch, and prayers—all of which are powerful when in the hands of medicine men. Prayers are said for water and living things like ducks and horses. The horse has a sacred name which is used when one is praying for it. These prayers, songs, tools, and other things pertain to the essence of our lives and have been handed down from many generations. They are also part of our physical body and bring rain.

When there is no rain, people start to pray. Snow is also prayed for, and to show appreciation for it, one takes snow baths early in the morning. This is the good way. The people pray to the heavens, and when the snow comes, the people say prayers of appreciation and give thanks that they will harvest various kinds of crops the following year. All of these things that a Navajo does and prays for are also in the physical body and are part of one's journey through life. It is like this.

---

45.   During the Enemy Way, a scalp, bone, or some other part of an "enemy" is sung over and later shot with a gun and destroyed as part of the exorcism. This object represents the alien ghost afflicting the patient.

Young Navajo riders in Bluff in the early 1900s. Groups like this formed hunting and trading parties. (Photo courtesy of the San Juan Historical Commission)

MORE SICKNESS

After I got well from having the ceremony performed on me, I wanted to look for work, but my older sister and mother asked me to stay around our home. I remained for a whole year. It was in the fall that I went to Dennehotso. This was where my mother had moved. When I arrived, we planned to go rabbit hunting. I borrowed a horse from a person who lived just west of Dennehotso at Red Water Point.

There were about eight or nine of us that summer morning who were on horseback chasing rabbits. We were out on a plains area, covered only by shrubs of gray greasewood. The people chasing the rabbits used a club to clunk the rabbits on the head. I did not kill any that day, even though I was confident in my every move. The other hunters had killed some jackrabbits. This was sometimes a main source of food. Some of the hunters had jackrabbits tied onto their saddles. Toward evening I finally got two rabbits.

In the custom of hunting rabbits, whoever gets one keeps it, even if someone else killed it. There was no fighting over the rabbits. No one said that he hit a certain rabbit; it just belonged to the first person who picked it up. So I got two rabbits. We ate them for supper. We had gravy on the rabbits, they tasted good, and we were happy to have a good meal.

We all went to sleep, but I suddenly woke up at midnight. There was an unbearable pain in the upper part of my body. My mother started the fire and brought out herbs that came from around a tree that was struck by lightning. She sent word to our closest relative, who came over and held a meeting about what was wrong with me. They said that maybe it was the ceremony that I had just recently had. Then one of my brothers named Tłʼahii [Lefty] came riding in. He saw that I was sick and asked my mother what we should do. The pain was unbearable, but I listened to what they were talking about.

They thought that somewhere in the ceremony there was a mistake. Then my mother said maybe it was because when she had given birth to me, she did not have a Blessing Way performed. She said the corn pollen had not been given to me in the Blessing Way. Some ladies came and said it was the Evil Way that was still bothering me. My mother said it could not be, that it was because she had just given birth to me without a ceremony, and that was the problem. She asked if I would like some water and if the Blessing Way was bothering me. I said yes. My relative said that he would go to where my brother's wife's relatives were living and start the preparation. In Dennehotso we did not really have anyone to help with the ceremony. There was no one at my mother's place who could help with it. My relative said that we would get this ceremony underway somehow. Maybe it was really this ceremony that was giving me a hard time.

He took me with him. Riding toward the trading post, we saw Dághaałbáhí [Gray Mustache] nearby. My brother went after him because he knew the Blessing Way ceremony. He asked Gray Mustache at the trading post to perform the ceremony. My brother returned and told me the medicine man would be over that afternoon if that was all right. I said it was better to leave it in his hands because a person usually understands what he is doing without asking a lot of questions. He came to our place that evening and said a prayer for me.

The next day, my hair was washed with yucca root, and I was dried off with cornmeal. Again the medicine man said a prayer for me. Many people came to my ceremony when they heard I was ill. I tried to stretch myself, but it seemed better just to hold onto my chest. I told the medicine man to sing the songs to me that he loved. Some medicine men keep the best songs hidden away. My uncle said he wanted him to do this for me and not to leave anything out of the songs. The medicine man said that was fine with him and that he was pleased that I felt that way.

It was after midnight, and there were a lot of people there. The blankets and fabric were laid out for the medicine pouch to sit on until morning. The medicine man gave me corn pollen and told me to take it when he told me. The songs came in sets, each one moving us closer to dawn. It was near first light, and I do not know if I went to sleep or what happened to me. All I remember was the singing. A small, fat man came into the hogan and approached me. His hair was beautifully done in a knot, and he had red ocher on his face. He fell on his face in front of me. I recognized the person as I looked up and heard people singing. I sat up straight.

It was the crack of dawn. The last song was sung, and I felt better, like a plant that was growing. Then I told about what I had seen and asked my uncle why a man had come in. The medicine man asked me if I recognized the man, and I said yes. I asked why it was like that. He said that if what I had just said was true, then I would get well, and that this man I recognized would die, even though he was usually very friendly to me and treated me like a relative. He had no reason to do this to me. This man lived in Bluff City, and about the same time I was ill, I heard he was, too. He was crying when he died.

This man was of the Tábąąhá [Water's Edge People] clan and lived in the area called Red Rock. He was married into this group of clans that stayed in this area. I knew him only by sight, when we would meet traveling. He would say Water's Edge People is the extended clan of Tódích'íi'nii [Bitter Water People].[46]

I even herded sheep with him one time. When I was moving the livestock to the plains on the other side of Monticello, I was with a Navajo man who told me that things were not going right and that we needed to get another man to take my place for five days. He returned with this man who was from the Water's Edge clan. We exchanged clan relationships, then I said that I was going home. He said that was fine with him, so he stayed there and used my things, like blankets, to witch me. What ceremony he used, I do not know.

The man who took my place in caring for the sheep was the one who came in with his red ocher. He was with me for two days and then five days on his own to do whatever he wanted. The medicine man told me that some of these people would do anything to do away with a person's good circumstances and leave him lying there sick. He could use little scraps of things from my belongings, from the fuzzy balls on my blankets to hair on a brush and small clippings of cloth from clothing.

---

46. An important part of greeting strangers is establishing clan identity. By learning clan affiliations, one understands family, social, and sometimes economic responsibilities and relationships.

Perhaps he did something to me during this time, like using witchcraft through Blessing Way, where he changed some parts of it, to affect
me in an evil way.[47] This was what the medicine man told me. The medicine man said he suspected that something like that might have happened, and so he sang the most powerful song in this ceremony to send
the evil part back to that man, where it had come from. When I had this
Blessing Way ceremony done on me, I found out the powers of the corn
pollen [to heal and protect].

After the song was finished, the medicine man told me and the people
who lived in this household to take the corn pollen out and offer it to the
dawn. I went outside, sprinkled the pollen to the east four times, and said
my own prayer. I passed the corn pollen among the other people; then we
went back inside while the medicine man packed his belongings and left. I
recovered from the illness rapidly. I was happy about being well again.

Two days after the ceremony, I went to my brother's home.[48] My
older brother, Gambler, was going to come and visit me to see how I was.
He was just getting ready when I rode up to his place. I told him what I
had experienced in the ceremony. He said that one cannot trust any man
and that it had always been like that. He also said that a person should not
talk of another person in a harsh way. One never knows what the other
one may know. I agreed with my brother, but I also know that I had not
tried to bully that man, and yet he still did that to me.

HELPING FAMILY MEMBERS

Later I remembered my mother had no firewood and wondered if she was
cold. She still had corn on the cob when I left, and she had a son living
close by, but I told my older brother I was going to help her with the corn
if it was not yet prepared for storage. I went back to her place, and as I

---

47. One way to invoke the power to produce evil is to take a prayer for health and well
    wishing and reverse the words and insert evil thoughts against an individual. Oshley
    believes this man took an object that belonged to him and used sorcery to make him
    sick.
48. Oshley spent a lot of time with his older brother, Gambler, whose camp was located
    near Totem Pole Rock by Sand Spring in the heart of what is now Navajo Tribal
    Park in Monument Valley. There were three large hogans and corrals in this camp,
    which supported only part of Gambler's livestock operations. He kept the remain-
    der of his animals in various camps, one of which was southwest of El Capitan in
    Cane Valley. The main camp was approximately fifteen cross-country miles from
    Dennehotso. Ray Hunt, who for some time owned the Mexican Hat Trading Post,
    traded extensively with Gambler and provided the description of these camps.

rode up, she was sitting in the sun. She looked funny, like she was gnaw-ing on the corn; it was the first time I really had a good laugh in a long time. She said she was getting the corn off the cob, but now her hands had gotten really sore from doing it. She was happy to see me and told me to get a blanket from inside. We got the corn off the cob by pounding each one with a stick while the corn was in a blanket, hanging on posts.

Just as I was going to help my mother, my youngest brother rode up. When she had been by herself, it had taken her a long time to get the corn off the cob, but now with both of us helping, we were done in no time. My mother thanked us for our help and said that she was tired and needed rest. We started to remove the chaff from the corn, but my mother said not to do any more because she could do that herself.

About three days later, my mother moved again. I went to her place, and she was sitting outside with her things, away from the hogan. I asked her why she was sitting there since the hogan was not far away, but she told me she was tired and could not get firewood. I took her dull ax, then gathered any sticks that were lying around. I also made a fence for her. I told her she had to move into the hogan soon, but she wanted to wait until my younger brother came and fixed the hogan before moving in. I went to one of my brothers and told him our mother needed his help. Then he went to another brother in Dennehotso so they could both work on the hogan and haul wood with a burro, before my mother moved in.

When I got to my mother's place, I saw smoke coming from the chimney. She said she was not feeling well, and I knew it was going to be hard traveling by horse to get the medicine man. I thought of my older brother, who, even at this time of the year, seemed to always have a pretty good-looking horse. I told my mother she needed to move to Red Grass, where there was plenty of firewood and water nearby, and that she should ask one of my brothers to help her move there when one of them came to visit.

I went to my uncle in Dennehotso and told him of her situation. He replied that she had been sick when she was still living over here and working on the corn. My uncle said that she had only one Wind Way ceremony done on her and that this was probably bothering her.[49]

---

49. There are several different forms of Wind Way chants, but all help cure a patient who has come in contact with whirlwinds, snakes, or cactus that are malevolent. Ailments may include stomach trouble, eye irritation, itching, and infection, as well as heart and lung disease. The different forms of the ceremony include various sandpaintings and may take up to nine nights to perform.

He told me to get a medicine man for her as soon as possible, before the snow started to fall, even if I had to go on foot. He then gave me a blanket to put under the medicine pouch during the ceremony. By the time I got back to my mother's home, she had moved again. I told her that my uncle had said she needed to move to another location, so she asked me to tell my brothers because that was the only way she could do it.

As I was riding, I saw one of my brothers herding sheep. I told him about what was happening. Right after telling him this, he took the sheep back home and drove the burros to my mother's place. It was a cold time to move, but they did it. My older brother told me that I was not an old man if I could be riding anytime during the night. "When you are as young as you are, you don't even think about it being night; you just ride," he said. "Life is very precious so one should not loaf when life is in a critical condition."

My brothers were bothered by our mother's situation so I went out and roped a horse, then told my mother I was going for a medicine man. I ate with her and then left Bullsnake Spring, went past a place called Where the Sheep Perished [Drowned] to El Capitan rock [in Monument Valley], where the medicine man lived.[50] His name was Bee'eldǫ́h biye' [Gun's Son] of the Kin yaa'áanii [Towering House] clan. He agreed that we should leave immediately, even though the sun was low on the horizon. Then he changed his mind and said we would go the next day, and that I was to sleep there.

We left that next morning and arrived late in the afternoon. A sheep was butchered, and my younger brothers had gathered a lot of firewood. They had gone to get a medicine man, too, not realizing I had already gone for one. After they had gathered the firewood, they asked their mother if they could butcher a sheep the next day, and my mother agreed. By the time I arrived, there was a lot of firewood and plenty of meat. My brothers loved their mother dearly, and that was why all of this was done for her.

That evening they did *zaa'nił* [literally, "objects are put into mouths"], and the next day, the drawing on the body was done as part of

---

50. "Bullsnake Spring is located north of Totem Pole Rock in the Monument Valley Tribal Park. Where the Sheep Perished is in the farthest canyon in Mystery Valley [located southeast of Promise Rock]. There were some deep and steep watering holes there. They say one winter, when the water hole was frozen over, some sheep got on top of the ice to drink. Because they were all standing on one side, the sheet of ice flipped over, spilling them into the water. The ice came down on top, drowning all of them. That is where the name came from." J. II.

the Wind Way ceremony.[51] In the evening, *zaa'nił* was performed again, then again the next day. A yucca root was brought back to wash my mother, and the drawing on the body was done. The medicine man sang most of the day. During the night, there was a continuous set of songs sung in order. The next day, the horses were brought back, and I thanked the medicine man for doing a fine ceremony. My mother said she was a lot better, and that now I could go where I pleased.

I went back to my older brother's place for five days before returning to my mother's home. She looked fine, like there was nothing wrong with her. It had been that ceremony that was making her ill, and now that this was done on her, she was cured. That is why I believe in the Navajo ceremonies, because they cure a person. My mother got well when a medicine man performed a certain ceremony. I know that these ceremonies are truly powerful healing tools. Medicine men keep them really sacred.

I went back to Gambler's place. He had two wives, and the first one said she was not feeling well. She was of the Kin łichíi'nii [Red House] clan from the Mexican Water area and was the daughter of 'Asdzą́ą́ woo' niteelí [Woman with Wide Teeth].[52] My older brother wanted to get a medicine man, but he also wanted to move that day. He told me to gather up the cattle, and that he would take care of the moving. In the evening, I went to their new home and watched my older brother's family settle in. As I ate, my brother asked me where the cattle were, because his son had looked and could not find them. I knew where the cattle and horses roamed, but it took me a whole day to round them up. My brother was pleased with me.

Gambler thought that his wife might have caught a cold, though she said she had not because she always wore her blanket. She moaned all through the night, and the next day, she said she wanted to have a five-day Evil Way ceremony. Family members were suspicious of this illness. The medicine man, my aunt's husband, was of the Within His Cover People clan and did not live very far away. Gambler's second wife went for him; he agreed to perform the ceremony and said he would come in two or three days.

---

51. *Zaa'nił* is part of the Wind Way and other chants. Herbs are mixed with water and then drunk or rubbed over the body. Thus, the patient and other participants receive internal and external protection from the disease and evil that afflict them.
52. "Woman with Wide Teeth lived where the San Juan River and Dennehotso Wash meet—a place called River Water that Rises. She was Oshley's aunt on his father's side, or Oshley's father's sister. She had a big peach orchard, and people used to haul fruit from her place. There was a large waterfall close to where she lived called Water Coming Down so people called her by that name too [Lady Waterfall]." J. H.

My older brother asked me to go to the trading post to get some coffee. It was snowing and very cold so I asked him if he could go, but he was cold and wanted me to go over for him. I said that I could do it that very day, but I had to find the horses first. His oldest son went looking for them while I stayed and helped around the home.

VISIT TO A TRADING POST AND CEREMONY

The next day, I got up at dawn, found the horses, and by sunrise, had them in the corral. After breakfast my older brother told me to pick whichever horse I thought was best for the trip. There was a good horse called Red Mane that ran pretty fast so I picked him. Gambler gave me less than fifty dollars, but this was when the price of things was very low. As soon as he gave me the money, I saddled up and left. There was snow on the ground about four fingers deep.

The trading post was owned by a man named Charlie [Charlie Ashcroft] but was being run that day by another man who understood the Navajo language.[53] He asked me where I was from, and I asked him where he was from, and he pointed this way. He said that where I was from was a long way and that he had been there one time with Charlie. He told me he was not a good cook but gave me a little bit to eat. I greased my feet and legs with the grease from the food I had just eaten as a symbol of giving them food, too.[54] Greasing your shoe has a story related to it. Now the people who go to school do not do this, and if they see what I am doing, they look the other way.

I bought food and fabric, but it cost a lot more than I had expected. Two dollars were left over. I got back on the horse. It was really cold, with a strong breeze blowing, so I kept the horse walking at a fast pace. When I crossed Laguna Creek, I almost got stuck in the mud, but the horse hurried across, and the mud did not have a chance to hold the horse's feet. It started snowing. I was thinking of spending the night in the home of Hastiin Łitso [Mister Yellow] at the foot of the mesa so I hurried the horse along, but it was still nightfall when I arrived.[55] I built a fire, brought in the things I had bought, and tied the horse to a pole.

---

53. Charlie Ashcroft ran the Dennehotso Trading Post during the 1920s.
54. Rubbing grease is a type of prayer or blessing for both thanksgiving and continued health and strength.
55. "Mister Yellow used to own a lot of horses. He would herd them into a big canyon called Among the Rocks and would fill it up—there must have been at least a thousand horses. Oshley and I have helped herd these horses, and it was always a lot of

Aneth Trading Post, 1920s. (Photo by Milton "Jack" Snow, courtesy of the Navajo Nation Museum, Window Rock, Ariz., #NE 18-14)

Nobody was there. Mister Yellow was of the Honágháahnii [He Walks around One] clan and married to one of my relatives, an aunt named 'Asdzą́ą́ Tsé łichíí' haa'áhí [Lady or Woman Red Rock Standing Up]. So I was not hesitant to stay there, because if it was my relatives' home, it was my home, too. When I was unsaddling the horse, I saw ice on it. My grandmother and older brother had taught me to take care of the horse, for I might be traveling in the dead of winter sometime and face this problem. The fire inside the hogan was burning, so I took out some dry, warm dirt and sprinkled and patted it against the horse, which made it happy after I was finished. It kept rubbing its nose against me.

I tried to gather some more firewood, but I was getting cold. During those times, a person was not supposed to burn the logs from a hogan.[56] I tried to find some other firewood, but it was snowing. After drying myself, I went outside to warm the horse, which by then had snow piled up on its back. Again I got warm dirt and put it on the horse, then ate

---

fun. Oshley would sometimes ride after them—especially the wild ones—all day. He never gave up on those that ran away; he'd chase them until he caught them." J. H.

56. A person should not burn wood from an abandoned hogan because someone might have died in the dwelling. By taking the wood and disturbing the structure, the person could summon a ghost and invite trouble.

A section of the "terribly rough road," Where Dynamite Made a Road, as it appears today. (Photo by author)

supper. It was still snowing when I went outside to see how the horse was doing. Steam poured off of him, but when he saw me, he made a sound with his nose. I think he felt warm.

At dawn I saddled the horse, and although the snow was as high as his knees, I let him trot in some areas. I rode past Red Rock to where my older brother had moved, called Ripened Fruit. I arrived home while people were still eating breakfast. A sheep was butchered, and all of my relatives were happy and came out to see me. My older brother told his children to get the things inside and unsaddle the horse because their uncle was cold. I ate.

The next day, the medicine man came. His name was Hastiin Nii'ditł'oii [Mister Furry Face].[57] Everything was ready—we had the firewood, and the fabric had been torn to a certain size. The ceremony ended with the lighting of four fires. On the fifth day, some people who lived a long ways away came to the last day of the ceremony. Some came from

---

57. "Mister Furry Face was married to my grandmother Lady's Horse. His face was hairy, and so that is how he got his name. He was a medicine man who knew many ceremonies and was always going places. After my grandmother passed away, he was given a very young girl for a wife and lived in Dennehotso until he died." J. H.

Douglas Mesa, others from Mexican Hat. The patient was very sick at the beginning of the ceremony.

Just watching a person made one see how beautiful and sacred a ceremony really is. There was the tying of yucca on the patient's elbows, knees, and other joints.[58] This untying of the yucca is tricky, but it looks simple to a bystander. I was really good at this. Two people took care of the untying of the yucca, and just as the knot separates, one says, "Aiyo." The two people were in front of each other, with one facing the patient and the other right behind. The person standing next to the patient unties the yucca and says, "Beibei aiyo," while at the same time, the other person says, "Beibei aiyo ahihihiyo aihiyo" [with emphasis on the last *yo*].[59]

The helpers then went outside and ran around the hogan but did not go inside, because they had to turn around when they got to the north side of the door. They go all the way back to where they came from, then went inside from the south side of the door.[60] The same thing happened with the pressing of the spearhead. This time one says, "Aihihihi" [with the emphasis on the *ai*]. The other person says, "Paah." I was really good with the "Aihihihi" so was usually the person next to the patient saying it. Now I have become an old man, and I do not do those kinds of things. The ceremony ended and she was well again. Everyone in the family was happy that she had recovered from the illness.

TRAVELS AND MYSTERY

I stayed around there for the winter. My older brother said he was going to see the cattle. He was always saying that and was always looking for

---

58. The yucca in the Evil Way ceremony both cleanses the patient and casts the evil out. It also serves as a shield to prevent the evil from reentering the body. Untying the yucca removes the harmful substance because evil, as a personified essence, is afraid of yucca (a lily) and cactus. Some Navajos say that if a person has to spit, do it in a cactus because evil cannot get at it.

59. Evil is afraid of all of these sounds in this section; it flees when they are said. Intrinsic in their meaning is the certainty that whatever the evil came to do will not happen because the speaker is stronger than the evil. The "paah" actually "blows" the evil away.

60. When going around the hogan, those helping with the ceremony are careful not to complete the circle and trap the evil or sickness in. Clockwise movement from east to south to west to north is standard in all Navajo ceremonies and etiquette. In this part of the ceremony, the people who go outside take a bullroarer (a piece of lightning-struck tree carved into the shape of a spear point) that makes a sound that scares the evil away.

Chilchinbeto Trading Post in 1956. The left side of the structure was the original post, while the right side is an addition made in 1944. Behind the post sits Black Mountain. (Photo by Joe C. Hunt)

them. The next day, he brought back a gray male horse. My brother said that things had ripened in Dennehotso and that we should move over there. I was told to bring in the horse. This was near Comb Ridge where there was a terribly rough road going over it. The next day, we got the horse over the ridge, but the sheep were a real problem. It took us a long time to get them safely over this rock formation. In the meantime, the other people started to move, and I was left alone with the sheep.

My relatives had already settled in at Dennehotso when I finally arrived with the sheep. The corn had ripened, and the people were making kneel-down bread, while others were playing cards east of Charlie's trading post.[61] Many, like my brother Gambler, were heavily involved in playing cards. I did not participate even though I knew how. My mother told me not to play with cards because she got worried when I did. I always thought of the good things in life, and that was one of the reasons I stayed away from cards. My older brother won beautifully made rugs

---

61. Kneel-down bread is made from a ground-corn-and-water batter that is poured into green cornhusks, wrapped and tied, and then placed in a heated pit from which the live coals have been removed. The husks are then covered and allowed to bake. When removed from the pit, the husks are taken off and the moist bread eaten.

that he put on his horse's back. He also won two fine horses, which he gave to me. One was spotted, and the other one was black with a white spot on the tip of its nose. He almost always won.

When the corn was harvested, the family moved back to Comb Ridge, but I stayed there. This was the time when people hunted mountain lions and coyotes. I had set a lot of traps and caught three coyotes and a big mountain lion. I took its skin but not those of the coyotes. Other people told me to do it, but I did not because my older brother said it should not be done. There was another man who skinned the coyotes.[62] I took the lion pelt to Mexican Hat and got three dollars for it. I just bought some things and stayed there for another winter.

My mother and Woman Who Owns the House were living where the road was blasted down. They had sheared the sheep and had many other goods to exchange at the trading post. Somehow they had heard about the Chilchinbeto [Sumac Springs] Trading Post paying more for the wool, sheep, goatskins, and rugs.[63] They got the horses in and roped a good-looking reddish brown horse. My brother asked me to go to the Chilchinbeto Trading Post—that was the place where the traders paid more for the goods. I said that I would go with my brother. The wool was tied up with two blankets and placed underneath me. The sheep and goatskins were tied, along with the rug, on the back of the saddle. The horse was in really good condition. I just let the horse trail after me.

I went through a place called Tonalea, then past Where the Horses Hop Up,[64] over Gray Hill, and across Laguna Creek, which comes from

---

62. The hunting and trapping of coyotes and lions make an interesting comment on Oshley's views. Many traditional Navajos believe coyotes and lions play an important part in the origin story and have strong supernatural powers. To those people, avoiding these animals is best, unless a person understands how to control the powers associated with them. Oshley has no fear; in fact, he seeks them, showing the range of responses possible among the Navajo.

63. The Chilchinbeto Trading Post is located twenty-five miles southeast of Kayenta, Arizona, on the northeastern flank of Black Mesa. The first owner of the trading post was George Washington Sampson, who had it operational by at least 1910. See Frank McNitt, *The Indian Traders* (Norman: University of Oklahoma Press, 1962), 251. According to Ray Hunt, a veteran trader in the Four Corners region, subsequent owners included Frank and Lee Bradley. During the 1920s (around the time Oshley was visiting), Howard Wilson was probably the trader; he was followed by a man named Garcia (Ray Hunt, interview by author, tape recording, January 21, 1991).

64. Where the Horses Hop Up is also called Short Uphill and is just beyond Tonalea. It received its name because the trail was rough, forcing the horses to hop up the rocky slope.

Kayenta. My horse drank some water, and I washed myself. I thought I would drink some water, too, but it tasted salty so I just rinsed my mouth. By this time, the sun was setting very low in the sky. The crows were flying back to their resting place. As I got back on my horse to leave, birds were singing, and a mourning dove had come for water. I rode on, noticing rocks that I had not seen before. This was new territory to me so I was just following the directions I had received.

The sun was setting. All I could see were hills and Black Mesa, while in another direction the land leveled out. The sun went down, and there were many horses that probably belonged to Navajos. I followed a trail, wondering where the trading post was. It became dark so that all I could see were hills with trees. There were sheep tracks so I knew some people were living nearby. The horse carried many things but remained high spirited. I wanted to settle down for the night so I kept looking for a good spot. As I was riding along, the horse raised its head and walked close to a deep wash. It was very dark. I wondered what my horse had heard, so I stopped to listen for dogs barking.

At first I heard other horses, then someone singing very close by. I thought there was a ceremony going on, and so I thought I would spend the night there and then be on my way the next morning. In the wash, there was a corral, and the singing came from that direction. There were horses making their snorting sound as I rode by them. I tried to get my horse to go where the singing was coming from, but it would not go. The singing was very soft, so I thought perhaps someone had died here, and I was at a burial site. I thought this because my horse was rooted to one place and would not go any farther. It was hard to maneuver the horse because of my bulky possessions packed on it. My horse jumped backward because it was scared, so I just let him take me back to the flat area. We got back on the trail, and my horse just kept going.

I was told that I would see a white mesa and that on this side of the mesa was the trail to the trading post. As I was riding along, there was a small valley with a trail going through it, so I took it. I knew the post was somewhere around there so I thought I would spend the night where I was. Then I saw a light reflecting on the side of the hill; it was the trading post. Even though it was dark and I did not know where the trading post was, I found it.

I walked in and met the trader for the first time. He asked me where I was from, and I told him Tonalea, just this side of Plain with Reeds. The place was called Red Grass. He asked how far away it was, and I told him I had started off when the sun was just warming up. Then he said that

The typical interior of a trading post with its high counters, stocked shelves out of the reach of customers, and the "bullpen" with stove where Navajos could visit and warm themselves. (Photo by Milton "Jack" Snow, courtesy of the Navajo Nation Museum, Window Rock, Ariz., #NE18-134)

there was a hogan over there and that was where the Navajo people slept.[65] I asked him if he had food to eat. He said there were some cooking utensils here that the Navajos used to cook with. I told him I brought some wool, sheep and goatskins, and a rug. Then we went outside after he gave me coffee, sugar, flour, and water, and told me there was firewood at the doorway of the hogan.

The horse was still scared. I unsaddled and tied it to a tree, then cooked my supper. I took out some meat I had packed away and ate it. I got my things together inside and hobbled the horse, then went to sleep. When I got up, it was light enough to see so I built a fire. The drinking

---

65. Many trading posts, as a convenience for their customers, maintained a guest hogan for people who had traveled a long distance. Traders also loaned pots and pans, provided wood for cooking, and enticed customers with a few free gifts such as tobacco, a can of tomatoes, or a little candy. A reputation for hospitality and fairness in trading went a long way to ensure that a good post would have a steady flow of customers.

water made me suspicious. I thought maybe a skinwalker had put some of his corpse poison into it. I just threw it out and got some more water from the trader before I cooked my breakfast and ate.

I saddled my horse, tied it up, and took the things to be traded to the post. The trader gave me a good price on the rug and the goatskins but not much for the wool. After I finished trading, I bought flour, coffee, sugar, and other necessities as well as a pair of pants for myself, because my mother had told me to. I also purchased some crackers and candy. I had bought so much, I had to put the flour underneath me with the coffee on the back of the saddle, and many other things in a sack on top of my lap.

When I got back on the trail, I started to wonder who had been singing the night before. Even though I was lazy, I turned my horse in the direction where the chanting had come from. It was a ways off. Where I thought the sheep corral was, was just the wash that almost made a complete circle. Where I had heard the singing, there was no hogan. The horse, however, still snorted as I went toward the place. There was a spot of hard flat ground that looked suspicious so I searched for a clue of what was going on.

I found a person's footprints in one direction. The shoe was too small for a man so it was a woman's footprint. She had walked right onto the flat hard surface that had some leaves on it, but the tracks that left the hard surface were those of a coyote. The human footprints did not leave the hard surface, while the coyote tracks went toward the trading post. I believe it was a skinwalker that I had encountered the night before, and this was the spot that she had put on her skin. Her singing was very soft, almost as if it was a secret. I still did not want to believe this, so I rode around again to see if her footprints came out somewhere. I saw it with my very own eyes. The footprints showed that she was a very old woman. There were some hogans in the distance where I thought she lived. I rode off, thinking about what I had seen. I was a little bit scared after that experience.

When I got to Where the Horses Hop Up, I ate some things that I bought, gave my horse a rest, then started again. When I arrived home, people were happy with the things I had brought. They built a fire, and the women started to cook. Then my relatives wanted to know about my journey so I told them about my encounter with someone singing. The younger people did not believe such things and did not understand how witchcraft could work like that. My mother said that what I was telling them was true—that there were skinwalkers. She said that when a person becomes a skinwalker, he or she travels long distances fast, and my older brother agreed with her.

Spencer Trading Post at Mexican Hat, Utah, in 1917. The large man in bib overalls is probably Arthur Spencer, Big White Man. (Photo courtesy of the San Juan Historical Commission)

My brother started telling about how skinwalkers work together. I asked what the cure was for them, and he said that only arrows and whips were used. When a skinwalker starts to bother you, you slash the whip toward it or else shoot an arrow at it. Once the skinwalker is injured, you can see it the next day. If the being that is shot is a ghost, there will be a mouse lying there.[66] This is what my brother said.

DAILY BUSINESS

It was close to summer when the sheep had their lambs. I was expert at castrating them. My older brother had good, fat lambs. His two wives and children had their sheep and my mother's sheep in the same herd. I started to herd the lambs to Mexican Hat with the understanding that my older brother would follow me a little later. There were four of them riding behind me—my brother and his two wives and Woman Who Owns the House. We crossed the wash that comes from Monument Valley. They had brought my lunch, and while I was eating, the others kept on herding the sheep. After I finished my lunch, I took after them. They had already gone quite a ways and were close to Mexican Hat. We crossed the river, where a white man named Bilagáanaatsoh [Big White Man—possibly Arthur Spencer][67] was running the trading post, but the person who bought the sheep looked like a Mexican.[68] I bought a pair of blue jeans but do not remember how much money I had received. The trader said that the lambs were big and fat and that he had not seen lambs that big. My brother said he bought a ram from a white man, and the trader said no wonder the

---

66. Some Navajo people believe that mice are associated with the deceased. They are said to crawl into graves and nibble on buried goods and so should be left alone.

67. According to Ray Hunt, Arthur Spencer is a likely possibility for the person named Big White Man. Another person who plays a prominent role in this narrative and is also known as Big White Man is Jens P. Nielson, who lived in Blanding. The exact identity of this first Big White Man is unclear.

68. John Holiday remembers this early post: "The Navajos were living around that area back then, in the red rocky hills west of Mexican Hat Rock. We used to live there, too. The store was small but nice. The people made an irrigation ditch all the way from the San Juan River by the Hat Rock to the store so that they could have a supply of water. He [Spencer] used to buy sheep and goats from the Navajos so he kept his store well-supplied with flour, potatoes, and other groceries. I only bought striped candy canes since I was still a little boy. People bought things over the counter while the trader stood behind the counter. The store was quite large and built with rocks. There was also a guest hogan for the Navajo customers. The hogan was built halfway up with rocks, and the rest was made of logs, bark, and sand." J. H.

lambs were fine looking. Some people had come to see the sale, and one person asked my brother how he had gotten such a good price on the lambs. The trader said it was because the lambs looked very good. We settled in for the night right there, and the women started to cook.

We had used five horses to get the lambs to Mexican Hat. I hobbled the horses at Mexican Hat Rock for the night. The next morning at dawn, I brought them back. There was pressed hay provided by the trader for the horses near where we slept. He probably bought his hay in Blanding because it was hard to grow things in the Mexican Hat area.

When we got home before sunset, we had a lot of goods. Woman Who Owns the House bought a shawl, fabric, and food, some of which my brother's children ate. When we were still in Mexican Hat, my older brother had asked me to buy some food for my mother so I purchased a fifty-pound sack of flour, which cost $3.50, and took it to her. I also bought her coffee and $.25 worth of sugar. She was thankful for the food and for the way I acted. Then one of my younger brothers, Little Dove, came to see her because he thought maybe she was running out of food. My mother said she had plenty of food since I had just brought some to her. My younger brother thanked me for it. At other times, I would herd sheep for my mother or bring her firewood, as did my younger brother.

I stayed there for the summer, throughout the winter, until late spring, when the sheep were sheared. My older brother had a lot of sheep, a good set of rams, and was always wanting my advice on subjects. We packed the wool on burros and took it to the trader named Charlie at the Mexican Water Trading Post because the price was higher over there. I bought a pair of cowboy boots that ranged in price from only $5.00 to $9.50. The pair of boots that I got was $8.00. I thanked my brother for buying them for me. The leftover wool was taken to Mexican Hat. I did not go with them that time. When they came back, they brought a lot of food, shawls, and many other things.

About a month later, my older brother said he was going on a journey to his father's relatives. He was away for many days, and the food supply was running low. His family butchered a sheep in the hopes that he would return anytime. I was lying down one day, and my older brother's wives told me they were down to drinking only the soup from the mutton. Our food supply was gone. They asked me to round up the horses so that we could go to Mexican Hat. I asked them if they really meant it, and they said yes.

When the horses came in for a drink, I took my rope and approached them. Some were tame, but others were still wild and ran away when I went after them. I got one of the tamed ones, rounded up the rest in the corral, brought two of the horses to the hogan, and told the wives to go by themselves. One of them said not to say that. It was not good to have only women traveling by themselves to such places. She asked me to accompany them, and I agreed to go. I had a beautiful black stallion that may have been a white man's horse. Some people even offered to buy him from me, but I wanted that horse for myself. The women packed some meat for our journey.

First Experiences in Blanding

When we got to Mexican Hat, we bought some food. The next day, we were getting ready to leave when I got an idea. I would go to Amidst the Sagebrush [Blanding] and see what was over there. There might be some jobs, and if there were not, I would come right back home.[69] As we were about to leave, I told them I would be going to Blanding to look for a job. One of my brother's wives did not give me her okay for quite awhile, but when she did, she gave the rest of the cooked meat to me before I rode off. They took the purchased food back with them.

The road over Comb Ridge was in an awful condition so I wanted to eat there before going any farther. There were some people returning from Blanding camped there. They had just eaten, but when I arrived, they put the coffee pot back on the coals. The man asked me where I was going, and I said to Blanding. He said that work was scarce, that I could not just ride in there but had to be prepared because it took time to find employment. I said that might be so. They had only bread to eat so I brought out my meat, which we ate with their bread and coffee; then I started on my way again.

I was close to Bluff City when I saw Utes standing on the edge of the cliffs having a dance. At the time, I did not know about their dances. I passed Bluff City and camped close to where the Utes live now [White Mesa, eleven miles south of Blanding]. At dawn I went for the horse, but it ran away. At that time, I was a fast runner so I ran beside it. Pretty soon,

---

69. "Navajos came from different places to go to work in Blanding. They would say, 'We are going to go and clear the sagebrush,' which meant they were going to Blanding to work. Some would come through our homesite from Dennehotso with their packed donkeys and horses. Several weeks or months later, we would see them headed back to Dennehotso, chasing their overpacked donkeys. They would load the packs with food like flour, potatoes, coffee, and so forth. The men would say, 'I'm returning from clearing the land.' They worked for food." J. H.

Blanding in the 1920s. The large stone building on the right is Parley Redd Mercantile, where Oshley often traded. (Photo courtesy of the San Juan Historical Commission)

we were in Bluff City, and I was still chasing the horse until it ran into the midst of a herd of horses. There was a Ute there, and he asked me where I had slept. I told him, and he said that the Utes had been dancing last night. I wondered what dance they did and thought that maybe it was the Navajo ceremony called the Enemy Way. I found out much later about their dance and that they did things differently. I got the horse and rode back to where I had slept and saddled up. I got it to run hard to Blanding because I was upset with him for running away from me.

I arrived at the town I came to know as Blanding and went to a white man called Biníyol [The Person Who Is Windblown]. I had worked for him once before so he was happy to see me. He understood the Navajo language and told me to bring all the firewood inside, which I did. He fed me meat and bread. Whatever the meat was, it was not cow's meat because of all the fat. After we ate, he asked me different things, like what I was doing here and where I was going. I told him I wanted to do work like chop wood and herd sheep. I had chopped firewood for him before, so he asked me how many people were with me and where my horse was. I told him that I had come by myself. He said he had some horses, but they were down where he was going to drag out some firewood. He asked me where I would sleep, and I said any place I was working. He said that there was a Ute and also a Navajo living close to town.

Navajo gambling was a favorite pastime for many and a real temptation for Oshley. (Photo by Milton "Jack" Snow, courtesy of the Navajo Nation Museum, Window Rock, Ariz.)

The sun had just gone down so I went back to my horse and went to the Navajo's place. I knew him and that he was of the Within His Cover People clan so I went inside.[70] He asked me where I came from and called me his grandson. I said I had come from In the Midst of the Reeds and was looking for work. He told me that they had been there about two months now, had chopped wood for a white man, and had received sacks of potatoes for pay. I stayed around there and worked in exchange for food but was not offered any extended employment.

GAMBLING

Many of the people living there just wanted to play cards, so I thought to myself that I would play cards, too. I stayed around there for many days. The first thing I lost to gambling was my horse's bridle, next my saddle blankets—two good ones and a worn one—then my chaps and a blanket

---

70. The importance of clan relationships—even between people who have never met before—is illustrated in this incident. Oshley's father was from the Bit'ahnii clan, and because of this kinship tie, Oshley now had relatives in the community upon whom he could call for help.

which my mother had given to me. I had only two possessions left—the saddle and the horse. It took a couple of days to gamble away the saddle, but I lost it. By then I was wondering what I was going to do. I asked the person who won the saddle if I could buy it back from him, but he said no. I watched other people playing cards and thought maybe my luck had changed, so I sat down and played cards again.

At that time, the price of a horse was about twenty dollars. I said that this horse was top quality and I wanted fifty dollars for him in the game. The people who were playing agreed. It took three days to lose the horse. When the winner took it, I just hung my head for a long time and thought how I had just been in it for the game and what I was going to win. I did not have anything, and I was at someone else's home. The person that I stayed with told me that I had lost it all but that I should not feel embarrassed and that I could stay around. I felt depressed because of my actions. This made me ask myself why I did this. I shouldn't have even gotten the horse involved. I kept thinking about it.

A man called Naakaii yidíits'a'í [One Who Understands Mexican— Grant Bayles],[71] son of Bila' díí'í [Four Fingers—O. Hansen Bayles],[72] wanted me to herd sheep for him. Another man named Billy lived in Kayenta and was also asked to herd sheep. I was to take care of the garden or corn/wheatfields, or I could take care of the sheep at fifty cents a day. I told him the pay was too low and to raise the price. He did not want to but finally agreed to pay seventy-five cents a day. This was during the time the sheep were lambing.

We gradually moved the flock toward the area east of Blanding. Even though we watched the sheep closely, eight of them went into the hay. The owner knew these sheep were really stubborn so we moved them into the canyon. Two months later, all the flocks were put together and taken back to where the Mexicans were herding sheep. I was paid a little over forty dollars. The other person got the same amount. He bought things for himself, and I bought only a hat, a pair of shoes, and a shirt. I got involved in more gambling and lost more money. I thought about what I was doing and realized it was not good.

---

71. The One Who Understands Mexican was Grant Bayles, a local Mormon stockman who first learned to speak Spanish from the Mexican workers who herded sheep for his family. In 1926, he was called by the Church of Jesus Christ of Latter-day Saints on a mission to Mexico, where he became even more fluent in the language. When he returned to San Juan County, he was well equipped to work with the herders and cowboys from the Hispanic community in Monticello.

72. See note 108 for an explanation of the way O. Hansen Bayles received his name.

I had a really old quilt that I slept in at night just about anywhere. Sometimes I even slept under a tree. One time there was no food at all, so with what little money I had, I went and got a little bit of coffee and bread. I was thinking that night that this small amount of food would not last and that the next day, I would go home. My older brother and the rest of my relatives had heard of my misfortune. They heard that I was somewhat of a hobo in Blanding and that I was living off of other people. These stories about me were not good ones.[73]

I told 'Asdzą́ą́ ałts'iisí [Tiny Woman] that I was going home that day, and she told the Ute. The Ute told her to pack some meals for me, but since they did not have food for themselves, I was only given bread. I had a little bit of money but no horse. It was almost noon when I got to Bluff City, where there was a white man called Naakaii yázhí [Little Mexican—John Hunt]. He sometimes was in Mexican Hat. He asked me about my horse, and I told him what I had done. He gave me some bread and jam and a little meat; I ate and then left.

It was late in the afternoon when I got to Mexican Hat. Arthur Spencer was there, and he told me that my brother had told him what I had done in Blanding. He asked me when I had started off, and I told him that morning, that I was in Bluff at noon, and that now I was going home. He told me not to because I might die trying to do it. I said to him that maybe he would die but that I was strong and healthy. He let me go, and I started off again, getting home when the sun was almost set.

My brother hugged me, and the rest of the relatives were happy to see me. My relatives got together and asked why I hadn't started for home earlier if I had lost all of my things to gambling. Some of them were really hurt by these stories. One of my great uncles said that when they talked about one of his offspring like that, they were laughing at him. They all said that I was not a poor person, but I was in no condition to do anything. They told me what they had heard about me, but I had never thought that I would be poor.

---

73. Oshley's concern about his family's and community's response to his gambling, poverty, and seemingly unproductive lifestyle is central to traditional Navajo values. Richard Hobson in *Navaho Acquisitive Values*, Reports of the Rimrock Project Values Series, no. 5 (Cambridge, Mass: Peabody Museum of American Archaeology and Ethnology, 1954) details at length the importance that Navajo people attach to making a good living, having lots of property, taking care of things, working hard and not being lazy, and looking after the family. These values are an important theme running through Navajo Oshley's life.

My older brother heard about my return and came back two days later from a horse-buying trip in Rough Rock. He came with no saddle on his horse. The people were making fun of us and talking nonsense. He told me to stay around awhile, to not think about the horse, that I could always get another one, that we had burros, horses, and cattle, and that I had many things to do around home. He warned me not to think about my past mistakes. After he said this, I felt better. I stayed there, helping my immediate family.

Family Help

During the winter months, I gathered firewood for my relatives. In the spring, the lambs were born, their ears were marked, and the lambs taken to Mexican Water to be sold. My older brother bought a saddle, bridle, and blanket. He told me that there was a reddish brown horse with saddle, bridle, and blanket that I could use, although I might lose it to gambling again. He said it was all up to me to decide. He talked to me for a long time, told me to ease up on gambling, but that he did not have the right to tell me to stop playing cards. He also told me to take extra care when I did play cards because I was still being laughed at, and that I should be aware of these things. When I was among the people, I was not to say anything but just look respectable, and then the people would get embarrassed about what they were saying.

My older brother really loved me. He and I rode among the people. They stared at me and looked at my new things, thinking I still had the items I had lost. I heard people say that it had been a lie when they were told I had gambled my possessions away. There was a man who told me he never really believed anything that had been said and that I had not really lost anything in gambling. It seemed everyone was looking at me or my horse, saddle, bridle, and blanket. When we were at the store, the trader, Charlie, told me that these people said I had lost everything I had to gambling.[74] Some people were in the trading post when he said that if I was a gambler, how could I have a good-looking saddle and bridle and a horse? The white man was usually not embarrassed about such matters so he spoke what was on his mind. Some people were laughing about what the trader had said.

---

74. According to Ray Hunt, the trader Charlie is most likely Charles Ashcroft, who at different times during the early-to-mid-1900s owned and operated the Dennehotso and Mexican Water trading posts.

People said that they were thankful that I was back with them. My uncle came there and told me that people were making fun of me, and he was embarrassed by it. He said that what he thought was that I had a fine-looking horse, some cattle, and some sheep, and that when they were making fun of me, to think nothing of it. He said that he was also very thankful that I was back. We ate outside, and my uncle told me that if I was just drifting around, I ought to get myself a wife. He invited me to spend the night there, but I was going home that evening. I thought of going to my mother's place, but I went to my older brother's place instead.

The next day, I went to see my mother. She was outside when I came along. She and my little brother cried as they hugged me. She said that people had told her that I was like a tramp in Blanding. Even though we were not working, we were better off. My mother asked me if I was using my older brother's saddle. Then I told her that he had bought me the saddle, bridle, and blanket, and given me the horse. My mother told me to value my decisions in everyday life because the family trusted my decisions. She told me to slow down on card playing, that I looked good on fine horses, that she always remembered me driving the cattle and horses, and that those were good qualities in a man. My older brother had cattle, and he had given me important responsibilities. When he was asked about his cattle, he would tell them to ask me. My mother said that was a big responsibility and that was why I needed to ease down on the gambling. Now I knew what card playing did to a person. She was crying when she was saying this to me. I agreed not to gamble anymore. She said that was all she wanted to hear from me.

My mother was the youngest in her family. My aunt came in, embraced me, and cried. She asked me what happened because I had not been into gambling before. I told her that I did not know what had happened to me, other than I was gradually enticed into losing all of my things. She said that I probably knew what playing cards would do to me, that I should not mess with it, and that we were not poor because we had sheep to take care of us. It seemed like I did not even know what I was doing.

My aunt told me that around where she lived, there was nothing to entice me away from my daily work and that she had a blanket at home that I could come and get, but I told her my older brother had bought me a blanket, saddle, and bridle so I didn't need another blanket. She probably thought that I didn't have anything. A couple of days later, I decided to take the beautiful blanket my aunt had offered me. A man named Dinédííl [Heavyset Man] gave me a brown horse in exchange for it. It

May and Eugene "Thin Hand" Powell belonged to a family that for three generations traded on the Navajo Reservation. (Photo courtesy of LaVerne Tate)

seems that my relatives put my thinking back in the right perspective because they understood life and what it was about. They gave me the desire to live a strong, healthy, stable life. I thanked them many times.

HERDING SHEEP

Soon a white man came and asked me to herd sheep for him. He said he had set a date for me to come in, but I had not come so he came in person to ask. I took a mare with a colt. My older brother told me to just let it go when I got to Mexican Hat. Before I left, my relatives again cautioned me about gambling; my older brother said this only because he loved me. Even though I had some money, my older brother gave me three more dollars. He told me that it was for a meal on my way to work.

After I let the horse go, I went to the trading post and then to
another trading post run by the same man. He knew me and gave me food
and a place to sleep. The next day, I left and went to Bluff City, then to
Blanding and Bilagáanaatsoh [Big White Man—in this case, Jens P.
Nielson], the man who had asked me to come.[75] He said he had expected
me to be back a long time before. He had told people who came looking
for work that I was returning to work for him. Now he had a Mexican
working for him. The white man called Bila' sighaní [Thin (skinny and
hard) Hand—Eugene Powell][76] was herding sheep at White Mountain,
and there was also a Navajo herding sheep in another place, and another
Navajo in a different place. One of the herders was scared to herd sheep at
White Mountain because there were bears there. The white man told me
that in one month, he would pay me five sheep or four sacks of flour and a
sheep. I said that it was up to him. He said that I would earn five sheep.
These sheep that I was to receive as pay had once been Navajo sheep that
he had bought, but they did not have good wool when they were sheared.
I agreed to the payment.

When we got to the worksite, the sheep were out in the meadow,
while the sheepherder was just sitting in the shade. Hastiin łigai bich'ah
ádinígíí biye' [The Son of the Man with a Light Complexion Who Has
No Hat][77] was the man herding the sheep, and Powell said that he did

75. Jens Peter Nielson was born in 1862, was a Hole-in-the-Rock pioneer, and lived in
    Bluff for many years, but by 1910 he had moved to Blanding. His nephew, Norman
    Nielson, estimated he stood between six-foot-six and six-foot-eight, had a large
    chest and wrists, and was noted for his strength; hence the name, Big White Man.
    He died in 1935.
76. Reuben Eugene Powell was born in Monroe, Utah, in 1872. As a young man, he
    worked at the trading posts in Tuba City, Arizona; Kirtland, New Mexico; and
    Cortez, Colorado; then in 1908, he moved to Bluff, Utah, where he worked in the
    post called the San Juan Co-op. All of his sons (June Powell was one who also dealt
    with Oshley) worked in trading posts throughout the Four Corners region. By the
    mid-1920s, Eugene earned his livelihood by sheep ranching. He died in 1942.
       Eugene Powell received his Navajo name of Thin Hand from an accident he had
    as a young boy. A runaway horse dragged him and broke his wrist, which never
    healed correctly. The wrist remained bent inward, and the hand had limited use
    (LaVerne Tate, granddaughter, telephone conversation with author, May 17, 1998).
77. "The Son of the Man with a Light Complexion Who Has No Hat was hard of
    hearing. There is a funny story about him that is told by others. Some folks met him
    when he was on his way back to Fry Canyon [near Natural Bridges, Utah] to herd
    cattle. Someone asked him, 'Hey grandpa. Are you going where there are plenty of
    piñon nuts?' [This was during a year when there was a good harvest in the moun-
    tains.] He replied, 'Yes. I'm going to look for the horses.' 'So you are going to pick

that all the time. Powell took care of things and shifted things from one
place to another when the sheep were moved. The person who was there
was told that I was going to be the sheepherder and that he could go back.
He gladly accepted this and went back with my employer.

I took the sheep up into the mountain. Powell was very proud of me
and said that I really knew how to take care of them. He was very happy,
told me to take care of the sheep the way I wanted to, and, on occasion, I
would hear him laugh out loud. Another man came, and they were happy
that I had the sheep up in the mountain. The sheep grazed beautifully,
and the only thing I did was walk around where they might roam off. My
coworkers were pleased with what I did. Every two days, I took the sheep
to water.

BEARS

One of the other herders came to visit me. He said he did not realize that
it was me who was herding the sheep, and he wanted to know where the
other sheepherder was. I told him that he had gone back and that he had
been scared to take the sheep on the mountain, was afraid of bears, and
that was probably why I replaced him.

It was just two days after I arrived that it rained one night up on the
mountain. I heard yelling and thought it was the Mexican who was herding sheep, so I yelled toward the sound. It was actually a bear growling,
but I thought one of the sheepherders was lost so I yelled that I was over
here. Bears closely resemble man. There were a lot of tracks around, and if
one was frightened of bears, this was not the place to be.

I had a good dog and rifle, and I was close to a semicircular ravine
where a bear had killed some of the sheep. She had cubs so the dog and I
surrounded them in the ravine. The cubs were making sounds almost like
a goat and were trying to escape, but the dog and I were always in front of
them. I thought I would catch them, but these little things moved fast. All
of a sudden, the dog came tumbling out with a whimper of pain. Even
though they were small, these bears were ferocious, pawing at me when
they were cornered. The dog was now frightened of the cubs as they ran
away up the mountain. They looked like pigs when they were walking
away from me. I was told later that if a bear scratches you with its claw, it

---

piñons?' 'Yes. I'm going to herd sheep to the water hole.' 'So you are going to pick
piñon nuts?' Then No Hat's Son said, 'Why don't you shut up? You will probably go
to hell yourself.' [The words in Navajo for "picking piñon nuts" and "going to hell"
sound almost identical. No Hat's Son's deafness confused him.]" J. H.

is not very good.[78] They are very dangerous, but I was told that all I had to do was to plead to them.

I was there for two months, and the wild berries were ripening. At night the bears came to eat the berries, and I could hear them snapping branches. One evening I went out and told them not to eat on this side of the meadow because that was where the sheep were. For the rest of the night, they stayed on their side because they listen when they are talked to. A couple of days later, Powell came to see me and said he heard that Navajos talk to bears and the bears hear what they say. He then asked me to butcher a sheep and said that the next day, he would return to get some of the meat.

Although he was our supply man, he wanted meat from me so I selected a nice, fat sheep. After the butchering, I took a small piece of meat, and the rest I packed and hung in a tree. I left to gather the sheep, but when I came back to camp, the meat was gone. I thought perhaps the supply man had come and gotten the meat, but the only tracks I found were those of a bear. The sack of meat had not been ripped but neatly untied and left on the ground with all of the meat missing. I wondered how the bear could do such a neat job; in fact, I did not believe he had.

The supply man returned two days later looking for his meat. He laughed, said bears would do that, told me to butcher another sheep, and this time, to put the meat way up in the tree. I butchered another fat one late in the afternoon, just before it was time to check on the sheep, which I did every couple of days. As I hung up the meat, I said that whoever took the meat the last time maybe ought to try to get this sack this time. I got back to the campsite and again found the meat gone, the rope on the ground, the tracks of a bear, and the sack without bite marks. I thought that the supply man had come and gotten the meat. I began to realize that bears were like human beings.

Two days later, I told the bears not to eat on this side, and they listened to what I said to them. They stayed where I told them they could. Now I am not frightened of bears. I just tell them to leave me alone, and they do. My maternal grandmother told me that if a bear should block my way and does not move, that I should take my shoes off and throw them

---

78. To many traditional Navajos, bears are powerful creatures which are assigned by the gods to live in the mountains. The origins of different species arise from mythological stories, such as the one about Changing Bear Maiden, whose supernatural qualities caused her to become a monster. When she was destroyed, parts of her body engendered other bears. Usually bears are feared for their power, which is often considered evil.

to the bear, and that would get it to move. A couple of days later, this happened. I asked him, as I took off my shoe, what he was doing in my path. Then I told him that here was my shoe, and the bear took off into the bushes. So what my grandmother said about throwing your shoe at the bear really works. If I had not done that, I do not know what would have happened to me. This was the rule that a bear would obey. After the bear left, I got my shoe and put it back on my foot.

About two days later, when I was still quite a distance from my campsite, I saw the bear where I usually hung my food. I shot, it growled at me, but I missed him. I thought about what had happened that day before I went to sleep. In my dream, a tall man with a bushy mustache came to me.[79] He asked why I was shooting at him, and I told him he had brought it upon himself, so he walked off without saying anything. The white man told me to kill the bears, but I said no. I remembered what my grandmother and my elders had told me, and that was why I did not kill bears. The next morning, I offered the bear corn pollen. I called him grandfather and told him I was thankful that he was talking nicely with me. I told him from then on I would not shoot again. I had already said I would not harm them, and I kept my word, even though at times they got very close.

I stayed there for six months and was paid sixty-one sheep. I told my employer that the sheep would be kept here until I got back with some help. He asked me when I would return, but I did not know because it all depended on what it was like at home. I had just arrived at my older brother's place when I learned there would be a work project under John

---

79. During the creation of the world, animals received their outer forms, which at certain times and places can be put aside to disclose the human form or spirit residing within. When Oshley talks about communicating with animals, he means it in a very real, very human sense.

John Holiday tells a story about the way Woman with the Four Horns was saved by such relationships. "Her survival when escaping captivity [from Indians in Texas, probably Comanches] depended on her belief in the sacred ceremonies. One night, when she got very cold from a blizzard of snow and winter weather, she prayed to the owl to keep her warm. The owl came to her and covered her with its wings, and this kept her from freezing to death. Then the next morning, the owl gave a call [hoot], and she awoke and went on her way. She walked all day, and by evening it was cold again. She looked around and dug a hole under a bush and crawled inside. She prayed for warmth again. Then she heard some noises; she looked up and saw a coyote above her. The coyote stomped on the bushes and lay down on them. This kept her warm all night until dawn. The coyote let out a cry, which awoke her. She then followed the direction in which the coyote howled and went on her way to Fort Sumner."

A display of local weaving obtained by the Spencer Trading Post. (Photo courtesy of the San Juan Historical Commission)

Collier in three days.[80] I bought from the Utes a beautiful black horse that ran pretty well. The Utes wanted to exchange the sheep for the horse, but I told them no and paid cash.

Indian CCC Work and Travels

When I got home, I told them I was going to the work project. My older brother said that maybe the horse was tired and that I should not ride a fat horse too much. I said I would not go racing over there but just ride it slowly. The horse was not used to going over rocky places, so when I reached Comb Ridge, I had to get off and lead it over. In some places, the horse slipped on the rocks. I got to my uncle's place in Dennehotso and

---

80. John Collier was the commissioner of the Bureau of Indian Affairs between 1934 and 1945. Although Navajos generally refer to Collier in connection with the very negative experience of livestock reduction, he was also instrumental in providing many New Deal reforms through the Indian Reorganization Act. Self-determination, changes in tribal government structure, shifts in education and training, and the Indian Civilian Conservation Corps were just some of the programs he introduced on the reservation. Subsequently, wage income became a welcome relief from problems of unemployment.

was told the project was to build dams and wells, that the people were now meeting at the trading post, and that it started that day. The work lasted twenty days, until a new group of people would come to work.

So it was after forty days that I told my older brother about the sheep I had earned. He told me to get the sheep back over here as soon as possible because by then, Powell would have probably earned some of the sheep back. Those white men were very greedy. I went to my aunt and told her I needed help herding the sheep back. She said that she and her husband would help me get them. Her husband was my brother by our fathers' clan, and so that was why we were brothers. I thought he was just bluffing me about going over there, but the next morning, he gathered his horses together, and we set off. We slept in Mexican Hat, where we bought some food to take with us. The trader there, Atsiiya hochxǫ'í [Ugly Back of the Neck—possibly John Oliver], gave us some firewood, water, and hay for our horses.[81]

It was getting cold. I had a good strong horse, and I led the way. We let our horses drink some water at the Valley of the Gods since this was the only water until we got to Comb Ridge. My aunt wanted to eat because the next water was a long ways, but her husband said he was not hungry and assured her that they would not starve before they got there. We got on top of the hill, and there was Comb Ridge with two trails

---

81. The chronology of the Mexican Hat trading posts and their traders gets confusing quickly. Ray Hunt tells that there were a number of posts at different times. The first post was located about a mile west of Mexican Hat Rock, away from the San Juan River. Another post's remains are found beyond the old trash dump in Mexican Hat, west of the old airstrip. The post by Mexican Hat Rock was built in 1911 by John Oliver and operated by Arthur Spencer. It had one bedroom, a kitchen, a small storage room, and the store. In 1926, Hunt leased the facility from Oliver for fifty dollars a month. He intended to buy stock from the reservation, while his goods came from Aiken Mercantile in Dolores, Colorado, the same place where he sold his sheep. After five years, he withdrew from the business, and John Oliver tore the store down for its lumber.

In 1937, a third Mexican Hat Trading Post, beside the San Juan, went into operation. A man named Dan Tyce established it on the ledge of the rock overlooking the river. Norman Nevills, a river runner and entrepreneur, placed enough pressure on Tyce that he sold his ownership in the one building he had constructed. Merritt Smith next owned the store, but when his wife died, June Powell, son of Eugene Powell, bought it. He sold the post to Ray Hunt in 1940. Hunt remained there for four years before moving on to Chilchinbeto. Jim Hunt next bought the post, added a motel and a restaurant, and enjoyed the increased business as the uranium industry became prominent (Ray Hunt interview by author, August 22, 1995, notes in possession of author).

before us. They asked me which road we would take, but I let them choose. My aunt wanted to know where the water was, and I told her it was ahead of us, so she said we would take the shorter road into Bluff City. We got to the water which was good, because it was not salty or bitter and flowed from the mountain.

After we ate, we saddled the horses and went over Comb Ridge. I told them there was water a little farther, and if there was firewood, that we should spend the night there, to which they agreed. It was sunset when we got to the water left by the rain. There was plenty of grass so we unsaddled the horses, hobbled them, gathered firewood, built a fire, and boiled coffee. We told each other of our adventures and stayed up late into the night. I told them I used to herd sheep with Mexicans for the same person, but the sheep were divided into two herds. The Mexican kept the sheep on the mesa, and I kept them in and out of the canyon. Later we went to sleep, but at dawn we built a fire and put the coffee on. My aunt's husband said that as soon as we ate, we would leave again, then asked how much farther we had to go. I said that if we hurried, we would get there about noon.

We crossed Allen Canyon, and I told them this was the only good water that we could get. On the west side of Allen Canyon, there was a home lived in by a Ute called Yidlohí [Smiley]. I told him I was coming for my sheep, and he knew about them. He nodded his head and said to give him one of the sheep. I said that if I had the sheep with me, I would give him one, but that they were over there.

EMPLOYMENT

At noon we ate, then left to find the white man I had worked for. We got to his place in Blanding and found Jens Nielson sitting outside of his trading post working on ropes.[82] He gave my aunt a big hug and told me I was past my due date. I told him that I had said I did not know when I would come back. He laughed and said he was going to drive southwest

---

82. Jens Nielson's store, called Nielson's Cash Store, was thirty feet wide and sixty feet long, with a pitched roof that had a ridge pole running down the center. The store had a big front so that the name could be painted on it. Another building next to it was provided free of charge for the government to use as a post office. This encouraged customers to come to Nielson's store rather than its competitors. The store owners sold groceries on one side of the building; clothing, shoes, and dry goods on the other side; and saddles, harnesses, and tack in the back. See Howard Kimble, "Reminiscences," San Juan County Historical Commission, Blanding, Utah, pp. 13–15.

of Blanding where the sheep were. He gave us some food to eat and asked where we were going to spend the night. I told him any place would be fine, then asked what corral we could drive the sheep to for the night. He said we would use the corral where the sheep were usually sheared on the south side of Blanding, toward Bluff City. The next day, he would have the sheep there.

My uncle asked where we would sleep that night, and I told him we would sleep at Smiley's place. We got there when the sun was about to set. The white man had given us some food, which my aunt carried. We were told that there was room inside, but we preferred sleeping outside. My aunt built a fire and cooked supper, while my uncle and I hobbled the horses, then ate. It was cold, but there was a lot of firewood because my uncle was not a lazy man. He built a big fire. It was very early in the morning when my aunt woke up, said it was dawn, and that we should build a fire, since the white man said he was going to have the sheep in the corral. We finished eating before the sun came up.

After breakfast my uncle went for the horses and brought them back, and by sunrise we were mounted. We arrived at the white man's house, and he mentioned that when the sheep came, he had told the herders to put them in the corral. We went to the corral and separated sixty sheep from the flock. There was only one black one and one ram. I told the white man we were a little short of food, and he said we would go back to the trading post. We rode our horses to the trading post and left the sheep in the corral. He gave me a hundred-pound sack of oats for my horse and some coffee to me out of the kindness of his heart. He called me his brother and said that he wanted me to help with the sheep again. I thought I would have to take the sheep back up there. I thought about it for awhile, then I said it was fine with me because he had kept my sheep with him for a long while. I felt like I owed the man many things.

I told my uncle and my aunt what the white man was saying to me, and I asked them how they felt about it. They told me that what he was saying was really good, that he was giving me sheep and wanted me to continue working, that he had given us food, treated us well, that I should not say no to a person who has been so nice, and that they would take the sheep back for me.

I herded the sheep a little ways, and then I turned back to the white man. I worked with a Mexican from the Monticello area.[83] I did not know

---

83. Monticello is known in Navajo as Mountain Coming to a Peak because it is located at the eastern foot of Blue (Abajo) Mountain.

Sheep at Hookatow Wash, ten miles south of Mexican Hat. (Photo courtesy of the San Juan Historical Commission)

his name, and he was not good to work with. He was a very stubborn [willful] person so we would get mad at each other. One time the sheep were going in the wrong direction, but he would just start walking and did not bother to chase them back. He would climb to the top of a hill and sit there like a scarecrow.

I decided to just let him be and keep the sheep in one general area near the Bears Ears to feed, then down into Allen Canyon for water. The Mexican would just watch me do all the work, which I thought was his problem, not mine. My employer got after him when I told him what was wrong, but when he left, the Mexican got mad at me. He said that I had lied, but I told him that it was true that when he herded sheep, he just sat on the hilltop.

We were told to take the sheep eastward to the corral close to White Mesa. We moved them there, but nothing happened so we took them out of the corral to the place we did the shearing. We got the sheep in the corral, and I started walking toward Blanding, where I spent the night at a Navajo man's place. Early the next morning, I went to my employer's house, where I met the Mexican. I told my employer the Mexican got mad at me and that I wanted to go back home, but he said no. My employer told me he wanted me to stay and let the Mexican go. He had been suspicious of him, but now he knew. I still wanted to go back, even though he kept telling me he wanted me to herd sheep for him. But I told him I had sheep at home that I was supposed to take care of, and so the Mexican remained, and I left. My boss and I shook hands, and he said that when I needed employment to come to him, and he would always need my help.

I walked over Comb Ridge and was going to spend the night by the road near Mexican Hat, although I felt scared.[84] The next morning, I started walking until I arrived at the Mexican Hat Trading Post, where the trader gave me a little bit of food before I was on my way again. I arrived home late in the afternoon. I thought of how I used to make that trip in one day and decided I was getting old. The sheep were corralled at my aunt's place. I told her I was thankful that she had done that for me, and she was really happy about the whole thing. She cooked some food, and we ate. I got the sheep out and let them graze for awhile and did not return them to the corral until very late in the afternoon. I was happy to see such good-looking sheep. In the evening, I told my relatives of my adventures with the Mexican.

The next morning, I thought of what I wanted to do that day. My older brother was living near Kayenta, close to Baby Rocks, so I decided to go over there. My aunt said that my horse was with their herd of horses, which my uncle got. Gambler was not there when I arrived, but his wives and children were, so I stayed around. He later came home; I remained there for many days, helping him with various things. We were told that the sheep were to be treated at Salt Water Spring, near Mexican Water.[85] I decided to bring my sheep there, too, so I went to my aunt's home and said my older brother had asked me to help take his sheep there and asked her to drive my sheep to Salt Water Spring. I went back to my older brother's place, and we drove his sheep over Comb Ridge, past Dennehotso to Red Sitting One, where we spent the night. The next day, we crossed the Logs in a Semicircle Wash, drove the sheep toward the north, spent the night among the gray hills, and arrived at Salt Water Spring at sunset. My aunt's family had not yet gotten my sheep there.

---

84. Many traditional Navajos avoided being out at night because that was when malevolent spirits and people practicing witchcraft were about.

85. Oshley is referring to the sheep-dipping program initiated around 1905 in the Northern Navajo Agency. The process included having the sheep swim through a narrow trough filled with a nicotine solution, which was later upgraded to a more effective sulphur solution. Scabies, a contagious skin disease caused by a mite, was the main target of this program. Since this disease could reduce wool production in some cases by as much as half, the government launched a major scabies-eradication effort across the reservation in the 1920s.

John and Louisa Wetherill's post in Kayenta in 1916. (Photo from the O. C. Hansen Collection, Utah State Historical Society)

The next day, the dipping of the sheep started, but it took us two days to have our turn because the people had a lot of sheep. My aunt's husband came to me and said that they had gotten there the day before. We had the sheep treated, and my uncle said that they would be right after me. My older brother had my other aunt's sheep and my mother's sheep. My aunt was finished, and they left. The next day, we returned home. We spent the night somewhere near Logs in a Semicircle, and the next day got the sheep home at sundown.

I was herding them with Gambler and his second wife so there were three of us. His son was with his in-laws. We were driving separately, but we were all going the same direction. I told my older brother that I wanted to go back, and he said not to say that and to stay around and help him. I was riding the only horse, and I was wearing him down so I just hobbled the horse and went about on foot.

I went to Kayenta Trading Post a couple of times, spent many days with my older brother, and traveled to the trading post for him. I either took wool, sheepskins, or goatskins to exchange for food since the trading post was close by. I also decided to go to my aunt's place and spent many days there, then I went to my mother's and my other aunt's places. I went among them and ate at their homes but got embarrassed about what I was doing. My aunt asked me why I was saying that, because I had sheep in her herd as well as some cattle, and that I should not talk about myself that way. I told her I needed a wife who could take care of my things for me. I wanted a home to go to without embarrassing myself. I said I knew that this was my home, but I was not comfortable with it. I wanted a place that I could really call my own.

MARRIAGE

My aunt said that it was fine with her. Then she asked me what my mother thought about this. I said I hadn't spoken to her yet. Just then my oldest aunt, who was kind of deaf, came on her burro. While I was outside, my aunt told my oldest aunt about what I had just said. My oldest aunt asked me if I had really said that, that it was good, and that I had my possessions spread all over the place. If I had a wife, I could take them to one place and be more organized. She told me to tell my mother and see what she had to say, and that they would get a wife for me, and that I couldn't go back to work before they did. I went to Woman Who Owns the House's place and told her of my need. She said they wanted that for me and that was how I was to live. I had not told my older brother so my aunt went to see him, and he agreed that I needed a wife.

I stayed in Dennehotso and married a woman from Kayenta. I was older when I took her as a wife. Nowadays, boys get married younger. This lady was from the upper part of Kayenta. She was of the Many Goats clan and had gone to school in Tuba City and knew English. I liked her, but she had a husband called Ólta'í Sání [Old Teacher]. Her husband knew the ceremony of Akéshgaan [Hoof or Claw Way]. This was why I was afraid of what he might do to me. Most people were afraid of him because of his knowledge of Claw Way.[86]

When I went to her place, there was a ceremony going on at the woman's relatives. They were cooking and helping with various tasks, and she told me that she had to help her relatives. As I went outside, she

---

86. This ritual is not very well known and little has been written about it. Some Navajo informants provided some information. The Hoof or Claw Way is a three-day ceremony held for people who have concussions, fractured skulls, and broken bones. It is designed to restore the strength for recovery and takes its name from the buffalo-hoof rattles, as well as deer hoofs and bear claws that may be used in the ceremony. The bear claws are particularly powerful because teachings tell that a bear was once in shock and had a ceremony to restore its mind and strength. This blessing and power can now be used by the People to heal in a potent way.

Oshley seems to fear that Old Teacher may turn this healing knowledge against him through a curse that will produce similar injuries. Depending upon how he is witched, Oshley could become crippled in the hips or joints, lose his mind, or sustain

followed me and told me that she would be my wife, but I told her she already had a husband. She said not to say that and that she had heard my relatives had asked her family near Black Mesa, and they already were planning to say go ahead. I told her she still had a husband, but she said that she would get separated from him. Everything was already set [arranged] over there [home]. I was afraid of her husband because he was a medicine man and might do something to me, but she told me not to say that.

The ceremony she was attending was over so I got my horse and saddled it. When I was ready to go, she ran after me to where my horse was. Her father found out about the incident, thought it was a great idea, and said that we wanted each other. Her brother, whose maternal clan was Many Goats, found out about it. He lived near Kayenta.

By this time, a lot of people knew what was going on. My brother did not approve of this, but by then it was all set. We saddled two horses, but before we started off, my brother told me that her husband was a medicine man and that he was frightened at the thought of what the ex-husband might do. My mother said to go ahead and go through with it. We set out for my bride-to-be's place and got there at nightfall. My brother went in, but I paused for awhile before going inside. The people there were preparing food. Word had gotten around. My brother-in-law-to-be told me to go out with him and build a fire in an old forked hogan. I took my horse over there and built the fire. It was late in the evening when the sheep and goatskins and blankets were brought in. That was how I got a wife, and we stayed together there.

Three days had passed when I went back to my mother's place and was given food to take back to my bride. My wife told me that she would take the sheep in the direction of my home and that she would be waiting when I returned with my horse. It had wandered and grazed a long distance, but I finally found it and went to where my wife was herding sheep. Her ex-husband rode up and was mad. He whipped my wife. I grabbed his rope, and he jumped down from his horse. At that point in my life, I was really good with a rope, at handling horses and cattle, and was physically strong. He ran toward me and was going to hit me, but he missed. Then he seized me, and I grabbed one of his arms and a leg and threw him on the ground. He arose,

broken bones or a concussion. There is also the possibility that part of a claw or some other foreign object could be supernaturally "shot" into a victim, which would require it being "sucked" out by a medicine man.

John Holiday commented, "Old Teacher knew this ceremony which could affect a person with mental illness through witchcraft. Oshley was suspicious that he might cast a bad omen on him. He hired a medicine man named Continuous Hill, who knew how to ward off any evil."

but I told him not to do that again so he ran toward the woman. She ran behind me; then I asked him what he was trying to do. He calmed down, but would not talk to me. He started back for his horse, which was a little distance from where we had fought, and rode off. We got the sheep back, and my wife told me what had happened, but I did not say anything about it.

That evening something hit my toes, and just as I said, "Paah!" something hit hard against the door. The next morning, I went to look for my beautiful spotted horse and found it dead. I untied its hobble, then went to my mother. She was a good hand trembler so I did not tell her of the things that had happened. She used hand trembling and told me there was something intended to harm me and that this harmful thing had just bumped me but killed my horse. She said this was all the doing of the medicine man, Old Teacher. She also told me that I had felt and heard something, which was true, and that is why I kept repeating "paah" when I woke up. This event happened.

My wife was sick and coughing but was told by the doctor that she had a bad cold. Later I decided to go back to my mother's home; my wife said she wanted to go with me. I told her it was fine with me so we arrived at my mother's place in time for shearing the sheep. My mother hugged her daughter-in-law and called her "daughter." Then my mother asked her why she married me when she already had a husband. My wife said that he was always jealous and that every time a man came to their place, he thought that she was doing something with him, and he would beat her up. That was why she wanted to get away from him. My mother said that her family was thankful that she had come to them. Mother had many things to do around there, like shearing the sheep, so we helped.

We had a son at my mother's place, then later we had a girl. After my son had grown a little, a white man came and told me to herd his sheep at Mexican Hat. He asked me if I had a wife and a child, and I told him that I did. Even the white man was thankful that I had a wife.

SHEEP, COYOTES, AND WOLVES

I went to Dichinii's [One Who is Hungry—probably Merritt Smith] trading post where people were trading their sheep for goods.[87] The trader told me that he could not be in several different places at one time and that he really needed my help to herd sheep for him. I asked him if he

---

87. "Merritt Smith was very nice. He would open canned goods for weary travelers who spent the night at his post and give them some food again in the morning. He was a kind person, and the Navajos really liked him. He wanted to adopt me as a little boy but did not. If he had taken me, who knows where I could be now?" J. H.

knew me, and he said he sometimes saw me in Bluff City. I asked him how much I would be working for, and he said forty dollars a month. I told him I had a family now—a wife and a son. The trader asked me what his [the son's] name was, and I told him Ashkii [Boy]. I asked him if he knew my name, and he said he did. He asked me what my wife's name was, but I told him that I did not know her name. She was my wife, and she was just that, but that she could probably tell him herself.[88]

I told him this job was not very good because I needed to have my family with me. He asked me how much food I wanted, and I said it was up to him. He thought for a moment, then he said that if I brought my family, I had to buy my own food, but that I would be paid fifty dollars a month. We went over our deal again, and this time I asked him to get a pair of shoes for me. It was a little over a month when he sold his sheep, and we moved back to my mother's place. Now we had some money and food and were doing pretty well.

Eventually, our food supply ran out so I went back to see Gaandilch'aɫii [Swinging Arm—Ray Hunt].[89] He had a trading post in Mexican Hat and some sheep that he needed herded for forty dollars a month. He asked me if I wanted him to pay me for my food. I just told him to pay me sixty dollars a month, but he said no because there were only a few sheep, and that fifty dollars would be more fair.[90] We agreed, and he gave me food to bring back to my family. I told him that I would be back in two days, and that was fine with him. He also had a brother or friend who was deaf who took care of the sheep for him.[91]

---

88. Many Navajos use kinship terms and nicknames far more than a regular name. Since names hold power and are personal, they are not used just to identify people as in white society.

89. Ray Hunt was born in August, 1902, into a family that was already involved in trading with the Navajos in the Four Corners region. The vast majority of his life was spent in this profession. At the age of three, he was afflicted with polio that crippled his left arm and hand and caused him to limp. The Navajos, quick to name for a physical trait, called him Swinging Arm. Hunt spoke the Navajo language fluently, often served as a translator in both an official and unofficial capacity, was highly respected by the Navajos, and continued in the trading business until his death in March 1998. He was a good friend of Oshley's and always spoke kindly of him as a customer and an honest individual.

90. Hunt estimates that Oshley worked for him about a year. The trader loaned a tent to those who herded for him because they had to move about constantly searching for feed and water. There were also cattle belonging to the Cory, Dan, and George Perkins family from Bluff also ranged in the same area, increasing the competition for resources.

91. According to Ray Hunt, Oshley is probably referring to June Powell.

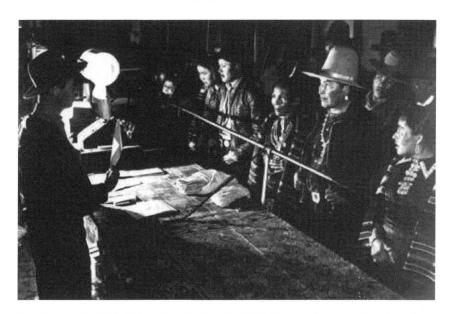

Ray Hunt at the Chilchinbeto Trading Post in 1946. Hunt spoke fluent Navajo and was well respected. (Photo courtesy of Grace Hunt)

My wife and I lived and planted our crops in the Dennehotso area, but we continued to herd sheep around Mexican Hat. I do not know how many months I herded, but it was enough to earn a saddle. I also got some groceries and all my clothing. I worked for the one with the swinging arm, and life was pretty good. Later I bought a saddle.

That summer I took the sheep out early in the morning to the river to drink. Then another white man [Taylor Norton] brought more sheep that he and my employer had agreed I would herd. So we moved to another place with the sheep. Then one month later, they separated their sheep again so we returned to where we were first living. My wife and I were herding sheep west of Mexican Hat. We were told to live there with the sheep because there were plenty of shrubs and plants for them to eat. In a small canyon, there was a little spring we used for water, but the sheep drank from the San Juan River.

We stayed there a long time. There were many cows and horses around that belonged to the Navajos. There was also a wolf that was killing off the calves, but I did not know this at the time. I herded the sheep, at noon went back to the camp to eat, then went back for the sheep. As I left, I said that there were probably some coyotes roaming around, and that was one of the reasons I stayed close to the sheep throughout the day. The flock had been grazing in a small canyon.

A coyote that was coming toward me ran to a lamb and seized it. I threw rocks at it, but they did not seem to bother it. This really big coyote ran through the flock of sheep and they, in turn, ran to the edge of the canyon. Even though I was there, it tried to get to the sheep. The coyote ran to the unprotected sheep and separated them from the herd. I threw rocks at him, but he just sat down and waited. So I sat down and watched for quite awhile before he started walking away from the sheep. I waited some more, then got a stick to beat him if he tried to chase the flock again. I started moving the sheep back to camp and arrived at sundown.

My wife, who understood English pretty well, told me that when we were living in Mexican Hat, she overheard the traders talking about a wolf that ran through this area killing calves.[92] She had not remembered to tell me this before. This wolf was large, his bone structure was big, and he looked strong. When I studied the tracks left by what I thought was a coyote, they looked like those of a very big dog. My wife told me to tell the Anglos, even though it was about nightfall.

I was scared to go but went and told them anyway. They told me that if someone killed that wolf, there was a large reward for it. They gave me a rifle and bullets and said that its skin was also worth money. The people at the camp were scared. The next morning, I walked to the highest hill around us and saw the wolf stalking my children, watching us from a bush. This time the people I was living with were really frightened. The boy, who was oldest, went off a ways to play, but this time we kept a close eye on him. My wife said that we were fortunate that the wolf wasn't around that other time. I eventually took the sheep out again just in time to see the wolf going over the hill. It acted like it was human, because it probably saw the gun and had learned to fear it when white men shot at it. Later I told the trader about it, and he said that I should have hidden the rifle.

---

92. Wolves enjoy a folklore all their own in southeastern Utah. Briefly, by the start of the twentieth century, the wolf population had increased dramatically. Sheep, goats, and cattle became their targets, and so bounties, in some cases as high as $150, were offered. In one instance, a notorious wolf known as Big Foot was said to be worth $1,000 when all the bounties presented by livestock and state and local organizations were added together. He was known to frequent the area where Oshley was ranging his sheep. Big Foot was supposedly trapped in September 1913 and again in March 1920. Whether the wolf that Oshley is talking about is Big Foot is difficult to determine because of problems with chronology. The last wolf in San Juan County was reportedly trapped in 1939. For more information, see Annette Carroll Cashin and Janet Wilcox, "The Phantom Wolf of Westwater and Other Wolflore of San Juan County," in the local publication by the San Juan County Historical Commission, *Blue Mountain Shadows* 5 (fall 1989): 7–13.

The next day, just as it was getting warm, the wolf was there again. It looked at me, then turned away. Everybody was scared. At home there was a big stick and a knife waiting for him. I said that if he showed up there, they should use the stick on its head. I would stay close with the sheep on the hilltop, and if they needed help, to wave a piece of fabric. It seemed the wolf knew we had a gun, kept its distance, and never bothered us again.

I do not know how many months I worked there, but my employer sold all his sheep in Bluff. Since there were only a few sheep left, he wanted to lower my monthly wages, but I wanted to move back to my home. He said that was fine with him. He had a saddle there for seventy-five dollars. There was another one for sixty dollars. It was a hard decision to make. I thought to myself that if I bought the seventy-five-dollar saddle, I would not have any food to take home. Then he said that he would give me credit on part of the saddle, and with that, we went home.

STUBBORN SHEEP

The summer days were gone, a good corn crop had ripened, and everybody was there eating the corn. There was a man who wanted my saddle, but I told him that I was not finished paying for it yet. He offered a very nice-looking horse in exchange for the saddle, and so I agreed. I picked a tan horse instead of a reddish brown one because it had more meat on its body.

Later I returned to Mexican Hat. The trader, Ray Hunt, was standing in the doorway with his brother, who was deaf. He looked tired, and he walked slowly back into the trading post. He had taken the sheep—there were only a few—back to the river. Hunt was very happy to see me, saying hello, calling me his brother, and shaking my hand. I took the saddle down from my horse and set it on the sand. I got some firewood, and he brought me some water, coffee, and food. It was evening by the time I had finished eating, but he stayed with me late into the night.

The next day, I got up and took the sheep out just as the sun rose. I let them graze and set the coffeepot on the hot coals. After I finished my coffee, I went after the sheep, which had remained nearby because they were satisfied with where they were. I tried to herd them to another place, but they would not budge. I went back to the trading post, and the trader asked me if I had eaten. I told him that I had, but he gave me some water then I took off again. When I got back to the sheep, it was hot, so I thought I should take them down to the river before it got really hot. I tried to make them move a little faster, but they just took their time.

Sheep crossing the San Juan River on a bridge built in 1909 at Mexican Hat. The suspension-cable bridge has since been replaced with a steel structure. (Photo courtesy of the San Juan Historical Commission)

When I got there, it was noon so the sheep went under the shaded area on the side of the rock where the hill slopes into the ground. The sheep stayed there, and I went back to the trading post, where I cooked my lunch and ate. Then I got worried that a coyote might go by the sheep, so I went back to where they were. I did not know that the sheep were used to roaming around by themselves, and here I was going back and forth while the sheep were staying there. I started washing my clothes and myself. When it got a little cooler, I took the sheep back to the river again.

After they drank, I wanted to have them go back toward the trading post, but they still wanted to roam around in the canyon. When the sun was about to go down, I had finally gotten them back to the corral. Then Hunt came to me and said that they just let the sheep out and let them roam around by themselves, and that all I had to do was keep an eye on them. I said that I was afraid of what might happen to them, but he said that he didn't think there was anything to worry about.

Since my wife was still in Dennehotso drying the corn, I just slept anywhere near the trading post. I was doing this work to pay off the debt on the saddle at the rate of one dollar a day. I was well taken care of and was there for many days. There were some Mexicans working in the same area.[93] They planned to get a sheep from me by either asking for it or stealing it. They told me to give them a sheep, and they would not tell. I did not do this sort of thing, and I did not like it. They offered $2.50 for a sheep and said I did not have to tell the owner anything. I laughed. These were not my sheep; I was herding the sheep for the owner to pay off a debt, and they should go ask him themselves. They just looked at each other. All my life, I have never liked to cheat and lie. They left me alone.

About two days later, I told my employer what had happened on the hill. He asked me if I had given one of the sheep to them, and I said that I had not. He said those Mexicans were not good, were better left alone, and that I should not let them trick me into doing something for them. I replied that I had my principles and that I did not think they would do anything to me. One time my employer asked me if I wanted to fix a sack lunch to take with me, and I said that it was up to him. He made my lunches, and I tried my best to take care of his sheep because he really took care of me. He thought I was a very good sheepherder. He never told me which way I should herd the sheep, and if I asked, he would say that I knew the best place to take them, where there were plenty of shrubs and grass. He did not care if I herded the sheep where I wanted to. He told me that a man had recommended me, saying that I was a really good worker, and that was true.

The road to Bluff City was in poor condition in those days. I do not know how many times the trader in Mexican Hat went to Bluff to get supplies in his old vehicle, but I do know that it kept stopping on him.[94] He also had a telephone line, but it was in poor condition. One evening at sunset, I had gotten the sheep in and was eating supper when the deaf white

---

93. Throughout his narrative, Oshley tells of negative feelings and experiences with Mexican people. Historically, Hispanic peoples, both Spaniards and Mexicans, have been at odds with the Navajos, with raiding, slavery, and warfare characterizing much of their shared history. Even in Navajo mythology, they are portrayed as greedy and untrustworthy. Oshley's views, no doubt, have been tainted by the past.

94. Ray Hunt described his vehicle as a "stripped down Ford with a box on the back." Comb Ridge was so steep and difficult to traverse that Hunt had a bicycle pump

"The road was in poor condition in those days." The road in Mexican Hat as it appeared in 1916. (Photo from the O. C. Hansen Collection, Utah State Historical Society)

man who assisted the trader came out to see me. He told me to come in and listen, then handed me the phone.[95] My employer was making the call from Bluff and asked me to take the sheep out and head for Bluff the next morning at dawn. He said it would take me two days to get there, and he agreed that I should herd the sheep slowly and not rush them. I told him that if he wasn't joking about it, it would happen. I also told him that I had very little food left, but he said that the deaf person would prepare the camping food. I gave the telephone back and went outside to sleep.

The next morning, I took the sheep and food such as crackers, pop, and other goods, as well as my one blanket, and started to drive the sheep toward Bluff City. It was getting a little cold by this time. Across from Comb Ridge, there is a big hill, where I spent the night and kept the fire going. The following morning, I herded the sheep, then let them graze near Comb Ridge. By the time the sun was setting, I camped at Navajo

installed in the fuel system so that, as he drove, an assistant could hand-pump enough gas to the engine to propel the car up the grade.

95. By 1910, a telephone system extended from Monticello through Blanding and Bluff to Mexican Hat. All calls were routed by an operator in Monticello, who, through a system of long-and-short rings, identified which phone in a town should receive the call. The line constantly needed repair, especially the section extending to Mexican Hat. Ray Hunt remembers going outside his post and pouring water on the ground wire to improve reception.

Springs, where I spent the night with the sheep lying against the rock walls so they would not try to run off.

The next morning before dawn, I built a fire and cooked the little bit of food left. I got the sheep to Bluff just as the sun came up. My employer came out, told me that my debt was paid off, then got me some food. He wrote down on a piece of paper how I was to be paid and how much I had left to pay on the price of the saddle. I was very happy to go back to Dennehotso. I arrived at the trading post just before sundown. At that point in my life, I was a fast traveler. The saddle was paid off, and I had a little bit of money left over.

The following day, I went after my horses that had wandered over to another ridge. I chased them back toward the trading post into a small canyon that I blocked off. One of them approached me so I roped him, then drove the horses back to the trading post and saddled them. I shook hands with the trader, then took the horses back along Comb Ridge to Dennehotso, where I arrived in the late afternoon. My wife was with my mother, and although it was cold, we cleaned the corn off the cobs, storing it in three different places. I stayed with my mother and herded the sheep for her all winter long.

A Family Loss

In the spring, the corn had just come out of the ground when my wife gave birth to a girl. When I came inside from herding sheep, there was a small bundle beside my wife. The baby's name was Dzanbaa' [Polite Woman]. I stayed with my mother herding sheep until we moved to another place near Thin Rocks with Water Coming Out from Between called Water Coming Down.[96] My daughter was about two years old, and my son was four. My wife by now had gotten very sick, and she was coughing more.[97] The doctors, perhaps in Tuba City—I do not remember where—examined her and told her she was not going to live long. They

---

96. "This is far in a canyon south of the Vanadium Corporation mines [in Monument Valley]. There is a falls where the water streams off the rocks and flows into a well." J. H.

97. Tuberculosis was one of the major killers that stalked the reservation during this time. Crowded living quarters, a lack of understanding about the way communicable diseases all spread, and unsanitary conditions allowed tuberculosis to kill men, women, and children. One study found that at least one of every ten Navajos was infected by tuberculosis following World War II. Another study determined that prior to 1952, when new preventative measures began to be instituted, 50 to 60 percent of children

said her lungs were in very bad condition, and that she was only going to live a short while, although she actually lived longer than expected. We were together for about seven or eight years before she died.

I tried everything in my power to keep her alive. She became very thin, with no flesh on her bones, and spent two months of continuous coughing. She kept telling us the suffering was too great for her, and she wanted peace within her body. I had a medicine man named Chan dinihiiyee biye' [Son of Aching Stomach] perform his most powerful ceremony on her.[98] My mother brought some herbs, as did the medicine man. I even gathered herbs for her, but they did not work. Her brother, who knew how to do hand trembling, came and performed on her. He said that this sickness did not just happen. She was like this for a long time, and what he said was true.

This disease feels like your lungs are burning. In my hand trembling, I thought there was an eagle sitting on my chest. Maybe this disease came from the eagle, I don't know. Then I thought it was the witching of another person, but the hand trembling said it was not. Another hand trembling said the same thing. The sickness had something to do with the eagle. Maybe it was the owl, and it just looked like the eagle.[99] One medicine man said that we could kill the person who was witching my wife with only a small song and prayer that would cause him to die. I went for another medicine man, but I do not remember who.

This occurred at the start of winter, when the cold weather began to close in and her life was fragile. She was so sick that we felt depressed, but still there was hope within us. A hand trembler who had performed for my wife told me that there was nothing to be done, and that she had suffered from the disease for a long time. My wife told me when she was awake again that she was very sick and was going to die. My mother was sitting nearby and said that maybe in some way she would live with her daughter, then my mother started crying.

---

between six and ten years of age tested positive for tubercle bacilli. (See John Addair, Kurt W. Deuschle, nd Clifford R. Barnett, *The People's Health: Anthropology and Medicine in a Navajo Community* [Albuquerque: University of New Mexico Press, 1988], 19–20.) In southeastern Utah, the disease was not brought under control until the 1960s. For further information about health practices on the reservation, see Robert A. Trennert, *White Man's Medicine: Government Doctors and the Navajo, 1863–1955* (Albuquerque: University of New Mexico Press, 1998).

98. "This is my father; his English name is Billy Holiday. Oshley used to have Billy do ceremonies and sings on him. He used to go to Blanding and perform sings for the Ute and Navajo people from this area." J. H.

99. The owl is a bird associated with the dead, ghosts, and foretelling the future.

The debilitating effects of tuberculosis can be seen in this little girl, who is wasting away in the Shiprock hospital in the early 1940s. (Photo by Milton "Jack" Snow, courtesy of the Navajo Nation Museum, Window Rock, Ariz., #NK10-19)

My wife never said any harsh words to me, and I never said any harsh words to her. She told me that I didn't have any bad thoughts or feelings, that I was a faultless man, that there was no harshness in me, and that I should take care of our children. I told her that I would. When I remember this moment, all I can do is wipe away my tears. She said that whatever happened, not to worry about her, but I told her not to say that and to think about getting well. She had her arms around me when she said that she was getting worse. I brought back another medicine man, but she had just died that day.

Her brother was there when she passed away from the coughing. After she was gone, he talked to us, and I asked my brother-in-law and one of my brothers, Lefty, to fix her for burial.[100] She did not have much—a

---

100. Lefty was Oshley's father's brother (his uncle) and was a member of the Many Goats clan. Burial of the dead is a ritual that includes washing the corpse, dressing the body in new clothing, carrying the corpse to a site where it is interred with various forms of wealth (cloth, jewelry, tools, etc.), and observing a four-day period of mourning by friends and relatives.

blanket that was quite used and a sheep and goatskin that were not really in good condition, but her clothes were all right. My wife was dressed up and buried with grave goods that ranged from fair to good condition. My mother donated some of her things to the burial site. I was asked if I wanted her to be buried somewhere nearby and answered that I wanted her to be buried in the hogan.[101] I asked what else should be done after the burial.

It is said when a person dies, he or she reunites with their family that has passed on. This is what happened to her. She probably went back to her mother. This is how it was. Her brother said so be it. I was told again not to worry about her, and I wiped away my tears. That event has had a great influence on me. Because of this, when I see a big man crying, I do not say anything.

When something like this happens, you kill a sheep for food on the spirit's journey.[102] One of my brothers asked if it was just killed and left at the gravesite, but my mother said that everybody ate the sheep. We killed a big one that belonged to her. We ate it and did not let any of it go to waste. After four days, I cleansed myself. We did everything possible in a good way for her journey. My mother said, as she cried, that things were done correctly, to which her brother agreed. I told them that we had each other here to think about life and to go forward. I thought this was what should happen, to start again. My wife's brother, who lived in the Oljato area, was encouraged to visit us. He rode off, and we stayed there.

I tried to think positively, but I became depressed. My mother said these things happened, it has been like this always, so I just stayed around there and provided for my children.

My son wanted his mother and cried for her. He was not hurt in any way because his great grandmother took charge of him, and she did not let anyone harm him, but it was still painful to see a child crying without a mother.

We moved toward the south in the wintertime because when something like this happens, one does not move to the north.[103] We almost

---

101. When a person dies in a hogan, it is abandoned and considered the home of that person's ghost. Even the wood from such a hogan should be avoided.
102. There are different interpretations as to what happens to a person's spirit after death. Many believe that it takes four days for the spirit to travel to the land of the dead, which is said to be to the north, an undesirable place. One of the best and earliest studies concerning these beliefs is by Father Berard Haile, *Soul Concepts of the Navajo* 1943; reprint, (Saint Michael's, Ariz.: Saint Michael's Press, 1975).
103. Oshley is referring to the idea that when a person dies, the spirit journeys to the north. If the living traveled in that direction, there would be a greater possibility of contacting the deceased, something that should be avoided.

moved onto the Navajo Reservation, but the brother of Old Teacher, who was living fairly near to the place we had moved, kept pestering me about what had happened. The head man from this area came and talked to both of us, telling him not to say mean things, and that I had already been through enough. Old Teacher's brother did not even own the land, but the leader said that when many days had gone by, we should move back to the north.

I had to feed my children so we ate a lot of boiled corn. My mother did not grind the corn well because she was old and got sick from working hard. I told her not to do hard labor like grinding corn, so she just cooked it with goat or sheep meat. We mostly ate corn stew. Later we moved to another place back toward Water Coming Down.

Immersed in Work

I wondered how I could progress forward. I was living in the Dennehotso area by Red Water [near the trading post]. It was said that the land was getting cleared in Blanding. Smiley, Tóbijisteezhí's [Two Lying by Water—Bob Keith][104] brother, went there to help grub sagebrush, and when he came back, he had nice pants and shoes. He did not stay around that long before he returned to Blanding. I was told that life was pretty good over there so I went. The only work to be found was clearing the land and herding sheep. I did both.

At that time, pay for labor was low, but it still attracted me to the town. I might even get a pair of shoes. In those days, a pair of boots was $3.50, a pair of denim pants about $3.50, shirts $2.00, a fifty-pound sack of flour $2.50, and a twenty-five pound sack $1.25. It was like this back then, but now prices are so much higher. Coffee was $.25 and sold in grayish paper packages, not in cans. Sugar was $.50 and was weighed before it was sold. The price of shovels, knives, and axes was low. Blankets were usually between $20.00 and $30.00 with Pendleton blankets and quilts all different prices. Some were $4.00, and some were $5.00.

---

104.   According to John Holiday, Bob Keith had a number of names. When he was young he received his first one. A sandstone ridge extends all the way from Dennehotso to the Chilchinbeto area. Close to Chilchinbeto, where the hill ends, there used to be a spring. Keith and a friend were at this spring getting water and resting. While he was there, some people saw them, and that is how he got the name, Two Lying by Water; this place is now also known by that name. He got the name Darkness because he was always roaming around at night. Ironically, in his later years, he was blind.

There was a real heavy-looking quilt that cost $7.00, but I do not see that kind of quilt anymore. I wonder where they went. That type of quilt was so warm that it was enough even when sleeping outside on winter nights. The stitches on the quilt were pretty good. This was what I was aware of at that time.

The Blanding area was the only place I went. I have hardly ever gone anywhere else. When I first stayed around Blanding, there were only a few white people, the road was horrible, and I saw only wagons—no automobiles or airplanes—being used to carry things around. All I did was clear the land or else herd sheep.

The more I came to Blanding and watched the town grow, the more I saw how the people lived. There was alfalfa everywhere, making it a beautiful place. The Anglos used horses to cut the alfalfa, and at this time, rain came often. There was a lot of vegetation, and the alfalfa was good grass for horses. In the early days, the place was just beautiful; everything was green. Also there were many rabbits and prairie dogs, and the birds made a lot of noise. There were many kinds of birds that had different calls, and one type sounded like it was laughing.

Over the years, the rain started to decrease, and the water in the reservoir and ditches was lower. I wondered why it did not rain, what was happening to the water, and why there was less alfalfa. It seemed like the planting area was shrinking. The water level appeared to be continuously going down. This was what I was aware of during those times. The irrigation used to go down to the end of White Mesa, where the white men used to plant crops.[105] As the water gradually decreased, the farmers could not get anything to grow except weeds, and the water only reached close to town.

What I think happened is that the white man was doing everything to Mother Earth and caused this. The Mormons were digging into the ground for minerals, causing a lack of rain. Even though there was water flowing down, they would say that there would not be anymore. If they practiced the sacred ways, we would have had rain and snow. They should offer prayers instead of drilling into Mother Earth.

These Anglos had wells drilled for them, but they are stingy with the water. When Navajos dig for water and find it, they are not stingy with it. They share it even if there is a small amount of water. They let everything use it: birds, Anglos, and many other living things. But white men have all of these rules I do not understand. The Navajos tell each other this is the

---

105. The distance Oshley is talking about is approximately twelve miles.

Parley Redd, "Horned Toad," in 1911. (Photo courtesy of
Ada Rigby)

way you do things, and that way there are no laws. We don't tell each other
that this is my land. People just live where they please.

Anglos are not like that. When they say it is their land or water, they
start building fences around it. I do not know why they do this. On this
earth, everything is made for the Navajos. In the past, the Navajos have
utilized the land, and it was still in good condition until the Anglos came
and started tearing it up and claiming that they owned the whole place.
This is not the way the earth should be treated. It should be viewed with
respect.

This thing called water is for everything that is living. The people
in Blanding say that the water is to be paid for. I do not like this,
although some people feel all right about it. I am aware of what is going
on around me. The Anglo is doing all sorts of things to this earth we live
on, and this is the reason there is no rain. They drill into the earth; the

Mormons do not take the sacredness of the land seriously and are ruthless toward the land.

When I first came to Blanding, there were only a few houses and two stores. There was a small man called Dich'ízhii [Horned Toad—Parley Redd], who had small children and took care of the store.[106] The other store was run by Jens Nielson.[107] There were no schools and no churches at that time. The Anglos probably worshiped, but there were no buildings for that purpose. There were not many people there. Water from Blue Mountain came in a ditch that ran between the hills to the east side of town, right next to the buildings where wheat was ground to make white flour. The water was used to irrigate the land. A lot of smoke came from the building where the flour was made, so I asked what was going on and was told that wheat was taken there in sacks. That is what I saw.

When I came to Blanding, the white man called Four Fingers [Hansen Bayles] had sheep.[108] His son was One Who Knows the Mexican Language [Grant Bayles]. Although the pay for a sheepherder was very low, two of us—me and a man from Dennehotso named Little Deswood—were hired for seventy-five cents a day. I think we were insane to work for that little. I had worked two months, and Little Deswood worked for almost two months during the summer, when it really started to get hot. A Mexican came to take the sheep to the mountains where it was cooler, and I was asked to stay on but declined.

Another time my younger brother and I drove our burros to Blanding. It was just the beginning of winter so the people were chopping down trees. We spent one night there, and the next day, we were asked to

---

106. Parley Redd got the name of Horned Toad because he ran so fast, just like a toad. His store, Parley Redd Mercantile, was in direct competition with the Nielson Cash Store. Eventually, the Mercantile outlasted its competitor. Parley Redd died in 1955.

107. Another Navajo name for Nielson, in addition to Big White Man, may have been Loincloth, because he always wore an apron when he worked. John Holiday visited this store, located at the main intersection in Blanding.

108. O. Hansen Bayles received the name of Four Fingers from the Navajo because of an accident he had while living in Parowan, Utah. According to family members, Hansen was very handy with a whip, which he often secured to his middle finger. One day, as he was "popping" the mice and rats that were fleeing sheaves of grain being fed into a threshing machine, the whip became entangled in the blades and drew Hansen's hand into the machinery. The first two joints of the finger were removed initially, and after a few days of suffering, Hansen's father removed the remaining stump with a chisel behind the woodshed. Eventually, the other fingers moved over to replace the missing appendage, and the hand became very strong. The Navajos, always observant, were duly impressed and gave him the name (Finley Bayles, grandson, telephone conversation with author, April 5, 1996).

cut firewood in exchange for a sack of flour and a little bit of money. We were told a wagon full of wood was worth $2.50, which was good since the usual price for a wagonload was $2.00. The white person that we were going to work for took us with some supplies, a wagon, and the burros we had brought, to the upper part of Blanding. I asked him if our burros could have some hay, and he said yes.

For days we chopped down trees for firewood until a deep snow covered the earth. The white person came with his wagon to our shelter, which we had made from logs pulled to a tree, then covered with juniper bark. It was not very good. We received nine bags of flour, which I had agreed to, and told him we would leave the next day. We packed in the firewood, and the white man gave us food. The next day, we went to the white man's place. He cooked for us again, then gave us the flour so that we could leave early the next morning.

The following day, close to noon, we were at Navajo Springs, where we unloaded the flour for awhile to let the burros' backs rest. We built a fire and cooked our lunch—I made bread while my brother kept the fire going and peeled potatoes. We were happy that we were taking some food home. We ate, then headed for home once more. We spent the next night at Mexican Hat, the following night at a place called Between the Mesa Rocks [west of the prominent Alhambra rock formation toward Monument Valley], and by midmorning we reached home.

In-law Problems

There was no food there when we arrived. No one had gone to get the stored corn, even though one of my younger brothers was there. I did not know what was wrong with him. We heard someone singing. My mother had told him to bring some of the stored corn because the only thing they were eating was meat and milk. My children came out crying to me because my wife's relatives and some other people were there. They wanted my wife's sheep, as well as her eight-year-old daughter, Baa' sinééz [Tall Warrior], who she had given birth to when she was with Old Teacher. The girl was crying, but I told her not to.

One of the main spokespersons for this group was a woman called 'Asdzą́ą́ tł'ízí łání [Lady with Many Goats], who wanted both the girl and the sheep.[109] I told her the sheep were going nowhere except here because

---

109. "She lived between the Mittens in what is now the Monument Valley Tribal Park. She was a really good weaver, was very kind, and always happy." J. H.

they belonged to my children. As for the girl, she had always called me her father, had said Old Teacher was not her father, and insisted to the group that I was her parent. She also told them that I was a good provider, never harmed any of the children, and they never went hungry.

Even before I had arrived home from chopping firewood, these people had come to our home to claim the sheep and the girl. They said that this girl had told them there were five sheep, but that one had been killed for the funeral. My wife's relatives then went outside, tied up four sheep, and got one more. That was when my brother, Lefty, went out to see what was going on. They almost got in a fight over these sheep, when he let the last one go and told them that only four of them belonged to her. They tried to take another one but were told they could not. Then they tried to take five others that belonged to me in addition to the four they claimed. Lefty told them the five belonged to his brother, and that if I found out they took the sheep, he did not know what I would do. My wife's relatives had asked my daughter how much I knew about witchcraft.

They also wanted to take my son, but Lefty said that they could not take him until they found out how I felt about it. My brother was a heavy-set man and looked strong, whereas I have been thin all of my life. He stood in the doorway and scared them off so no one got the boy. He said that if they wanted to fight about it, to go ahead, and that even though there were many of them, he would not let his relatives assist him in the fight. He would be the only man to deal with them.

In Oljato there was a leader called Hastiin yázhí [Little Man], whose brother was a policeman. This person was away working when this happened. Another man came and told me to tell about my misfortune and said that my wife's relatives would have to give back the sheep. He also said for me to be strong, for that was the only way I could keep these things. I do not know how the people from the Oljato area found out about this, but they said that people should not just yank sheep away from other people. Many of these sympathetic people were of the Salt clan.

I was told to go to Kayenta, where my wife's relatives were, to tell my side of the story. I went to these people and told them that there were five sheep and I killed one. As I told my point of view, they were silenced. I said that when we were first married, she had only three sheep, and we butchered some of them. These relatives had tied four and were getting another one when my brother said no more, and there was almost a fight. I told them I did not like this kind of harassment.

Before I went to Kayenta, my older brother came to me, saying to leave them alone because we were not impoverished and should not make a big issue of the incident. There were more sheep if I needed them, but that I should not let the children go. If these people kept harassing me, I should take all the sheep and the children back. One of them interrupted, telling me to return the children, but he was shushed and told he could not say that.

I said the children were mine, my son and my daughter, and that my wife had another girl who I think of as a daughter, too, but that I did not have much to say about her. If they really wanted to take care of her, then for her sake, they should give her to me and let me raise her. That was their choice. If they kept bothering me, then they would have to give me the sheep back, too. I asked them what they thought about what I had said. They just said so be it, ending our property dispute.

Caring for Children

I spent time at home, then went off to work to bring home food for the children. One time when I came back, my son was very sick. I asked Son of Aching Stomach, the medicine man, to perform a ceremony for him, which he did. The ceremony included putting *ntł'iz* in the coyote tracks and saying a good prayer for my son.[110] After this he got well. When he had recuperated, I returned to Blanding and herded sheep for Floyd Nielson for two months.

During that time, my mother really took care of the children. She milked the goats for them, and when the food ran out, she would butcher a sheep or goat. In late autumn, when I got paid, I thought that my children were probably out of food. Grant Bayles let me borrow a mule, although he still wanted me to herd sheep for him. But I thought my children might be hungry so I started home on my mule. When I arrived, there was no food except corn and a sheep they had butchered earlier that morning because the children were hungry. My son said he was starving, but that he felt I was coming home. It is said that children are apt to know what is going to happen, and my mother said that was probably true.

When I found there was no food, I decided to ride to Dennehotso and bring some back, but my son said he felt lonely and did not want me to go off again. I told him that I had to go and that he would get over this feeling. I bought some fabric for my daughters and a pair of pants and boots for my son. This took all of my money because I had not gotten much pay.

---

110.   *Ntł'iz* is a sacred offering made of ground turquoise, jet, and shell—materials used in most ceremonies and associated with supernatural powers and the four directions.

Before I left Blanding, I had told my employer that I would be back in seven days, and I was. I spent four nights with my family and then started herding sheep again. One day a person came by and told me that I should see my daughter in Dennehotso because she was sick. The next day, it was snowing when my employer came to where I was herding sheep. I told him my child was very sick, and that I wanted to go see what I could do. He said that I could, but that it would take a long time to find my replacement. I told him to get one as soon as possible, and the next day, he brought a Ute. The white man told me and the Ute that when the child was well, I would return to work. When I got back to Blanding, my employer drove by and asked which way I was going. He was heading to Mexican Hat so I caught a ride with him. From there I set out on foot.

When I got home, I found my little girl very sick. I do not remember who performed the hand-trembling ceremony, but he said that she needed herbs and roots for her to drink and bathe in. I went out and gathered some for her, and she got well. My son also said that sometimes he felt sick and other times fine. I asked him if he really got sick, and he said no; he just did not feel well sometimes. I told him I would try to come back as soon as possible and bring some food. At that time, there was only one sack of flour left, which would not go very far, although there was plenty of the other food. I saddled the burro and traveled to Dennehotso with a friend named Charlie for another sack of flour. Charlie brought it back to my mother, while I went on to Blanding.

I had set a date with the white man in Blanding to return to work at a certain time, but I took one day longer than I had planned. I started working again, and the Ute went home after I thanked him for herding the sheep while I was attending to my sick child. I asked the white man if he would rather have the Ute herd the sheep, but he told me he did not want to let me go now that my children were well. For two months I worked, then told my employer that I was tired and to get another person to herd for him. I knew my children were well, but I still wanted to be with them.

To the Railroad

I came to Blanding when another white man asked me to herd sheep for him. At the same time, there was a man from Dennehotso who had been there two or three days before and had seen my children with their grandmother at the trading post. He said they looked fine to him so I felt happy about the news. I went back to the white man and told him that I would work for him again. I herded sheep in the Monticello area from that spring to the next until they were moved to the east side of Blanding, where the sheep were lambing. The castration took place, and the lambs were separated from their mothers to be taken elsewhere. I was asked to take the lambs to Sunshine Mountain [La Sal Mountains] but declined, saying I would rather herd the sheep.[111] There were two Mexicans and two Navajos herding at this time, but my employer did not trust the Mexicans to take the lambs to the La Sal Mountains. He told me he preferred that I take the lambs up there so I said I would do it. Herding the lambs was very hard work because some of them would not travel on their own, so we had to push them along. We crossed a canyon toward the La Sal Mountains and herded them through places I had not seen, over the hills and out to the open plains. There were three of us taking the lambs there. One hauled our food in a wagon while the other two herded.

There was no water so the lambs got thirsty, but there was a white man who lived near where we were going, who had dammed some water in a pool. The person driving the wagon wrote a note to this white man, asking if the lambs could drink some water for ten dollars, and if we could rest and eat nearby. The man living there slowly gave his permission. We ate, cooled down, then ate again before we started off. The lambs arrived at the La Sals, where there was a train [Thompson, Utah] and a place to buy livestock. There were other herders there with their sheep and lots of Mexicans.

In the morning, when we counted the lambs, there were five missing, probably stolen out of the corral by the Mexicans or Anglos. There were so many people there that I do not know who did this. The white man that was buying the lambs had counted them before, and he told us we should wait until morning before putting them on the train. He counted them again, and that is when we discovered five were missing. He said that it was probably the Mexicans because they were very good at this sort of thing. Once the lambs were on the train, Floyd Nielson was going to leave so I got a ride with him back to Blanding to start herding sheep again.

After a month, I told my employer I kept thinking about my family, and that I wanted to go home for awhile. He said it was all right to go, and that a Ute called Braided Hair could herd sheep while I was gone.[112]

---

111. The Navajos call the La Sal Mountains Sunshine Mountain because it is one long, continuous ridge that does not cast shadows—the sun is always shining on it. It is also known as Five Mountains because "it has several peaks, and so it is several mountains combined." J. H.

112. "He was [later] an official for the Ute tribe at Towaoc and was part Paiute." J. H.

As this photo taken in 1916 in Monument Valley shows, transportation in those days was tenuous at best. (Photo from the O. C. Hansen Collection, Utah State Historical Society)

There was a man from Dennehotso looking for work, who brought word from my relatives that my daughter was sick. He asked me if I had been told about this, and I said that I had not. I thanked him for this message and said that I would tell Floyd Nielson about it, then go home. There was an Anglo driving in that direction so I caught a ride with him.

Sadness, Sickness, and Death

The roads at that time were in horrible condition. I got off at Bluff and started walking again, spending the night in Mexican Hat, then leaving early the next morning. Around noon I was close to home, when I saw a woman named 'Asdzą́ą́ Tsénteelí [Wide Rock Woman], who greeted me by saying, "My brother!"[113] She was crying and told me that my daughter had died and that death had come very fast. My daughter got sick one day and died the next.

When I got home, my sister told me to spend the night there, but even though sunset was approaching, I left for where my daughter had been buried. The sickness had come in such a rush that I wondered what

113. "Wide Rock Woman was my maternal aunt—a real sister to my mother; they came from the same mother. She was a sister of Oshley's, too. I used to work for her and plant corn for her at Dennehotso and her other home around Comb Ridge. She was wealthy, had livestock and expensive jewelry. She was a pretty woman, tall and slender." J. H.

had killed her. I think she died from the same disease that had killed her mother. Coughing was also weakening my son. While I was there, I gave him herbs, but he said there was nothing wrong with him so I left again.

I went back to the white man I had been working for, then in a month or two, returned home for a short while to see what was going on, and then returned to herd sheep again. I told my boss, Dághaa' łichíí' [Red Beard—Kumen Jones],[114] that I was tired, but he still wanted me to take care of the livestock.

Different white people wanted me to herd sheep for them so that was what I did. I would herd the sheep all day, then build a fire for the night. I might find a log on the ground and use that for protection. The log would be on my backside and the fire in front of me. Sometimes I would feel scared, and sometimes I would not.

As winter approached, I was herding sheep on the other side of Monticello, almost behind Blue Mountain, when Floyd Nielson came to tell me my son had died. At first I thought he had said that the boy was well, but the Navajo with us told me that my son had died. I asked him again if it was true. He said that it was. My son and daughter had died four or five months apart. I told my employer that I wanted to go to my family for awhile, but just as I was getting close to home, I saw my son riding a burro. People like my employer probably did not understand that the Navajos were saying the boy was only sick. He had been really sick, but now he was all right.

My relatives went to the Dennehotso Trading Post while I stayed home. I gave them money to buy food for the family and some clothes for my son, but I did not have enough for the hat he wanted. My mother was not feeling well, either. My son asked me to get some herbs for his grand-mother so I did. I asked him how he felt, and he said fine. Since he did not act sick, I left in three days.

I herded sheep for Floyd Nielson again. He asked me if I went home, and if my son was dead. I told him he was well, and he said that was good. I herded the sheep through the summer and during the winter months in the Cahone Mesa area, then back to Blanding for shearing and lambing time.

It had almost been a year when a person came to tell me that my son was very sick again. I started for home, and when I got back, I found he was very sick, though walking around. Soon his head started to hurt, and

114. "Kumen Jones was a very kind man. He had a lot of cattle. If people asked, 'May I have one of your cows to eat?' he would say, 'Sure.' He would shoot one for them and say, 'Go ahead and butcher it for some food.' He was very generous. O. Hansen Bayles was like that too—very kind. He [Bayles] was also named Missing Tooth because of a front tooth that was gone. He later had it replaced with a gold tooth." J. H.

he died instantly. This time it seemed like something hit me in the head. I do not remember what happened, or who fixed the burial, but only that I cried. My mother said I almost died, too. After my children passed away, I thought about what might have caused their death. I think it was tuberculosis. I also thought about the possibility of witchcraft because there were people who did not have kind thoughts about others.

My mother had recently returned from the clinic, had tied strings and pieces of fabric on her head, and just lay there coughing. I watched her, thinking about how old age was getting to her, causing her suffering. She had lived a long time and had always been there for us. A lot of times I saw people crying, and I wondered why. Now I know. When I think of my family, I cry because they really loved me and never exchanged any harsh words. When I think of them, I feel awful. I had stayed in Dennehotso for four days, but after my children died, I knew I could not do anything about it so I went back to Blanding.

For one year, all I did was think about what had happened. I did not herd sheep but just hung around. Not until midwinter did I start herding for Kumen Jones's son [Tom Jones] for about two months. My thoughts were always going back to my family. Tom Jones asked me why I was like that, so I told him about my wife and children and that I did not feel like herding sheep. He told me some comforting words, and that I was welcome to be among the people of Blanding. Even though he was a white person, he spoke kind words to me and said there was no need to say harsh things. After this I felt better.

Some people do not like the Christian beliefs. I go to church with them, and they tell me about it and explain the things pretty well. What I have observed about the Christians is that they are well-behaved and speak good words. Their prayers are true, too. The Christian people are helpful. When they see you need help, they help you, and with this, life is a little better. They taught us a way of life, and what they say tells of a good way to live. I wondered where they came from to be so nice and kind with their help and words. They gave us food. I just wondered how they could be so wonderful—I am talking about the people in Blanding. They are the Christian Mormons.

There was another man, Bila' díí' biye' [Son of Four Fingers—Hanson Durham Bayles], who wanted me to herd for him.[115] He had

115. "There were at least five [actually six] boys from that family [Bayles]. They lived in Bluff City. One of these boys was called The One Who Burned His House Down. [This refers to the youngest son, Scott Lyman Bayles, who, around the age of five, went with a friend to his father's large barn in Blanding and accidentally set it on

very few sheep, but they were down on the side of Blanding where the tall grass ends. I went to herd sheep for him for twenty-five dollars a month. There was not much to do except to walk around them once in awhile. I worked almost two months for him before he joined with another sheep owner. They asked me to herd sheep for them, but I told them no because I wanted to go to my mother. I spent five days over there before returning to Blanding. I told my mother to buy some flour, and although I did not have much money, I gave her seven dollars. She said that she would not forget me; then I said that I would not forget her, either. Whenever I went to her home, I felt all right.

Working Relationships

It seemed like I had no place to go. I did not say anything about how I felt since talking about it would not solve the problem. I just let it go at that. I did not herd sheep as much but just stayed adrift, not really working. I lived on or near Blue Mountain. I had only a circle of branches to call home. The people who worked came to visit me and slept there, and I was really happy to see them. I thought about how precious they were, and that was why I never hated anyone. Some of them did not have any money, so if they needed to eat, I usually had something.

There was a Ute who came to visit me very often to sleep at my camp. It bothered me to have him come so constantly so I moved to another place. Later I saw him at the store, and he told me he had come to see me twice, but that I was not there. He then asked where I was living, and I lied, saying I was chopping down trees at the edge of the canyon. I had never lied to anyone before, but I thought it was necessary. I had been told to chop some trees down there; I just had not moved there yet, so really I had not lied to him.

The white man, whose name was Bee' eskaalii [The One Who Got Batted (Hit with a Stick)—Morgan Nielson],[116] wanted me to chop

---

fire when experimenting with cigarettes. It was a total loss. (Finley Bayles, grandson, telephone conversation with author, April 5, 1996). I remember one time when we came to Bluff, these little boys were all tied to a tree because they were naughty. But now they are all grown up, and they are big strong men." J. H. When Finley Bayles, son of Grant Bayles, heard this story, he said it sounded highly probable since his grandmother, Evelyn Lyman Bayles, would restrain her boys in good-natured fun to keep them around.

116. Morgan Nielson is not a relative of Floyd and Jens Nielson. He was a jack-of-all-trades, who, in the 1920 census, is listed as a carpenter but also dabbled in trading

down trees so he went with me to the site. I had two big axes there, worked for one dollar, and chopped down so many trees that he added twenty-five cents to my pay. I told him I had enough money and chopped at my leisure. He brought me food as I worked, then he added twenty-five cents again to my income. I began to have a toothache caused by the vibration from chopping down a lot of trees. I was hurting all over, and my employer told me I probably was sore from chopping. I went back to where I was living, and the Ute started to visit me again, so I went to where a Navajo named John lived to stay for awhile. He had come to Blanding for work, but he eventually moved back to Bluff City.

Floyd Nielson came to me and asked if I would herd sheep for him, but I did not feel like it because I was still in mourning. He said that was all right, and he left me alone, but I did go to see Jens Nielson, who was looking for me. He gave me some food, asked where I was living, then said he wanted me to eat because that was why he had asked me to come. He also wanted to know how many people I was living with so I thought he did not want me to share with others. I told him I lived by myself and that I shared.

Later I went back to mother because I thought she might be out of food. She was happy to see me. When I got there, the family had just butchered a sheep since the food had run out, and they had only milk that morning. I started to wonder how we could get some flour, and even though I had money, I did not know what to do with it. I told my mother I did not know what I was doing, and that I did not have anything to look forward to. She said life was like that.

I had plenty of money—for one job I was paid sixty dollars, in another I had herded sheep and gotten seventy dollars, and at another place I was paid thirty dollars. I had all of this money but no children to buy things for, so I just had it with me. Even so my shoes were not in good condition. My mother told me she had no flour, coffee, or other basic food items so she asked me if I would buy some for her. I told her I

and handyman jobs around Blanding. According to John Holiday, "He [Nielson] was a boss in the Civilian Conservation Corps program, and we worked for him. This program was located in several different places, where the government set up white houses as their offices. One office was located in Kayenta, Arizona. The program used to provide recreational activities for its workers. The men would be bussed around to compete in basketball and baseball with other CCC camps. Once the men and Nielson went to play at Flagstaff at the Anasazi dwellings, where there was a CCC camp. While he was playing baseball, someone hit the ball, which struck him in the ankle, and he fell down. The men then called him The One Who Got Batted."

would go to the trading post for food, but that I had set a date with a white man to start work for him and so would have the food delivered.

My mother said that I always set a date to go back and I never spent time with the family. She asked me to stay with her for a year because she was very old, but I told her I felt better when I was going somewhere. I went to the trader in Dennehotso and bought my mother four sacks of flour, which cost $3.50 each, as well as four of every other necessary food. I asked someone to bring her the flour, then I was on my way back to Blanding. The people brought those things to my mother's place, and later, when I checked with others, they said it was delivered.

It seemed like I was gradually recovering, but I did not work as much and often told the white people no. It seemed I had more time to just be around. I began to think of who I was working and living for, since my mother had her own things. I was beginning to sleep anywhere, and I was in a poor condition. I bought a saddle and all the accessories, but I did not have anyone to take care of my things or anyone for me to buy things for. I talked with my mother about it and said that I would like to have a wife because I was just sleeping anywhere and did not feel good about it. Even when I came to her home, after two days, I was embarrassed to be there and eat her food. I did not know what to do with myself, going from one place to another. I said this in front of my relatives, who told me I should get a wife.

Marriage and Conflict

I married a woman from Chilchinbeto, the daughter of Bob Keith, who I first met at White Mountain.[117] I still herded sheep and rarely went back to my wife's place. My time was mostly spent herding with Mexicans and Navajos for the white man. Some of them were laid off, but I was not. Once I had had enough of herding sheep, I was let go. Jens Nielson wanted me to herd sheep for him. He paid me five sheep per month, and I earned sixty of them. I found out my wife was taken back to Chilchinbeto, but I did not go after her because it was best not to. We got a separation because of my working.[118]

---

117.   Oshley's second wife was Sarah Keith, daughter of Bob Keith, who belonged to the Within His Cover People clan and, like Oshley, was from Dennehotso. Keith arrived in Blanding around 1918. White Mountain or White Tipped Mountain is located between Monument Valley and Mexican Hat.

118.   Some informants (anonymous) said that Oshley told them there was also a problem with promiscuity and indications that their personal values were so widely divergent that bonds of trust and cooperation were never formed.

Sarah Keith (right), Navajo Oshley's second wife and daughter of Bob Keith, in the 1930s at Hanson Durham Bayles's home. (Photo courtesy of Carol Bayles Hurst)

I eventually went back to Dennehotso, where there were two leaders called Tó nichxoonii [Stinking Water] and Old Policeman.[119] Bob Keith, who I had been sharing our home with, said that he did not want to let me go. There was a meeting about this, but only a few people attended. Stinking Water and Old Policeman as well as my older brother, Gambler, were there. Bob Keith was told that I was not the one who moved out on him. I told him that I herded sheep and with the money I earned, I bought coffee, flour, and other things, and that he and his daughter had just left me. I thought they would move back, and that is why I didn't

---

119.   "Both these men were medicine men, who also did a lot of counseling. They talked to men and women who were divorced or trying to separate and counseled them to get back together and resolve their problems. They would hold meetings to do this. This is how I knew them." J. H.

Bob Keith's wife and children at the Peter Allen home in Blanding in the 1940s. The Keiths were good friends and relatives of Oshley . (Photo courtesy of Ada Rigby)

bother to follow them. I knew that one survived by working for the white man. So I said to just leave it at that and not to bother me. [I also said,] "Who knows, I might have another wife. Maybe one day you might come visit me and eat at my home, and I [may do] the same." My ex-father-in-law said that was all right with them. That is what happened.

After this it seems I drifted from one place to another. I started thinking again about how I could get food or blankets. I went back to my mother and told her I felt like my life was getting out of hand. I went to Blanding to herd for almost a month before going back to my mother's place. I thought by then my relatives must have found a wife for me. There were some people of the Salt clan living just outside of Kayenta. My relatives planned to ask for a girl from them. My other relatives asked another family near Mexican Water, so there were two places where my relatives had proposed.

One family had agreed to my relative's proposal, but I said I was going to go to Dennehotso to work for a farmer who had asked me. He did not give me a chance to think about it but just asked me to come for a few days, and so I agreed. But when I arrived at my aunt's place, I was told to get married then. My relatives said it was all right if I did not want to, but that there was a man called Áádóó yíní' [He Says "And Then"—Randolph Benally], whose wife had passed away.[120] He had two daughters. The

---

120. "They called him that [He Says "And Then"] because he always began and ended his sentences with 'and then.' It is just an expression. He married a Ute lady from Blanding. Her name was The Round Lady. He also had a brother who had a habit

oldest one was married to a man named Toohnii [San Juan River][121], and the youngest daughter, Mary, who was fifteen years old, was to be my wife.[122] My relatives said she could be my girlfriend, which at the time seemed funny. I said okay, that this was fine with me. The woman's family was from the Douglas Mesa area, but now they lived in Bluff City, where the [Saint Christopher's—Episcopal] church sits.

My brother-in-law-to-be came and told me to go with him to his family's place, where today the road is blasted down. When we got there, he told his family that the man who was going to marry the girl was with him. The relatives said they had already agreed to the marriage. We had no wedding ceremony, but the girl was told to take the bedding out for me. We talked for awhile, and she said she had seen me once. It was a happy moment.

The next day, the sheep were taken out, and I said I would herd them. San Juan River told me to get them to pasture before it got really hot. Water for the sheep was scarce so San Juan River wanted them moved to a water hole, but there I was, lying in the shade. People always used the expression that an in-law just lies around, and that was exactly what I was doing.

Shortly after my marriage to Mary, I wanted to go to an Enemy Way ceremony in Dennehotso. San Juan River had already gone over

---

of saying, 'that is exactly right,' after every sentence. Sometimes he would say just those words even when he was not talking. One time someone got tired of him saying that all the time and said, 'Why does he say that? Why don't you shut him up by hitting him on the head!' The brother replied, 'That is exactly right,' and everyone laughed." J. H.

121. The name Toohnii can be interpreted in a number of ways. Some translate it as Near Water or Edge of Water; others think it has to do with the motion of a river, while others say it is the San Juan River, and still others translate it as someone who lives near the San Juan—a river resident. Here it is considered the latter. This person's English name is Billy Water, and he was a member of the Red House clan.

John Holiday, a clan brother, remembers him well. "He was a medicine man who performed many ceremonies and moved around quite a bit. He stayed in this area until his wife passed away then he moved to Shiprock, New Mexico, where he remarried and lived until he died of old age. He got his name, Water—San Juan [also the name for Shiprock], because he married a woman in Montezuma Creek and had two children. He left [ran away] this family and returned home so everyone called him San Juan River, identifying that he was from that place."

122. "She was part Ute [more likely San Juan Paiute]. Her maternal grandmother was a Ute named The Woman Who Hears/Knows the Language. She was married to Dying of Thirst. There are still some descendants of the Ute [Paiute] tribe who live at Douglas Mesa." J. H.

Mary Oshley (the adult at far right) and her mother Sadie Benally (fourth from left) and the Oshley children: left to right, Franklin, Jennie, Floyd, Mary June, Joan, Jean (with dog), and Wesley (in Mary's arms). (Photo courtesy of Baxter Benally)

there. I told my wife about it, then she decided to go, too. I told her to take care of the home, but she insisted she was going so we started off. We met other people, one of whom was my mother's sister, riding their horses to the ceremony. San Juan River was there, watching me closely but keeping his distance. I wondered why.

We had just arrived for the second night of the ceremony. At home Little John and Toohnii biye' [San Juan River's Son] were supposed to be herding sheep, but they had come to the ceremony and left the sheep corralled.[123] I told my wife that they should not leave the animals penned up, and that we needed to go back. The sheep had gotten out through the fence, and so it took time for us to finally catch them. We got them back in the corral at sunset, at which time everybody was back from the ceremony.

San Juan River was mad. He threatened me with a .22 caliber rifle as my wife ran behind me. I grabbed the rifle, while his wife grabbed the rifle and took it away. When he calmed down, I asked him why he was doing this and who he was going to shoot. As he sat there, his wife became

---

123. The Little John referred to is John Holiday.

furious and was really yelling at him. She asked him if he had gone insane and said he was supposed to be the head of the household, but I did not say anything to him. What happened had happened so we all went to sleep.

The next morning, San Juan River went to work in Bluff City while I was working in Dennehotso, where a school was being built. I thought about what had happened and wondered how he could act that way. The people there were scared, but I was not. I thought he would do what he wished. The corn was ready for harvest when I went to the Dennehotso Trading Post. The trader asked me if I wanted to work cutting stones while other workers had the responsibility of stacking them and making a building. I do not know how many days I worked there.

San Juan River went home every day. Even though he was mistreating me, I still bought coffee, sugar, and other necessities for his family and my wife. Other men were doing things to him that embarrassed me. Even his son was having an affair with his wife. I kept telling my wife how embarrassing it was. She agreed but said San Juan River was blaming me for his wife's actions. I told her not to bother with this family problem, and I left. I decided not to go back over there because it was embarrassing but rather to just work hard at Dennehotso.

After I left, another man rode in and stayed in bed with my wife's sister. It was very early in the morning, and my wife told her that this was embarrassing so her sister got mad at her. The next evening, there was a different man sleeping in the sister's bed. My wife left the place and came after me. Someone told me that my wife was in Dennehotso, and I suspected that her sister had gotten angry at her. My wife had gone to one of my clan brothers, of the Many Goats clan.[124] I found someone to work in my place, then went to her. I asked why she had come, and she said that her sister was sleeping with a man and that she was mad at her for doing it. I told her that she would stay here with me and not go back over there, to which she agreed.

We were staying at my brother's place when San Juan River came by with a big stick. When I arrived home from work, he was still there. He got after my wife for not tending the sheep, but all the women rushed in to protect her. Just about this time, I came home. After this San Juan River calmed down. Before I returned, he was mad, but now he just told me that no one was tending the sheep. I told him they were his sheep, his family's responsibility, and that my wife was here to cook for me while I was at work.

---

124. This was not Oshley's clan but one he was related to.

He became angry again and picked up his stick. I thought maybe he was going to poke me with it, but I was strong so it did not matter to me what he did. Then he said all right, and we watched him ride off. I could see that he did not like me one bit. The men that I was working with knew what was going on with him and spoke to me about it, but all I said was that it was his problem. I could not do anything for him. These men agreed, saying that there was nothing wrong with me, and that whatever the problem was, it was not mine.

LIVESTOCK REDUCTION

The construction of the school was now finished so we started working on a different project, this time digging wells.[125] We were told that the well we were working on had not been constructed properly. After this I asked for a five-day leave. When I got back, I was assigned to another well. All of these projects were part of John Collier's program. I told the supervisors I only wanted to work for one month, but they insisted I keep working so I stayed for two. Because of these projects, many Navajos thought John Collier was wonderful, but something about this work did not sound right. I told some people about my feelings, but they still thought he was the greatest.

My next job was to take food, water, and hay to the workers and their horses. Sometimes I took firewood, too, but before long, I found myself again working on the project for a couple of months. Next the employment turned to the sheep, and we were told to sell the old sheep and old goats. This was the doing of John Collier, who, through this program, reduced the Navajos to the level of poverty.[126] He did this by having the sheep taken out and killed. Some [animals] were paid for, but most were just slaughtered.

---

125. This is one of the few verifiable dates to help mark the chronology of Oshley's life. The first Bureau of Indian Affairs (BIA) school, located by the trading post in Dennehotso, was completed in 1938. See Rodgers, *Chapter Images,* 50.

126. The livestock-reduction program that took place when John Collier served as the commissioner of the Bureau of Indian Affairs was one of the two most traumatic events in Navajo history, the other being the Navajo exile at Fort Sumner (1864–68). Livestock was literally and philosophically "life" to the people. When the government decreed that large portions of the herds had to be destroyed to save the land from overgrazing and consequent erosion, resentment and friction grew to new heights. Most of the reduction occurred during the 1930s as the American economy languished in the Great Depression. By the time this program had run its course, in many instances, the herds had been cut by more than half, forcing the

When people got money for the sheep, they thought he was a good man. I told them he was going to turn on them, but no one listened to what I had to say. I was not the wisest, most knowledgeable man, but I told them. Our leaders were all for him. I kept saying that somewhere he was going to turn around on them, but still people said he would not do that to them. After livestock reduction had been going on for awhile, I asked them how great they thought John Collier was now. They had changed their mind about him, saying that what he was doing was wrong.

The government bought old sheep for only two dollars a head, and for old goats, the price was very low. Trading posts such as the ones in Dennehotso, Kayenta, and Mexican Water bought many sheep and goats under the John Collier program. One time I was on the east side of the Dennehotso Trading Post, when one of our leaders came to the corral and said to kill all of the sheep that were in it. He had been told to say this and to tell the people that if anyone needed meat, that they could butcher the fat ones, but that we also had to dig a hole for all of the carcasses. I asked why we were doing this and suggested that at least we should do the butchering someplace else. There were people there just butchering away.

I butchered one even though I did not like the idea. All of these living things were going to waste. From then on, even though I did not like it, I participated in the project and felt the anguish. The digging of holes began. The people threw the heads, the insides of the animals, and feet into the hole. I did not like what I saw. A lot of older men and women died from this because the livestock was their life, and it was being taken from them.[127] They killed my sheep, too, and I can still feel the hurt.

Navajos out of economic independence into an off-reservation wage economy and dependence on the government. Collier's name became synonymous with all the hate the program created. For a view of the program's impact on Navajos in southeastern Utah, see Robert S. McPherson, "Navajo Livestock Reduction in Southeastern Utah, 1933–1946: History Repeats Itself," *American Indian Quarterly* (winter/spring 1998).

127.   Oshley is referring to the feeling of helplessness and despair that Navajos felt during stock reduction. The psychological trauma devastated many of the people, resulting in diminished health and, in some instances, death. Although no quantified study has been done to determine its emotional impact, and although it is difficult for a white person to understand, the Navajos' connection to livestock was as much psychological as economic. Each animal had its own personality and was recognized not just as food on the hoof but as a contributor to life. In Navajo thought, this whole incident was an attempt at enslavement similar to the Fort Sumner years. Because of livestock reduction, the Navajos were forced off the reservation into the dominant culture's wage economy.

There was one man called John Nakai, who tried to do something about livestock reduction.[128] He held meetings to put an end to this project. There was a big meeting at Willow Plain, where people talked about what was going on.[129] John Collier had asked us what we were doing with our sheep because they were messing up the land, grass, and water. We were also told that we had to kill certain plants. There was a man called Hastiin Tsé łichíí' haa'áhí [Mister Red Rock Sticking Out].[130] He was one of our leaders, and he opposed the project. When John Collier left, he said that what he [Mister Red Rock Sticking Out] said would be done, and that was what happened.

By this time, it seemed like the program was cooling down. Many of our leaders did not have anything to say about the matter because they were embarrassed that they were among those who had said John Collier was wonderful. The person who had told us to work for Collier was there, but he did not say a word. In Montezuma Creek, we heard that sheep were herded to the dipping vats to be treated. Nobody wanted what had happened to them to happen to the other people. I even voiced my opinion.

After all this happened, a man named Ta'neeszahnii nééz [Somebody Tall] and I left for another work project. We finished with one place and

---

128. "John Nakai helped the Navajos to keep their livestock during this reduction period. From my home, I had to take the horses and the sheep to the 'reduction' office near Montezuma Creek, where they were marked with red paint for extermination. Everybody was mad at me, including John Nakai. They said, 'For sure all of your livestock will be killed.' But instead, I was given a piece of white paper and was told that it would keep officials away from my animals, even though I had more than the allowed number. The government did not take any away.

John Nakai dealt with stock-reduction problems in the Montezuma Creek area. A group of stock-reduction policemen and representatives was sent out to the people at White Rock Point [Bluff area]. The Navajos, including John Nakai, planned to fight with them, but it did not happen. A man named Fat Banana [yucca fruit] was a messenger who rode his horse back and forth between the Navajos and the police, who were camped at Spring Water Coming Out. He told the police that the Navajos were given big guns from Salt Lake City to use against them. The policemen looked through their binoculars and said, 'Sure enough. We see the big guns sticking up from behind the volcanic ridge.' The Navajos had cut down some large tree trunks and laid them up against the top of the ridge so that the tip of the logs showed along the hill. Fat Banana had lied to the police about the big guns, and so they turned around and went back." J. H.

129. Marion Bidwell was in charge of the livestock-reduction program in the Kayenta area. He was known as Bald Headed to the Navajos.

130. "Mister Red Rock Sticking Out received his name from a prominent terrain feature near his home. He was quite wealthy with a lot of horses, cattle, and sheep, but he was not a medicine man." J. H.

moved on to the next. I thought that I should have my wife with me, but my aunt had said no. My aunt asked me if I knew that San Juan River really wanted to get me, and I said I didn't, but that if she learned anything more about it, to tell me.

One day we went rabbit hunting. Some of the men went hunting below the worksite while others went above it. Four of us went together in one direction, then two of us split off and went over to a rocky section. Everybody, including the farmer, was involved in the rabbit hunt. This reminded me of a long time ago, when the coyote first established the pattern for hunting. He boasted that he was really good at it but then had all kinds of trouble. My partner said he hoped we did not end up like the coyote.[131] I heard people chasing rabbits up higher. They had killed two, and we also killed two, but we did not come back until it was dark. We finished the project and moved to Sand Plain, where we worked for twenty days, then went home.

When I got back, my wife wanted to go to her father. It was getting cold, but she really wanted to go there because she had heard some rumors about her family. My aunt said that San Juan River said he was going to hurt me, but that she had hid this from me because I always got mad so easily. She said the family had told San Juan River not to say those things, but that he really disliked me. I said that was fine, that my wife wanted to go to her father, and that we would be going over there the following day. The next morning, I ate, packed and saddled the reddish brown horse, then we were on our way. The only thing we had for food was corn and a deerskin to trade, but we did not look poor. We had a good-looking saddle, saddle blankets, and blankets. I was on foot.

Life in Bluff

We spent the night at Red Area [about two miles south of the San Juan River near Mexican Hat], where it was cold and really hard to find firewood. The next morning, we ate the cooked corn and started on our journey again. We got to John Oliver's place, which was next to Arthur Spencer's trading post. I did not have any food so pawned the deerskin for $2.50. We left when the sun was high in the sky and got past Mexican Hat. I felt tired and hungry so I let the horse roam for awhile, built a fire

---

131.   Oshley is referring to the trickster tales of coyote who is either a tricker or being tricked. Even when he is successful in obtaining food, he still loses it through some problem that he creates for himself. See Berard Haile, *Navajo Coyote Tales: The Curly To Aheedliinii Version* (Lincoln: University of Nebraska Press, 1984).

Randolph and Sadie Benally carding and spinning wool in their hogan on the outskirts of Bluff, Utah. (Photo courtesy of Baxter Benally)

to cook on even though we had recently eaten, and wondered what was wrong with me. I did not know why I felt that San Juan River was coming, but as we ate, I told my wife that I felt like a man was approaching but did not say who. My wife just grunted to acknowledge what I had said. She wanted to get going again so we started.

We were at another spring in the Valley of the Gods, and I told my wife it would be quite awhile before we got to water again so we let the horse drink. On the hill, just before Comb Ridge, there was a pile of hay that a white man must have dropped beside the road. There was only a little bit, but I gathered it up, moved to the top of Comb Ridge, and spent the night there. I told my wife there was a spring called Navajo Spring closeby, and that we would cook our breakfast there. We took off for the spring.

When we were spending the night on Comb Ridge, I heard my horse make a sound like there was another horse in the distance.

At first light, I looked for tracks but found none, although there was a group of horses in the distance which my horse was probably neighing to. We did not have any water, but there was some at the foot of the ridge, so I saddled up and we left for the spring. When we got there, we cooked our breakfast, and the horse chewed on some grass. After we ate, we left again. I was really tired because I was walking on foot so we traveled slowly, and I told my wife what the various places were called. We were quite a ways from Bluff City, and I felt like the journey was very long.

I told my wife that I had heard that her father worked in Bluff, so we looked for him as we went through the streets and found him on his burro by the side of the road. He gave his daughter a big hug and was so happy to see her that he even cried. He also gave me a hug, saying he was very thankful that I had brought his daughter to him. He said, as he was crying, that a lot of times he was lonely for his daughter, and he wondered how she was doing.

We went up the river to where the [Episcopalian] church is now. He was living in a sunny spot among the cottonwood trees, which he used to make his home. The sheep stayed next to the cliff's rock walls, but there was no corral. As soon as we arrived, her mother came out and hugged her, but her stepmother just shook hands. They had two children, a girl and a boy, who [Randolph, Mary's father] supported by going every day to town to chop wood for the white man. Sometimes I would help him. He also took care of his sheep and goats, one burro, and four horses.

In Bluff, Kumen Jones was the leader of the white people. He was a very good friend to the Navajos and understood the Navajo language. The man who was running the trading post was Naakaii yázhí [Little Mexican—John Hunt], but other white people ran the trading post sometimes. The roads were in awful condition, the firewood supply was small, and there were few automobiles. Most of the white people got their firewood by wagon. Only rarely was an automobile used to bring in firewood. The Catholics [Episcopalians—Saint Christopher's Mission, approximately a mile east of Bluff] were not there yet.[132]

At the future mission site, there was only a fenced area where the people planted their corn, squash, and melons. My father-in-law lived on this land for a long time and planted a small field in the box canyon near a spring. He also diked the spring for the sheep and horses. He shared this

132. Father H. Baxter Liebler founded the Saint Christopher's Mission in the summer of 1943. It was generally well received by the Navajos because of his outgoing attempts to incorporate their culture into his services. He also did a lot to help combat illness and poverty among the people. Randolph Benally maintained his home on the outskirts of the mission and became a friend of Liebler's and a member of the church. For more information about Saint Christopher's, see H. Baxter Liebler, *Boil My Heart for Me* (Salt Lake City: University of Utah Press, 1994).

land with a man called Hashk'aan [Yucca Fruit]. Now the Catholics have moved there, so he had to move above them. He and his wife are gone, and now their children live there.

We stayed there throughout the winter. They were really nice people, the children loved us, and we were well taken care of. I herded sheep for her father, and he would chop wood for the white man. If I went to chop trees, my wife would herd the sheep. In the spring, the sheep were lambing, and we helped with that. In the evening, we would get a lot of milk from the goats, and when we were finished milking, we let the kids go to their mothers. At the end of the summer, it was time to sell the lambs in Bluff. Her father thanked me many times for being there to help him with the sheep while he made some money. My father-in-law said we had to get ready for winter; then he would go off on his burro to chop firewood.

The winter came and was almost over when I said I wanted to go home. I had not been there since we had left. As I rode off on the reddish brown horse, the sun was going down at Oliver's place, but I was told that some Navajos from the Oljato area were working on the road there, so that is where I wanted to sleep. I stayed there and was on my way again the next morning. I went to my aunt's place, spent seven or eight days there, and she butchered a sheep for me. My older brother came by and asked why they were giving me only one butchered sheep, and why they had not given me more to drive back to Bluff. I told them that we would return for the sheep. I started back to my wife and slept west of Oliver's home. The next morning, I left early and got back at sunset.

The family appreciated the meat I brought back. I told them what my relatives had said about the sheep, and my father-in-law urged that I get them as soon as possible. We went over there during midsummer and found that the corn and other things were ripe. We crossed the river above the church [St. Christopher's] and slept at Smooth Rock Wall. Some people were living there, and one of them was a leader. They gave us food; then we were on our way again. The next place we stopped was at John Hunt's. He was not there, but his wife and children were. They butchered a sheep for us, we ate, then traveled to Mexican Water before sleeping.

Early the next morning, we met people in wagons and told them where we had slept. One of the men was Tiyani yázhí [Small Person? (derivation unknown)] of the Water's Edge People clan. He said that they had slept just a short distance from there, and that there was an Enemy Way ceremony going on just a little ways off. He told us about the ceremony and how he and the others were going for firewood. We went up Laguna Creek, which comes from Kayenta, and came out in Dennehotso.

My sister, who was married to Hastiin Ntł'aa'ii biye' [Son of the Man Who Is Called Lefty] from Monument Valley, had a cornfield in Dennehotso. We stayed there for many days, then went a little ways to my older brother's cornfield, where we spent the whole summer. My horse knew how to pull a wagon, and they needed one to help haul firewood, which was mostly dried greasewood.

Herding and Wage Labor

In the autumn, we went to Comb Ridge where my aunt was living. I told my wife we would go back then. When we got to my aunt's place, she asked if I had come for the sheep. I told her that I had so we spent a few days there at Plain with Reeds. Late in the afternoon, she separated twenty-five sheep for us and started them on their journey to Bluff. In the evening, we were at Mexican Hat, where Oliver gave us some things to eat. We bedded the sheep along the cliffs of the San Juan River, and the next day, we herded them onward.

We stopped at the salty creek called Moving to Get Together, where there was sometimes a spring and sometimes not.[133] It was on the big hill [Lime Ridge] just before you get to Comb Ridge. Later there was a ravine with a spring in it. We got there when the sun went down. I told my wife we would spend the night on Comb Ridge because there was a good place to keep the sheep in a small box canyon. My wife liked it so we stayed there that night, letting the horse and sheep drink water, while we ate what was left from our morning meal and made camp.

In the evening, we passed the time away by telling each other of our adventures. Sometimes they were funny, and we laughed. I said that the next day we would drive the sheep slowly, and it would be close to sundown when we would get to Bluff. During the night, my wife realized there was no sound from the sheep, awoke me, and told me that they were gone. In my sleepiness, I had to ask again before realizing the stock was missing. Sometime during the night, they had walked by without awakening us, then gone a long ways toward home. We followed their trail, but I lost my direction. My wife said we were going one way, and I kept saying that it was the other way. She insisted so I just quieted down and thought

---

133. "Moving to Get Together Creek got its name long ago when Navajo men went hunting. They used to gather there before they moved toward the Bears Ears or Cedar Mesa to hunt. A group of hunters would make plans to meet there. One group would show up, then another, and another until everyone arrived. The creek is also known as Water Coming from an Iron Pipe and also Glass Rock." J. H.

to myself that it didn't matter if we were going the wrong direction. To my surprise, she was correct. Right in front of us were our saddles.

We found the sheep and drove them into the box canyon once more. The next day, we saddled our horses and drove them out again. It seemed to take forever to get through the area between Comb Ridge and Bluff when herding sheep on foot. We arrived at my father-in-law's place at sunset, and he was very happy about the sheep. We stayed there throughout the winter.

In the spring, the sheep had their lambs. Although we did not have many, we sold some, but my father-in-law sold a lot of his. I told him about how I usually worked for the white men in Blanding. He said that he could not do all the work by himself, that he needed my help taking care of the sheep, that he worked for the white man, and that his children were still small. But I was embarrassed to continue to eat his food because I wanted to bring home my own.

So I stayed there until the start of winter, then went to Blanding. I caught a ride from Bluff to Blanding and there chopped wood for a white man for only four days. I earned enough money to buy coffee, sugar, and flour, which my wife's family appreciated. As I was about to leave Blanding, I saw my father-in-law, who was also going to Bluff. He was happy to see me and asked if there was more work in Blanding. I told him I had been chopping wood awhile for a white man, and he said he also had been chopping firewood and had bought some food. There were three of us who returned to Bluff.

When I arrived home, my wife was happy that I had brought some things for the family. She had been taking care of the lambs, which my father-in-law appreciated. He told me that the white men in Bluff liked to have their firewood chopped, no matter what it was like, so I told him I could work in the Bluff area. If they did not want the wood, we could keep it for ourselves. The next day, after breakfast, I took out the sheep. As I was herding them, I thought about what I had said and decided to chop up some firewood to sell. If they did not want it, that was all right with me.

In the evening, I had the sheep at their sleeping place, my father-in-law was back, and he said a white man offered him three dollars to uproot a dried cottonwood tree just outside of Bluff City. I asked him how wide it was, and he told me it was not big, and that it could probably be taken out pretty easily. I asked him if we could both do the job, and he was excited about my going with him. We got there, and in no time we had the tree down and were chopping it into pieces, earning $1.50 each.

Part of the town of Bluff, looking north into Calf Canyon. Oshley traveled these streets often in search of employment. (Photo from the O. C. Hansen Collection, Utah State Historical Society)

We went to another white man's place and told him that we wanted work. This man was old and called Daghaa' néézí [Tall Mustache or Beard]. In the afternoon, I ate at his place. Sometimes my employer came to help, but it seems he barely did anything with the ax. He also had a field that he wanted cleared of willows. I earned $1.25 for doing it. He wanted me to work in a field where cockleburs had taken over. For the whole job, he paid $5.00 and a sack of beans. The cockleburs were still tender so they cut easily with a hoe and a double-bladed ax. I had a hard time with the ax, but the hoe was nice to work with because it was heavy.

While I was working, my wife herded the sheep out on the cliff nearby. When I had only a little patch left, my wife was thrilled. She went home and told her family that the patch was getting smaller. Each day she checked to see how close I was to finishing, because my getting closer meant we would be able to get food. Sometimes I felt embarrassed because I was not bringing in any food, even though my father-in-law told me not to feel that way. My wife was not like that because he was her father.

After I finished, I told my family to get the sack of beans while I went to another job. When I came back, the beans were boiling. I also received the five dollars so I bought coffee, sugar, and other essentials. My father-in-law was very happy about me going to work because I had bought some food, even though these things did not cost very much.

Time passed, and eventually the winter went by. I remained in Bluff because I had sheep in my wife's family's herd. My father-in-law spent most of his time chopping firewood for white men. I told him that I still felt embarrassed about living with him and eating his food. Even though I herded the sheep, it did not make it right. He was surprised that I felt this way because I was taking care of the sheep and working for the white people. He was very thankful for the help because it was hard to organize the daily activities without it. My wife also worked around the home so my father-in-law believed I should not feel uncomfortable. But when it got really warm, I said I wanted to go to Blanding to find work.

Whenever I wanted to go somewhere, I would tell him about it first. If he agreed, I would go. My father-in-law said it was up to me so I went to the trading post in Bluff, hoping to catch a ride from someone with an automobile. A white man I did not know, but who knew me, was leaving. He called out my name and asked where I was going. I told him I wanted to go to Blanding to do work, like chopping firewood. He said he was going there so I got a ride all the way to Blanding.

At this time, Biwoo' łání [Many Teeth—Harold R. Butt] lived in Blanding and had a lot of firewood piled next to his home. I went there, and he asked me where I was going so I told him of my intentions. Just then a white man, who wanted a Navajo to work for him, came in. The worksite, however, was just too far away so I did not bother to ask about what it was. Butt wanted to have firewood chopped for him so I went outside and looked at his whole pile of firewood. He wanted it all chopped for seven dollars, but I said that pile of firewood was worth more than that. We finally agreed on ten dollars for the whole pile. He told me I would eat at noon with him; in other words, no breakfast or supper. We agreed upon it, and I chopped for three days.

At that time, he had sheep in the Bluff area, and the person who was herding wanted to go home. He asked me to herd sheep for him for forty dollars a month. I raised the amount to forty-five dollars because I had experience with many sheep owners and knew about how much they usually paid their workers. We barely got the amount to forty-five dollars per month. I told him I would like to go home before I started herding sheep, so with the ten dollars I had earned for the three days of chopping wood, I bought some potatoes and flour and took them to Bluff.

I then herded sheep throughout the summer and into the beginning of winter, until he told me I had to move the sheep to the plains of

Monticello. He had bought grazing rights over there, but I said that I had had enough with herding sheep for awhile and did not want to go through the cold weather doing it. He hired a younger boy from Montezuma Creek, and I went home. I had worked for three or four months and gotten paid over a hundred dollars. I bought three fifty-pound sacks of flour and many other kinds of food, which was delivered to my home. My father-in-law was very happy. I stayed home and herded our combined flock of sheep through the winter while he chopped fire-wood and received food as payment. We had plenty of beans and did not buy meat from the store since our sheep were fat.

In the spring, Butt came and told me to herd sheep for him. I think he said he wanted to have the sheep in the La Sal Mountain area, and that the monthly pay would be forty-five dollars. I was herding our own sheep and did not go because our sheep had just had their lambs. We sold some of them and had only a few left. It was about midsummer when Butt came again, and the sheep were still there. Again he asked me to herd sheep, and this time I agreed. He told me that for one month he would pay me forty-five dollars, and that I could herd them on top of the plateau above Bluff. Nineteen days later, the man that I was substituting for came back so I went home after being paid more than $1.50 per day.

Whenever I was not working, I was at home herding sheep while my wife worked with the lambs, and my father-in-law chopped wood, cleared fields, and put in fence posts. When the white men needed my help, they would tell my father-in-law, who spoke very good English. With this kind of help, there was always work for me if I needed it. When I didn't have any more food, I would go into the trading post in Bluff and just ask for certain items, and the owners would give them to me. Once I was working, I would pay back what I owed, but it was easy for me to get credit. My father-in-law really loved me and liked to know where I was going. If I did not tell him, it would bother him. He also asked when I was coming back, and whenever I returned home, he was happy. He would say that I did not tell him where I was going and that he thought about me. When I was out working, he would talk to his daughter and tell her to let me go out and work since he thought about the food I would buy, and that there was always work for me.

Next I herded sheep on the wash near Cortez. It was there the sheep had their lambs. There were a lot of lambs and sumac berries and water, too. There were also beaver. As the ewes were lambing, I was made fore-man. Each herder had his own group of sheep with their lambs. I went from one group to another until all the sheep and lambs were back together. My boss said that we would now move onto the mountain. When we got there, some more lambs were born so we castrated them. I said that we were done now, that we had helped him, and now we were going back to our home. My boss was silent, so I asked him what he was thinking about. He said that I had worked really well for him, that we had no quarrel [hard feelings] between us, and that I was leaving now. We were paid and driven back from Cortez. My boss bought cooking utensils for us and said that we had worked hard for them.

After herding sheep for Harold Butt, I was paid separately, then taken back to Bluff City, only to find that our baby had been born prematurely. My wife and I stayed around Bluff for a short time, and then I was asked to herd sheep again. We moved back to Blanding with the baby, even though she was not feeling well. We herded sheep across Westwater, a little to the south of us, but the baby, whose name was Dzanibaa' [Woman Warrior], got worse.[134] My boss came out and got us and brought us into town while another sheepherder took my place.

We took the baby to Shiprock with a white man from Blanding we hardly knew. She was very small and in bad condition. We got her into the Shiprock Hospital, and the doctors told us that she was really sick, but that we should decide if we wanted her to remain there. We told them to do whatever was necessary so the baby stayed. We did not have a place to spend the night so the white man told us he would take us back to where the Utes were living at the place called Blue House [Towaoc], and we could sleep there.[135] He returned the next morning to Towaoc to take us back to the hospital, where we learned that the baby had died the night before. We took one last look at her and realized we could not do anymore, so I asked the hospital to arrange the burial, and they said they would. Everything was settled. We went back to Blanding with the white man.

We returned to Blanding, then went to my father-in-law's place. He had already heard about our child, and he tried to comfort us, but there was nothing to fill the empty space. These things happened, and they are

134. Many Navajo people have three or four names by which they are known in different circumstances and at varying stages of life. Both men and women may have a "war name" that is used during ceremonies, especially the Enemy Way. Usually women's names end with the word "war" and men's end in "warrior." Berard Haile in *An Ethnologic Dictionary of the Navajo Language* (p. 119), also notes that there were many Navajos who did not follow this practice. See also Gladys Reichard, *Social Life of the Navajo Indians* 97–100.
135. Towaoc is the tribal headquarters of the Ute Mountain Utes. It received its name because the agency was, in its earlier days, a regular house painted blue.

always happening. He said that together we would have more children, that if we had sons, we would have daughters-in-law, and if we had daughters, we would have sons-in-law, and there would be many grandchildren. We felt better after he said this to us; my wife and I thanked him. Jean, another daughter [belonging to Mary and Navajo], was born at my father-in-law's home in the summer when the sumac berries had ripened.

We stayed around there and helped him. There was a white man called Né'éshjaa' [Owl—Bob Wise][136] and the one called Long Beard, who I worked for occasionally. I would either clear or plant fields or hoe. Sometimes I herded sheep, and other times I just looked after my father-in-law's horses and burro. We stayed there, and within the next two years, Joan was born in the spring above Bluff City.

A New Home—Blanding

After two years, I told my father-in-law I wanted to work in Blanding for Floyd Nielson. I herded for him, but after awhile, I told him I wanted to go home because I was worried that there might not be enough food there. He told me it was fine with him, that his son was going to come the following day, and that I should be back in three days. So I rode back on a mule, slept in Blanding, and the next day traveled to Bluff.

Everyone was home when I got back, and I saw that there was plenty of food because the lambs had been sold. But my wife had gotten in a fight with her stepmother over the children, and she thought it was going to get worse. Her mother had jumped on her, taking her down. That was when her father came and asked his wife what had gotten into her. He scolded her, and she started crying, but my wife did not.

I told my wife that if she remained in Bluff, things were going to get worse so we should move to Blanding. Floyd Nielson had always been good to me so my wife agreed to go. Two days later, before leaving, I told my father-in-law that I was returning to work, taking my children with me, and that I would feed them any way I could. My father-in-law said

---

136.   "He used to make homemade brew close to Twirling Mountain [Navajo Blanket] by the San Juan River, way up in the canyon near Mexican Hat. My brother-in-law and another man from Monument Valley used to work for him and helped make the drink. While they were doing that, Mr. Owl would be down at the river panning for gold. I used to take them food and water by riding my donkey all the way up the canyon to their camp. That was Mr. Owl's small business—making brew. He got his name by copying the hooting of an owl when he saw you. He would do it at night, too, probably to scare the people." J. H.

Bob Keith, like Oshley, was one of many Navajos hired to chop massive amounts of wood for heating, cooking, and construction in the white community of Blanding. (Photo courtesy of Ada Rigby)

that it was fine with him. He mentioned that the women had gotten into a fight at the lamb sale, and that while he was still dealing with the white man, his wife jumped on his daughter. Now it was better for me to move on, but that we should remember each other. All we had were two horses and not many things.

We had lunch at the foot of White Mesa. The children were happy that they had gotten to come along. Even though it was summer, it was cold when we arrived in Blanding.[137] The first Navajos to move to Blanding were Smiley and his wife. Another person to move there in the early days was Bob Keith, but as I herded more in this area, I would see new Navajos moving in.[138] Now I was returning to live there with my own family, and I saw this again. Ch'ah 'ádini's [No Hat] daughter from the

---

137. What follows is a brief account of some of the first Navajos to move to Blanding and the establishment of the Westwater community. There was a tremendous amount of itinerancy that was fostered by economic necessity for many Navajos. Speaking of this time, older Navajos say that people were "like rabbits" or "grasshoppers" because they moved around so much. See Winston B. Hurst, "The Blanding Navajos: A Case Study of Off-Reservation Navajo Migration and Settlement" (master's thesis, Eastern New Mexico University, 1981), 86.

138. Bob Keith arrived in the Blanding area in the early 1920s and lived there permanently starting around 1924. He, like Oshley, was from the Dennehotso area and was of the Bit'ahnii clan. Hurst, 180.

Oljato area moved in, then Ch'ah 'ádini's son [Nez Hutchins], then Bitsii' łibahí [Gray Hair—Bert Atene], also from Oljato.[139] In Westwater Canyon, Bob Keith's children planted a small patch of land with corn, squash, and melons to live on. There was a man of the Kin yaa'áanii [Towering House] clan from Tsii' nazee'ai [derivation unknown], who always moved back and forth from here. Some Navajos came here to chop down trees because in those times, white people used firewood for everything. There were only a few white people, but they paid two dollars for a full wagonload of chopped firewood. This represented a lot of work, as did pay for clearing the land.

There was a Ute living there named Dagoozh [derivation unknown], who I asked to help me build a home because I was supposed to be back to work the next day. He said he would. Smiley was also living there, and we borrowed his ax and a shovel to make a shelter. The season got very cold. I didn't know what we were going to do. We got two axes and chopped down some trees—this is the same time Little Bobby came with his wife. We made a forked hogan. Little Bobby [helped], along with Bob Keith's son. This forked hogan was a male hogan.

After we finished that hogan, we started on mine. We built it near where Ałts'íísí [He Is Little] was living against a rock. It was a pretty good hogan that was finished in two days, but in some ways it was deformed. We made it into a round female hogan with juniper bark and dirt on it, and even the women helped with the building. When the logs were put into place, juniper-tree bark was spread over and chinked between the logs; then wet dirt was added on top. Back then it rained a lot so there was plenty of wet dirt.

When we finished, we gave the axes back to their owners. Later my father-in-law brought me an old, dull ax, and I did not ask where he got it but just got a file, honed the ax until it was really sharp, then let people borrow it. I do not remember how I got the shovel, but it was in terrible condition. When we were finished, I thanked the Ute, and he gave me

---

139. No Hat belonged to the Tábąąhá clan, arriving in the Blanding area in the 1920s. His son, also known as Nez Hutchins, came from the Monument Valley/Oljato area during the livestock-reduction period, arriving in Blanding around 1938–1939. His clan was the Táchii'nii. Gray Hair, also known as Bert Atene, belonged to the same clan, came to Blanding from the Oljato/Shonto area in the 1920s, was there in the 1930s, and moved there permanently in the 1950s. He came because it was the closest work. Nez Hutchins was his half brother. The histories of these three men illustrate some of the major forces that caused Navajos to leave the reservation: relationships, employment, and shifting economic conditions. Hurst, 176, 178, 175.

some medicine called Always Stumbling, which would help me become a well-mannered person.

Bob Keith's other son-in-law, who was from Chinle, also made a round hogan, but before moving in, he decided he did not like the way he had made it and so undid the whole thing and asked for my assistance. There were good-looking fallen trees lying around, which he used, so he did not have to chop down as many. Mine was not as good as his because I did not know how to make a round hogan, and the person who did had gone back home to the reservation.

Now, inside the hogan, we were in sad shape. We did not have any kind of bedding like sheepskins. Bob Keith was given two or three old quilts by the white men for bedding and already had some sheepskins, so he gave us some of each. Our bedding was made from what the white men no longer wanted. Many Navajos did not have doors on their hogans so they used gunnysacks sewn together. For my door, I had gathered many different types of fabric and sewed them together. It was ugly. Instead of having a stove, we just had an open firepit in the middle of our hogan. There was a lot of smoke, and the only way to get it out was to push the door blanket to one side. We had smoke, but we were warm.

We cooked on a small frying pan. We also picked up scraps of baling wire, fashioning them into a grill upon which we fried a piece of meat over hot coals. I often received flour as pay when I worked for the white people. My wife used a water pail she had gotten from her mother to carry the water from Westwater to our home. Her mother also gave her a bowl and cups. Our main meal was rabbit. We also hunted for muskrat and prairie dog. These are some of the things we ate when we lived there. We were in a poor state, and that is how we got our food.

At first I did not have an ax, so sometimes I just collected firewood by hand and broke it in two. If it was too hard to break, I would get a stone and hit it. This was our firewood for cooking and heating. Some people were living across Westwater, while the Mormons lived on the other side to the east.

After a couple of days, I went back to Floyd Nielson, who said that I was due back the day before. I told him what had happened, and that was all that was said. I started herding sheep, and the son who had been taking care of them went back. It was midsummer when one of Floyd Nielson's sons came and told me that a baby was going to be born. I told him I wanted to go home, and I did. My wife gave birth in the hogan that I built.

After this I was off to herd sheep again. My employer wanted me to take the castrated lambs to the market near La Sal Mountains. A Ute,

Floyd Nielson, and his two sons helped me herd the sheep to a place near Monticello, where there was a corral. The season was getting cold, so the lambs were to be separated from their mothers and sent to the La Sals, to be placed on the train. We took the sheep toward Monticello, camped close to the corral, and the next morning, we put them in the fenced area. I had a pain in my ankle so I told Floyd Nielson I did not think it would be possible for me to take the lambs to the La Sals. He told me to keep the sheep moving for two more days while he went to look for a Mexican to go the rest of the way.

Floyd Nielson's second son [Richard "Connie" Nielson] put up a tent when we were very close to Monticello. When it got dark, we heard the sheep become restless and believed the Mexicans were stealing our lambs. We both circled around the lambs; he had a rifle, and we sat in the bushes, but toward morning we went to sleep. The lambs had taken off and, as usual, I went and got them. The next day, we went past Monticello and by lunchtime were out in the plains area. Floyd Nielson had found a Mexican to bring the lambs to the market so I was taken back, even though my employer still wanted me to herd sheep for him. I told him I wanted to rest and stay with my family for awhile.

I got back to Blanding and stayed around my home for a whole year. We would haul firewood on our backs and sell it to the white people, but the snow got really high. One time my wife and I were coming back from town when something scared her. She jumped on my back, and we tumbled down a hill, but we had quite a laugh. We stayed around town, working various odd jobs and chopping down more trees, but we ran out of firewood around the place where we lived. The Anglos had cleared the land on the west side of Blanding, and as they were clearing the land, they also removed some of our medicine. They had bulldozers to pull out the trees, which crushed the medicine plants.

I have heard that those trees, shrubs, and plants were useless. I think all those things have purposes. Every living creature uses these things. For instance, an eagle will break branches to build its nest. Even the small birds build their nests in these shrubs. The white man has no right saying those trees have no purpose. Anglos and Navajos use them to build fires when they are cold. Now the land is cleared, and it is like that.

Deer Hunting

Before the trees were cleared, there were a lot of deer. Then the hunting season arrived, and some people from the Oljato area came to hunt. They went to my place and told me to help them. I left with them but was soon told that when hunting, there was a fee. At that time, I thought we had always hunted; why did we have to pay now? The people who we were going to hunt [with] should pay. I said that I was not going to pay, and that I would just be with the people.

All of these things [hunting] are sacred. The Anglo has no respect for the wilderness and its surroundings. When I went with this hunting party, I saw how the Anglo was ruthless with the wildlife. Deer were killed for no reason at all. I was there to make lunches and take them to the hunting party. There was a man called Bana' alyáhí [One Who Gets Paid Back], who had two sons. They killed some deer.

It is said that a deer is very sacred. The Anglos were not taking the deer apart in the right way, the way the Navajos do.[140] Because of the way the Anglos are taking the deer apart, there is no rain.[141] When a Navajo kills a deer, there is a song sung. The person who kills it gets branches and puts them in such a way. Then he puts the deer on top of these branches, and the deer is taken apart. The inside organs are fixed in a certain way. Everything is done just so when hunting, killing, and taking it apart.

Anglos have no respect for this sacred animal. They would just throw the inside organs away, make a big mess, and leave. I have seen this with my own eyes when all I did was take care of the food and did not hunt. These people that hunted gave me some of the deer meat. The deer is one of the sacred beings that are in close contact with the holy beings who control rain. The deer has an authority over the rain—this is what was said. The female deer is called Woman Who Leads in a Sacred Way, and it has the most power. The male deer is Man Who Leads in a Sacred Way. When Anglos hunt deer, they just go in there and tear up the holiness and respect. That is what they do.

A man named John Sání [Old John] told me this story. He said it happened somewhere on Comb Ridge, but who the story was about, I do not know. I just sat there and listened. The hunters there had settled in, and the following day, there was to be a ceremony. Just before daybreak,

---

140. Traditional deer hunting for some Navajos is heavily defined by ritual songs, prayers, and activities, starting from before the hunters leave their homes until after they return. See W. W. Hill, *The Agricultural and Hunting Methods of the Navajo Indians* (New Haven: Yale University Press, 1938) for a detailed explanation.

141. Deer are said to be mountain animals with sacred powers to control rain. Because deer eat medicinal plants found only on the mountain, even eating their meat is considered sacred and filled with health-protecting qualities. Black God and Talking God release a certain number of deer to humans and may be petitioned through song and prayer. Disrespect toward deer causes drought and dwindling success in hunting.

the fire was going out, and breakfast was finished. There was enough light now to see a ways off. Outside of the camp, one of the men was urinating when he saw a deer standing just ahead of him. He had to look twice, and both times, he saw a holy being with feathers standing there. The man really looked at this holy being, and there was no doubt about it; it was one. The man just went back to camp and told the leader who was there that they should leave for home. So the man in charge took his hunting party back.

Another man started telling a story. While hunting is going on, someone still had to cook. The person who was taking care of the meals was told not to go outside while the hunters had a ceremony going on. When it was midafternoon, this person ate, even after he had been told not to eat while the hunting party was out. No one was to eat until everybody was back together. A crow flying overhead cawed," ga ga—he ate, he ate." The hunting party heard this, and they said the person at the camp had eaten. The hunters went back to camp, and the person who was in charge asked the person who remained at the camp if he had eaten. The cook learned that the crow had told the hunters and admitted that he had eaten. The hunters had to perform another ceremony before going back to hunt. Hunting is very sacred, and it is real.[142]

Move to Westwater

Eventually, we made another hogan because the other one was too small. A Navajo man called Gene Longjohn helped us build it.[143] This was the time that Little Bobby visited us with his wife and asked us why we were living in a place where there was no firewood. He had gone across Westwater and found a lot of firewood there and so encouraged us to move. I did not want to so I said that some of those places were owned, that the people did not want anyone on their property, so we should not move. The next day, Little Bobby kept insisting that we move across.

---

142. The reader may question what Oshley means by using words like "sacred" and "real" since the sacred is real to Navajos. He seems to be indicating that there is both a visible and unseen reality that join together in the act of hunting. The two are inseparable.

143. Longjohn was one of the first Navajo residents in the Westwater community, arriving sometime between 1915 and 1920. He had previously established ties with the Mormons in Bluff, and it is unclear why he moved to Blanding. He, like Oshley, belonged to the Tódích'íí'nii clan (Hurst, "The Blanding Navajo," 178). "He was called Many Fingers and was from the eastern side of Navajo Mountain." J. H.

Finally, I gave in, and we started the very difficult task of crossing Westwater. With the help of Little Bobby and his wife, we made the move to our new hogan. It was a round one and poor looking because we used logs that were just lying around. We chopped off the branches and roots, then cleaned the bark. My wife and I made it ourselves. This time I used gunnysack fabric for my door.

We built our hogan in a place where we thought it would be good to live. But we found out that there was an ant's home near it, and that is the reason we moved our hogan to a different place again.[144] We also had medicine men who performed ceremonies for us. That is another reason we stayed across Westwater. There is also not much noise over there. These are some of the things we talk about when deciding where a good place is to put a hogan, before it is made and the people move inside.

We are also aware of the sleepiness that settles in a hogan. That is another reason a hogan is rebuilt in a different place. It must be felt that it is a good place, made in a good way, and has a good feeling. The doorway is always to the east, where all good things come before sunrise.[145] When a hogan has something wrong with it, a person can tell through dreams. For example, a person might be bothered by a spirit that used to live there. So the hand trembler does a ceremony over you. Maybe he'll tell you there is a burial site near the home, and this is when the family gets out of there and builds a new hogan.

In another hogan, a person might have awful nightmares, and the hand trembler is asked for his services again. The diagnosis might be that lightning had struck a tree nearby, so herbs found around the tree are sprinkled in the hogan, then outside. I have heard that people move because of lice but not because of bugs. The people then move the hogan to a different place. Either type of hogan—a round or a forked one—may be made. In a forked hogan, there are five places that are blessed with cornmeal for harmony, while in a female hogan there are four places.

Sometimes I would see a Navajo move out of a perfectly good home and move into a brush shelter, and I would wonder why. I asked the people,

---

144. In addition to the purely practical problem of building a home near anthills, these creatures are said to have powers and a relationship with Navajo people established in the worlds beneath this one. Respect is shown by leaving ants and their homes alone.

145. Navajo people say that the door faces east so that when the holy beings look into the home in the morning, they can tell if people are lazy and sleeping in bed. If they are, the holy beings will not bring blessings, but if the occupants are up and about, they will be helped.

and they told me that when a person dies, the people living there should move out because of fear of the dead. They would then make another hogan and move into it. When you are living in one place for a lengthy time, the firewood gets used up so they may move to a place with more firewood.

FRICTION OVER RANGELANDS

We worked and lived with the Anglos. There was this Anglo called Akałii Chxǫ́'í [Ugly Cowboy (remains anonymous)].[146] He and his family were the meanest of all the Anglo people there. They were always ready to pick on us. One very early morning, I followed my horse to their planting field. I knew my horse did not spend half of the night in their field, but he caught it there and wanted money. I told him my horse had just gotten into the field so he gave me back my ropes and I went back home. I told one of my neighbors about it. He said that that man and his family were very mean.

Later, as I observed them, they seemed to hate the Indians. This Ugly Cowboy was almost at war with the Utes. Recently the people helping Ugly Cowboy chased the Navajos' livestock at Montezuma Creek and gathered all of the horses roaming around in the Bluff area. I heard that all that land was claimed by Ugly Cowboy's outfit for his use. He told the people to move off his property. A man called Tsi'naajinii [Black Streak Across] was living just above Bluff and was told to move off the land. There was another man, Ńt'ę́ę́' [Could Have], living close to that same place. He, too, was told to move off and so went across the San Juan River. Later Ugly Cowboy's outfit gathered and herded some of Could

---

146.   "Navajos used to herd sheep for Ugly Cowboy. They would shear the sheep for him in a large corral that used to be at a place called Closing Gate on Montezuma Creek [McCracken] Mesa. Ugly Cowboy was mean. He received his name because of his characteristics and the way he dressed. His clothes were ragged and dirty. His leather pants [chaps] were all worn out, and he looked like he never changed his clothes.

I saw him and Oshley throw each other around one time. The argument erupted while they were castrating the lambs. Oshley took them [gonads] out one at a time, while Ugly Cowboy took both out at the same time by biting them with his teeth and pulling them out. They wrestled each other around in the corral [the one on McCracken Mesa by the windmill]. Oshley was very upset, packed his things, and started leaving. Ugly Cowboy ran after him and put his arms around Oshley's shoulder and apologized. Oshley returned to camp, and they made peace. This happened just before we herded the animals to Big Sheep Mountain [Blanca Peak, Colorado]. The day after the argument, we moved out with the sheep." J. H.

Have's son's sheep from Montezuma Creek, and he and his wife had to come to get them.

One time things got out of hand when this white man claimed the land and drove the Navajos' horses and sheep from Montezuma Creek. He kept the sheep belonging to Could Have's son, in a corral for almost two days. The owners came for their sheep, and the Anglo gave them a hard time before the animals were released back to them. They always tried to do things to a man called Tsék'izí [Crack between the Rocks], but his answer was always no. Up until these events, I really was not aware of this white man's ruthlessness.

He and his helpers gathered many horses. I had one reddish brown horse, and suddenly it was missing. I do not know what they did with the horses. Crack between the Rocks confronted these ruthless people about what they were putting the Navajos through. If this man had not stood up, I do not know what the outcome would have been like. They did not get him to do anything. He kept on saying no to whatever he was told. After this it seems things settled down, and the people that lost their livestock were paid back.

We stayed around Blanding and worked at various odd jobs. Then a white man came to see us and asked me if I could herd sheep for him, because of a trial that was going on about a man who had stolen some cattle. He was going to court in the next day or two. I told him I had a wife, and that I could not take her back to her father. The only way I could go was if she went with me. He said that was fine with him.

When we got there, there were two men. They were going to court, and I was told that there were three more somewhere else. The two men were taken, and we stayed there to herd sheep. This was during the summer before the shearing was started. Our camp was moved to a higher altitude behind Monticello; then we sheared the sheep. My wife took care of the sheep once they had been clipped, and I took care of the sheep that were to be sheared. When the shearing was finished, I asked if we could go, and the white man said that he wanted me to work for him. I told him that we were tired but asked my wife if it was all right. She wanted to know what we were going to do after this, then said that the work was all right. It was fine with her to work, and she was happy that my boss did not want to let me go, so I said it was all right with me. He said that when the lambs came, we would be near Cortez. We herded the sheep in that direction. My boss went back, and there was another white man, a cowboy, who was made the foreman. Near Cahone there was tall grass, and the sheep ran to it so the foreman got mad at me.

At that time, I was really in shape. The foreman got in front of me and between me and my wife. Why in the world he did that, I do not know. The horse was big so I grabbed the reins, and the foreman jumped down and told me to take my glasses off. I took them off and put a [bear hug] on him. He understood Navajo, and just when I really put a tight squeeze on him— and the sheep wandered off into the alfalfa field—my boss came.

As we settled down to make camp, I told my boss about the incident, and he told the foreman to leave. Before he went home, he tried to talk himself out of the mess he had created. My boss sided with me and said that the foreman caused the trouble. Then he fired him. He also told the foreman that he knew me and that I had worked for him for quite awhile. Even his wife agreed. Then we butchered a sheep and ate.

When I came back from herding, there were more Navajos that had moved in, like Red House and Shorty. Then Gray Hair, then No Hat's son, and then Lady with the Beads moved in. A man called John found a wife in Blanding after he was drawn here by the work. Another Navajo named Be'atsidí [One Who Hammers] moved here with his family of children and two wives. Sugar came with a woman, but they separated, and he found another lady, though he stayed in the area for less than five years. All of these people lived in the growing Navajo community on the west side of Westwater Canyon. People worked various, odd jobs in town on the east side; then when they finished their work, they would return to their hogans in the evening. This happened just like this.

There were also Utes who lived in Westwater. They did not make hogans for themselves but lived out in the open under trees, even though they had axes and shovels. At first there were not many Navajos, except for Longjohn, who lived over there. I asked about Smiley and was told that he had moved back to Dennehotso. The Ute called Always Stumbling was a mischievous, naughty person. Lehi's son-in-law was not like that. Those two Utes also helped me build the hogan. There was a woman called 'Asdzą́ą́ ałts'íísí [Small Woman], who was living where the road crosses Westwater. Sometime later a Navajo man who was herding sheep for Floyd Nielson moved there, too. I did various jobs but kept close to my family. My father-in-law told me to take care of them first, and that was what I did. Other Utes moved near us, close to Small Woman. One of them was called Gah yázhí [Little Rabbit].[147] It was getting cold when Charlie and Tł'ízí bidághaa'í [Goat's Beard] moved into Blanding.

---

147. "He was a slender Ute with gray/white hair. He was the kind of person who was
     conceited—too much self-pride. He was also a compulsive gambler." J. H.

Old sweat lodge in Westwater. Note the large pile of rocks to the north, indicating extensive use. Navajo beliefs say that spent or "dead" things go to the north. (Photo courtesy of Winston Hurst)

THE NATIVE AMERICAN CHURCH

One time there was a gambling game with cards on the rim of Allen Canyon. A person from Oljato named Tsé łichíí' bii' tohnii' [Water in the Red Rock][148] was winning, and the Utes and I were losing. This game went on for a couple of days until Tsin bikee'é [Wooden Foot][149] said that he was going to have a peyote ceremony at his home. I did not know anything about peyote so he asked me to come and see the ceremony. Just then Red Rock Spring was passing by. He said he wanted to see the ceremony but that maybe it was restricted, but Wooden Foot said it was not. I told Wooden Foot I would go, when in walked a man called Chiiłchin bii' to'nii [Person from Chilchinbeto]. He had recently won at playing cards, wanted to know if the ceremony was restricted, and was told it was not. Wooden Foot boasted about it and said that it was really a great ceremony,

---

148. "He was a medicine man from the Oljato area who married a woman from Water in the Red Rock, which is by Rough Rock, Arizona. That is how he got his name." J. H.

149. "Wooden Foot was a Ute from Blanding who had frostbite on his foot. He used to put a wrap around it with a wooden splint for walking." J. H.

and that when one eats peyote, the coughing will not come to you. Person from Chilchinbeto said he would come.

The next evening, I went to the ceremony, and all the people who said they would be there were. People were preparing a lot of food, and there were a lot of Utes, some of whom were from the Towaoc-Cortez area.[150] A lot of them I did not know. They were a handsome bunch, looked well fed, and their hair [was] neatly combed and braided. We all went in and began to smoke, after which the singing started. Both men and women sang, the drum and songs sounding really loud.

The peyote took effect and I started hallucinating.[151] The people looked as if they had big fat lips, their eyes were distorted and very funny in appearance. I thought they were looking only at me, and I felt like urinating, but when I tried, nothing would come out. I asked a Ute why I could not urinate, and he told me I should confess my wrongdoings and feelings; then I could. He also said that some other thing might be blocking it, and that I would probably come across it if I thought about it. Then I would get relief.

It was almost dawn when we went out again. I saw a red rock and a ceremonial tool, but for what ceremony, I did not know. The singing was very loud. This was when I started to relieve myself with urine splashing over the red rock. When I went back inside, the Ute told me my hat was up there. I got out my deck of cards while the people were still singing and the person named Red Rock Springs fingered his lips. I thought he did something to the cards to make him win. The cards were all set up when four things appeared to me, and then I turned the card over. It was a four of diamonds, which I had guessed correctly. There was money there so I took it and put it into my pocket.

Two days later, we were playing cards again, and I won twenty-five dollars from him; I just backed out of there, even though people were still playing and urged me to continue. This was what I was hallucinating about. I went out again [from the ceremony] and heard two people talking in the

150. Oshley's experience with the Utes and the Native American Church (peyote religion) offers an interesting commentary concerning the church's early days in Utah. David Aberle, in his seminal work, *Peyote Religion among the Navajo* (Chicago: University of Chicago Press, 1966), points out that the Utes from Towaoc were the prime influence in introducing the Native American Church into the northern part of the Navajo Reservation in the 1930s.

151. The alkaloid base of the peyote cactus button, somewhat similar to LSD, triggers auditory and visual images. The fire, fan, water drum, and other elements in the ceremony help a participant experience the visual aspects of supernatural power.

woods. The two of them appeared, and they looked like Utes. Right where they were walking, a coyote appeared. It was a big one, and he was standing in the direction of Ute Mountain, where the Utes were living. I thought it was like this, and I stood there and watched, but it did not change so I just went back inside. This was what happened in the peyote ceremony.[152]

At dawn I went outside again and said I wanted to go home, but the people told me I should not. A Ute called John took care of me because the peyote had really affected me. Little Rabbit's daughter also told me not to go home when I was still hallucinating. They were using dried [powdered] cedar leaves to cure me of these hallucinations. They put the powdered cedar leaves onto hot coals and prayed to it, but the peyote was still working me over.

I was standing facing the fire, and they put powdered cedar leaves on the coals. I pressed the smoke against my whole body. As I turned around from the fire, I thought someone threw a sheepskin on the ground before me. Again I was hallucinating. I picked up the sheepskin and tried to hand it to the Ute next to me. He said something to me—maybe he was afraid of it—I do not know. I threw the sheepskin back on the ground. When the peyote effect had worn off, I thought about it and came to somewhat of a conclusion. I decided that Wooden Foot was doing something to me.

Later I found out a fat girl was where the sheepskin was, and that she had died of diarrhea. I thought about the coyote that was standing outside, and it all went back to Wooden Foot. I went to him and told him of it. He said it was the same with Utes, that they know about witchcraft but are really protective about such things. At Wooden Foot's home lived his wife, a blind Ute, Gaabaaho [Ute name], and also a girl, who may have been the granddaughter of Wooden Foot. All the people that were there died soon after this peyote ceremony. Little Rabbit also died, as did all the people who went.

After this I asked Small Woman where she was from. She said she used to live in Oljato, and that her husband was called Naayízí bich'ahí [Squash Hat].[153] They were both really old and were living in Blanding. It seems like it had just been recently that the Utes moved onto White Mesa.

---

152. "Oshley said he did not believe in peyote. But when he got very sick, so sick that the hospital in Monticello released him to go home, my nephew went to pick him up. He brought Oshley back to Monument Valley, and there was a peyote ceremony for him. He got well after that ceremony and lived many more years. It saved his life. He might have changed his mind to like peyote. I do not know." J. H.

153. "He was a Ute who lived north of the White Mesa community. He was called Squash Hat because he wore a corduroy cap that had many colors." J. H.

All they did was play with cards and eat peyote. One could hear drums in their home. I asked them why they were always eating peyote, and one of them said it was good, that that was how to live the good way, and there was no sickness. I have witnessed this myself.

They prayed only for good things: for themselves, their neighbors of different nationalities, and even us Navajos that were in Blanding. I thanked them for praying for us, and they invited us to their peyote ceremony to pray for rain, growth of vegetation, fat livestock, and harmony within us. I asked a Ute who knew the Navajo language very well about where they really lived. He said that they just moved from one place to another for food and gathered the things in a basket. They used to go by Oljato, then into the mountains for piñon nuts. That was how it had always been.

Their real home was at Ute Mountain. There were two different groups. Tiny Woman was Paiute, and the other one was Ute. She said they were different, but they were the same.[154] I asked again where their homeland was, and she said at Ute Mountain. They just started moving from one place to another, and some got stuck here because there was work. She also said they made baskets and sold them to the stores for $3.00 apiece. If it was not made well, it was $2.00, but a really good one was $3.50. I asked her if their home place was in Allen Canyon, and she said no, that they had just recently moved to Blanding. She said they just migrated through here to gather various foods like big yucca and supplies for making baskets. They did not stay in one place but just roamed around and played cards. It was just recently that the white people saw what poor condition they were living in, and that is how they got houses. They used to live under trees. They had juniper bark for bedding and ate rabbits.

One time I visited a place and saw Utes and Navajos gambling but just went on my way. I went to Hastiin Yoo'í's [Man Who Threads Beads], where they were having a five-day ceremony. There were many

---

154. This is an interesting comment from a Native American perspective since the white men living in this area had similar problems distinguishing between Utes and Paiutes. The corner of southeastern Utah is a melting pot blending the two groups (Weeminuche Utes and San Juan Paiutes), who speak the same language and formerly shared a similar culture. As one travels farther east into Colorado, one finds more and more Utes with a Plains Indian culture. As one moves west toward southwestern Utah, there is a much stronger orientation to the Paiute culture, characterized by sparse resources and a simpler technology and lifestyle to allow hunting and gathering in the Great Basin. (See Donald G. Calloway, Joel C. Janetski, and Omer Stewart, "Ute," and Isabel T. Kelly and Catherine S. Fowler, "Southern Paiute," *Great Basin*, vol. 11 of *Handbook of North American Indians* [Washington, D.C.: Smithsonian Institution, 1986], 336–97.)

A Navajo woman from Westwater hired to do chores at the
Peter Allen home in Blanding. (Photo courtesy of Ada Rigby)

people there who were gambling, and some of them were Utes. After this
I went home. I wondered why they were putting all of their time into
gambling, if they had money to gamble with, and if they had enough
money to buy themselves food. I did not say anything, but it stayed in my
mind. Then I heard it was the last day of the ceremony, and there was no
gambling. All the people were just watching. I participated in the night
sing, and the next day, people were on their way home.

I heard someone had moved into town so I went over to find out who. The family was from Kayenta, and his name was Diné ałts'íísí [Small Man]. He brought his two wives and children and made their hogan out of fresh, chopped-down trees with their own axes. They borrowed the shovel. He did a pretty good job at supporting his children, and they hunted for rabbits and prairie dogs. There was another man called Red House, who did not gamble and so did a good job of raising his children. He had sons-in-law, and it seems like that family was good, really good together.

I heard there was another ceremony going on, but all I saw were people consuming alcohol. Some of them were angry. Even though I did not say anything, people wanted to beat me up. I asked them why they were going to do that, and so they settled down. I just observed what the people were doing and then went home.

Bob Keith moved back from his home in Dennehotso to Blanding. When he moved back up here, the woman that was once my wife had another husband named Shoodii [One Who Drags Around].[155] He had moved to the rim of Allen Canyon, and he had a daughter there named May Joan.

More Herding

I herded sheep mostly for Floyd Nielson, even though I did not want to. I herded sheep for only a few days and then was back with my family, when Dibétehí [Man Who Takes Care of Sheep] rode up in his wagon pulled by two mules. He was my brother-in-law and had come with his family for piñon nuts. They had just picked nuts for two days when it started to snow. The storm drove them to us.

Floyd Nielson's brother wanted some firewood so we chopped some for him. When we were finished, Grant Bayles asked us to work for him, clearing land and chopping firewood. We worked through the winter and into the spring. The pay was very low, but my brother-in-law kept telling me not to say that because it did provide food, and that point ended the discussion.

We kept working through the spring to planting time. I got tired of working there so I quit and went back to my family, but my brother-in-law still worked. Then a white man called Kayo told me to go help a white

---

155. "He lived in the Montezuma Creek area and was a medicine man. He was well known to the People and received his name because he was short in stature." J. H.

man in Montezuma Creek, who was cutting hay. He wanted two men for the job and would pay two dollars a day. I was on my way home when a person from Dennehotso from the Towering House clan met me. We knew each other only by sight. I told him about the job, and he agreed to work in Montezuma. Kayo brought us over there and said he might be back in two to four days.

We worked two-and-a-half days, but he did not come at the time he had set. We stayed there another night. At first I said we would just start walking, but the other man was scared to walk at night. I did not ask him what he was scared of. We stayed there, and early the next morning, we had breakfast, started off just as the sun rose, and walked all the way back to Blanding.

I had heard the Utes were having their dance, and the Navajo people in Blanding had all gone to it. My brother-in-law, his wife, and my wife had just returned home from Allen Canyon, where it had been held, and there was no food. The man that I worked with stayed at my home, although he wanted to go home, while I went to the store. I brought some food home, and two days later he went home.

I was to take care of some rams in Monticello for one day so I was driven there. A Navajo man named K'ai' bii [In the Willows] from the Oljato area was living there with his wife. I was told to drive the rams along the road, where the man and his wife would be waiting. I moved the rams very slowly because they were already hot and panting. In the Willows was waiting for me and told me to take the rams this way. I found out there were some houses there. Then I saw a Mexican let the rams go where they pleased and went back in the automobile to Blanding.

When I got back, some Navajos were chopping wood for Grant Bayles. It was In the Willows and two other men. There were many Navajos who lived in Blanding and then moved back. Only a few of them stayed here. A man called No Hat's Son was one who stayed on. His children still live here. He had about three or four boys who helped him when he worked for the white man. He had a light complexion and was called Tsii'łitsooí [Yellow Hair].

I was asked to take care of the rams for Grant Bayles. My brother-in-law was also asked to clear the land in a canyon toward the Bears Ears, where I was taking care of the rams. This was where Bayles had his cattle, horses, and planted fields. I fixed the box canyon to keep the rams in, then asked if I could also clear the sagebrush away. My employer said it was fine with him, and that he would pay $1.50 a day, which was very low.

Blanding in the 1930s with Parley Redd Mercantile in the background. (Photo courtesy of the San Juan Historical Commission)

Still, there were many people clearing the land, such as Yellow Hair, who was there. During the noon hour, we would all come together and talk about the different events that happened in our lives. When the people finished clearing the land, I stayed there with the livestock. The cold weather was setting in when Grant Bayles came and told us the rams would be put with the sheep. A young man and I drove them toward Blanding to a sheep corral, where a tent had been set up nearby for us.

That evening it started raining and continued throughout the night and next day. Half of the rams had run off so it took me the rest of the day to find them. Even though I rode a horse around to find them, it was very late in the afternoon when I finally collected the last ones. I was soaking wet. The other person who was taking care of the rest of the rams was also wet and hungry. We fixed the corral, got the rams back in it, built a fire, warmed ourselves, and ate. Bayles usually came often, but he did not come because it was raining.

We stayed there two nights. I said that we probably would have to move on to the corral, even though it was muddy and the soil was very sticky. We reached it late in the afternoon after the rain had stopped. The next day, no one came so we started to move out again with our things packed on the back of a mule. It was noon when we got to Yellow Hair's place with the rams. We ate lunch there and took them to Grant Bayles. When we arrived at his place, he asked me why I had not left when it started to rain. I said he had told us he would return, and that was why we had waited over there and almost froze to death. We all laughed about it, then we went home.

Later Life

Oshley was famous for his ability to communicate through pantomime. Spoken language rarely presented an obstacle to being understood. (Photo courtesy of the Oshley family)

The Later Livestock Years

ANATOMY OF A STOCKMAN

CLICK. THE TAPE RECORDER FELL SILENT, ending the last part of the interview. Chronologically, Oshley's life history so far had covered up to the early-to-mid-1940s (an estimate based on internal evidence). He spent the next fifteen to twenty years involved in the livestock industry and another twenty-five years in retirement, yet there is only a faint written record of anything specific that he did. Oral accounts of friends, family, and business associates remain the primary glue to cement together the anecdotal fragments of his later life.

These last years of Oshley's employment as a herder were apparently busy ones. The escalating market and prices associated with World War II and a subsequent recession created a pattern of continuous fluctuation, but the general trend was growth. For instance, in 1955 twenty-five sheepmen in San Juan County had a total of 72,000 head, which had yielded 720,000 pounds of wool the previous season.[1] Ten years later, 146 stockmen were running 24,841 cattle and 165,231 sheep on the same ranges.[2]

However, this picture of prosperity would change by the mid-1970s, and again, Oshley was a representative figure in the course of events. There were two primary reasons for the rapid decline in herding sheep in southeastern Utah. The most obvious one to livestock owners was that beginning in the late 1960s and early 1970s, the environmental movement that reached across the United States demanded changes in predator control. A poison called 1080, which had proved successful in eliminating coyotes, mountain lions, and other carnivores, came under close scrutiny. One of its bad effects, besides the fact it led to a painful death, was that its impact persisted. As different meat eaters in the food

---

1. "San Juan County Economy Strongly Stabilized by Sheep," *San Juan Record*, December 22, 1955, p. 23.
2. "Monticello BLM District Covers 5.4 Million Acres," *San Juan Record*, August 12, 1965, p. 2.

Floyd Nielson, friend and employer of Navajo
Oshley, as he appeared in the 1940s. (Photo
courtesy of the Norman Nielson family)

chain feasted on the remains of an animal, they, too, were poisoned. Some
people even believed that the decline in the eagle population in the
United States was connected to this cycle.[3] The government banned the
use of this poison, and the coyote population increased. Their numbers
grew dramatically as they preyed upon the flocks in general, and the
lambs, in particular. Norman Nielson remembers sustaining a 50 percent
loss of his lambs pasturing on Blue Mountain.[4] Other livestock owners
experienced similar losses.

The second problem, one that relates directly to Oshley's circumstances, is that many of the old sheepherders started to retire or die. There
was no one in the younger generation who had the time, patience, or
desire to practice the trade. Sheep need to have someone who will protect
and direct the herd, whereas cattle can be left alone for longer periods of

3. Jim Keyes, Utah State University Extension Agent involved with sheepherding
   projects on the Navajo Reservation, conversation with author, March 4, 1999.
4. Norman Nielson, conversation with author, March 4, 1999.

time to roam the range and are not as defenseless against coyotes. Thus, many of the people who worked in the livestock industry shifted to the easier animal—cattle—for their livelihood. Oshley's retirement presaged the problem of replacing these old, skilled herders and the move away from sheep.

Today the livestock industry brings an estimated twelve million dollars each year in revenues to the county, second only to the federal government.[5] Interestingly, this figure is based solely on cattle and a few horses, not sheep. In fact, there is not one commercial sheep rancher in San Juan County. People have tried solving the problem of finding good herders by importing workers from Mexico and Peru, but these arrangements have proven unsatisfactory.[6] Thus, the sheep industry in which Oshley had served so faithfully ended shortly after he left the ranges that he knew so well.

But until the mid 1950s, Oshley spent the majority of his time working for Floyd Nielson and his son, Norman, who continued to hire Navajos to herd sheep. Norman, interviewed in 1991 at the age of seventy, had a very clear recollection of Oshley's service to his family. He, like many other white people, held Oshley's work in high regard and so helped piece together the fabric of those years before he officially left the livestock business. The following information is derived, unless otherwise indicated, from that interview with Norman Nielson.[7]

He remembers first meeting Oshley when he was a boy of fifteen. Norman and his dad stopped to give Oshley a ride from Blanding to the edge of White Mesa, where the Ute community is located today. At the time, there were only sagebrush and junipers, but that was where Oshley believed he would find three horses he had traded with the Utes. Sure enough, they were right where he thought they would be. Nielson was surprised to hear that Oshley was going to move them to a corral, since the nearest one he knew of was a good four or five miles away. The horses had been broken to "lead," but none were ready to ride. Oshley let it be known that this was not a problem, got out of the car, thanked the two for the lift, then set out on foot, driving the horses from behind at a fast trot. His bowlegs maintained a long, even stride—down the mesa he went,

---

5. Jim Keyes, "Cattle by the Wayside First . . . Then the Communities?" *San Juan Record*, May 18, 1994, p.1.

6. Keyes, conversation with author.

7. Norman Nielson, interview by author, tape recording, May 1, 1991, transcript in possession of author.

across the valley floor, into Recapture Canyon, and eventually to the rock corral. Nielson was amazed at the stamina Oshley had, given the pace of the run (what he called "a wild gallop") and the distance to the corral.

That was the beginning of a relationship that would continue until Oshley's death in 1988. The two men spent a great deal of time together and shared memories that often brought a smile to their lips. One such incident, though not funny at the time, later became a joke between the two. Mary was about to have Oshley's third child. Although Nielson had spent part of the week with him and the sheep on the range south of Blanding, he needed to go to town a couple of days early to take care of business. Oshley asked that he and his wife be brought to town on a certain day and time because Mary would be getting ready to deliver. Nielson agreed but was a little late, though the sun was still in the sky. He helped pack up the camp goods, then moved the couple to Blanding, arriving just before dark. Minutes after the two had been dropped off at their camping spot in Westwater, Mary went into labor. No tent was up, no wood chopped, no water hauled—only a wife delivering a baby with no one to help. Oshley, modifying the traditional Navajo method of child delivery, had Mary stand beside a post, placed a rope over her stomach, and when the contractions started, tightened the rope to help push the baby. The baby arrived without a problem. Later, when Nielson asked Oshley how he had handled the situation and what he had done first, he chuckled, "Cussed the white man."

White people appreciated Oshley's sense of humor. Over the years, he had learned a little bit of English, and when coupled with his full-body descriptive powers, there was "no doubt in your mind what he was trying to tell you." At the same time, Norman and Floyd had learned some Navajo, which communicated both respect and friendship to their employees. Floyd Nielson, in an interview in 1971, told of another ranch hand's, Abe Navajo's, sense of humor. Abe never spoke a word of English. One day he was loading bundles of grain onto a wagon, and he began to sing in Navajo. Floyd recalls, "He was hollering and singing just as loud as he could. All at once he stopped and looked at me and said, 'Kid, that is damn good singing.' [Laughter] I'd never heard him say a word of English, and I just about fell off my wagon."[8]

Oshley enjoyed singing, too. Sometimes he and Floyd would start a song in Navajo around the campfire and keep each other racing through

---

8. Floyd Nielson interview by Gary Shumway and Kim Stewart, July 14, 1971, *Southeastern Utah Oral History Project*, (Salt Lake City: Utah State Historical Society and California State University at Fullerton, n.d.), 19.

Navajo and Mary Oshley butchering a goat. They spent many days on the range together, Mary supporting Navajo in his life as a herder. (Photo courtesy of the Oshley family)

the quickening tempo of the lyrics. One of their favorites was about a man, in the midst of trouble, trying to crank-start an old car. Gestures took as much energy as the verses, and by the time the car had been moved in song over a hill and out of sight, both men were laughing.

Oshley's humor carried over from employers to employees. Another herder, Sam Ketchum—a Ute—was a regular worker for the Nielsons and spent a lot of time on the range with Oshley. A windy night often evoked an accusation from Ohsley that his friend was the cause of the discomfort; he would implore Floyd to fire Ketchum so that the rains would start and the winds stop. Ketchum countered with charges against Oshley, swearing that he was the cause of the dry weather. Next both would break into song, each taking a turn at a verse, then singing the refrain together.

Yet life on the range was generally serious, often tedious business. The daily routine started early, ended late, and was hard work without a lot of creature comforts. Living accommodations were anything but plush. The Nielsons provided a tent, ten feet long and eight feet wide, for their herders. Although cots were available, most of the men preferred to get a couple of planks or posts to outline a bed, fill the area between with juniper

Norman Nielson saddling his horse in front of
one of the tents at a sheep camp. (Photo courtesy of the Norman Nielson family)

or pine boughs, then lay a sheepskin or mattress on top. Cots allowed cold
air to circulate underneath, making the sleeper uncomfortable.

A wood-burning stove with an oven heated the tent and allowed
cooking in inclement weather. Two portable cupboards held the dishes, a
few pots and pans, and some basic groceries. Unlike many herders who
kept a pot of beans or stew on the fire for quick meals, Oshley did not
cook ahead. When he or others arrived in camp, there was rarely anything
prepared to eat, and everyone was hungry. Once he got started, however,
he was a fairly good cook.

Nielson remembers that one of his herders named John Holley was
particularly skilled at cooking fry bread, and Oshley specialized in frying
meat. When large work crews arrived to help during the lambing and

shearing seasons, the two men would stack "a pile of bread a foot high" and meat to match, then set about consuming it with the other herders. By the time everyone had eaten his fill, not much was left.

A Typical Day on the Range

A typical day on the range started before sunrise. Getting up early never seemed to bother Oshley; the day was never too long, and "he was as agreeable in the evening as he was in the morning." Nielson remembers him going off by himself at daybreak, often to a hill or high point of ground, where he faced east and the rising sun to say his prayers. Next he wrangled the horses. A bell helped locate the hobbled animals following their night of grazing around the camp. Oats in a bucket or nosebag coaxed the animals closer so that a bridle and saddle could be slipped on. Oshley enjoyed this work as much as he did the breakfast that someone else prepared while he cared for the stock.

As with rising early, the weather never bothered him as it did others. It was a common topic for discussion around the camp, and everyone hated when the wind blew, but "Oshley accepted the weather just as it came. . . . If it rained—fine, if it snowed—fine, if the sun shined—fine, but I [Norman] never heard him complain . . . that's why I'd say he was at peace with himself and nature."

If he was unconcerned about the weather, he was vitally interested in taking care of the sheep. Nielson considered him a "top herder," taking his responsibility "very seriously" with "pride in his work." He knew where every sheep was and ensured they found sufficient grass and water. Nielson remarked that Oshley was not mechanically inclined, not too "handy with his hands," but he did have a "gift," and that was roping. "He could snake a sheep out there about as far as you could throw a thirty-five-foot rope . . . and that was the reason he was so valuable when working with a drifting herd." He also never had to ask for instructions about what to do with an animal in trouble. The answer came as second nature.

His even temper in the face of trials was admirable. He rarely became angry, though he might momentarily be disgusted when something went wrong. Some of the workers would hold a grudge and sulk around for days when things did not go their way but not Oshley. Nielson says, "I never did see him out of sort, though he had a lot of reason to be out of sort sometimes. I never saw him where he showed any anger. It just wasn't in his nature."

This attitude and skill guaranteed him one of the best horses in the Nielsons' remuda every time. They knew he would take care of it and that when man, horse, and rope came together, it would be an effective combination. Nothing pleased Oshley more. He loved to ride, for both work and pleasure. He often went off by himself to find water and grass for the sheep's next move. Especially in the summer, when the sheep would "shade up" during the hot hours of the day, Oshley was freed for four or five hours to scout the area. When he returned, he could tell you where the deer and the best feed were and where he would take the flock next.

The most critical time of the year was the lambing season, when the stockmen had a "dropping herd." As the ewes delivered their lambs, the babies were separated out in the evening and kept in a cluster. There were sometimes as many as twenty-five or thirty in a bunch. Herders moved the rest of the flock a short distance away so that the lambs could remain with their mothers and not get mixed up and lost. If they did get separated for too long and there were twins, one might be rejected by the mother and become a "bummer"—an animal that needed human help to survive.

The herders marked the twins by applying a design with a piece of oil chalk. Oshley would draw some "weird marks" on the sheep, but there was never any question about which lamb and mother belonged together. As soon as the ewe had dropped its newborn and licked it dry, Oshley would slip in and put a cross or arrow or some other mark on it. Other herders were sometimes rough with the sheep and bunched them too fast, which "doggied" the lambs, causing them to stray from their mothers. But "Oshley was just patient enough that he would work slowly with them [the sheep] and ease them off to one side before leaving them." If an extra lamb appeared and there was a question about its mother, the Nielsons would turn to Oshley, who could usually tell them which ones matched.

Another busy time of the year came when the sheep were sheared. Recalling these times, Floyd Nielson stated that he worked with more Indians than anyone else in the county. He estimated that his flock, plus two others herded with it, totaled about forty thousand sheep to be clipped with hand shears. Nielson employed a hundred Navajos to work temporarily for him during this hectic time, paying five cents for each sheep sheared. He noticed, "Indians are different than white people. They'd gather around together at night when the white people were usually grouchy or in a fight or something. But the Indians always had a clown among them. He'd clown, and they'd laugh and play cards. They

Norman "Skinny" Nielson in the 1940s, when he and Oshley rode the range together. (Photo courtesy of the Norman Nielson family)

would stay up nearly all night. It was a social occasion."[9] For forty years, Navajo Oshley worked for Floyd and Norman in this environment.

Paying tribute to Oshley's skill, Norman Nielson often refers to him as a "top hand." At one point, he says,

> You would just have to consider Oshley a top sheepherder, and that is just as much of an art as any profession there is. In this country, a good sheepherder has some skills that are as great and professional as any other skill. It was hard to find a good man you could put with that dropping herd and not have to worry about it. If you didn't lamb crop, you would have worked all summer for almost nothing, so it was very important. He [Oshley] was the man that we always put with that bunch.

By the end of the lambing season, there might be twenty bunches of sheep spread across the valley floors and in the canyons. A herder was

---

9. Ibid., 19–20.

assigned to a particular part of the flock and slept with it at night—perhaps a mile or two away from the main camp—and would return in the morning for breakfast. Oshley often stayed at the camp farthest out because of his ability to take care of different situations that might arise.

And occasionally, things did happen. One time when he was working for Grant Bayles, lightning struck a tree near Oshley's camp. In traditional Navajo beliefs, this is a sacred, powerful sign from the holy beings, something that should not be trifled with. He left everything—rifle, tent, all of his personal possessions—there in a pile and never went back to claim them.[10]

Traveling in an area where there were a lot of Anasazi ruins added another danger. Some traditional Navajos believe that ruins, artifacts, and burials of these people should be avoided. Navajo herders generally respected these practices, but those who transgressed ran the risk of having to pay for an expensive ceremony to purify themselves from harmful supernatural powers. Oshley avoided these sites, never picked up arrowheads, though they were plentiful, and refused to dig for objects.[11] But one spring after a wet winter, he and Sam Ketchum accidentally ran across a skull and part of a body protruding from soil that had washed away. They skirted the area from that time on.

Another time, Oshley had just left the herd, grazing twenty miles from Blanding up on Blue Mountain, under Ketchum's watchful eye. A large black bear wandered into the sheep and started to attack the flock. Ketchum, armed with a .32 Special on loan from the Nielsons, fired three shots but never knocked the bear down. He feared that the wounded animal would return at night and attack the camp so he saddled his mule and rode to town. When he got to the Nielsons at midnight, all he could say was, "Wow! Bear, bear, big one." The next morning, the Nielsons, Ketchum, and Oshley returned to the scene and followed the eight-inch-wide tracks and blood trail until they found the carcass. The men skinned the animal and put the hide on the back of the mule, making it skittish all the way back to town.

Nielson does not remember Oshley ever having any problems with either bears or lions, though both were plentiful in the region. Perhaps

---

10. Finley Bayles, telephone conversation with author, August 22, 1995.
11. "Oshley used to protect himself from the influence of the Anasazi. He used boiled juniper tree's juice, which he applied all over his body during a sweat hogan ceremony. Doing this ritual helped to cure his mind and any ill feelings that might be around the Anasazi dwellings." J. H.

Navajo and Mary Oshley working together to provide food for the family. (Photo courtesy of the Oshley family)

because of the experiences he had had earlier in life, it was now against his nature to harm them. Nielson recalls, "Oshley was not much to kill anything, and I don't remember him ever carrying a gun. The rest all did, but Oshley seemed to be a little more at peace with nature."

Many of the other workers for the Nielson outfit were seasonal. Some would come up from the reservation for a month and then get paid and return home. Others might stay for five months, but always there was a desire to head south and leave the job behind. This was not so with Oshley. He worked almost year-round, taking a couple of weeks off in the spring after lambing was over and perhaps a few weeks in the fall. Whenever possible, Mary and the young children accompanied him on the range. Mary normally cooked and tended camp, but during lambing and shearing seasons, she rolled up her sleeves and pitched in with the other workers. Once the children grew old enough to attend school, she remained in town, and Oshley traveled the range alone.

Besides vacations there was also the question of pay. Food, money, and horses were part of the going exchange. The herder's diet consisted of

Norman Nielson and Navajo Oshley, friends to the end, as they appeared in 1985. (Photo courtesy of the Norman Nielson family)

meat, potatoes, coffee, bread, dried and bottled fruit, beans, eggs, and bacon—all provided by the livestock owners. Sheep in the herd that could no longer bear lambs were marked with four or five dots on their back. These were available as camp food anytime the herders wanted fresh meat.

Actual dollar amounts of pay varied with the financial conditions of the time. For instance, during the Depression, when everyone was poor and livestock brought little cash, all the herders worked for low wages. But Nielson recalls, "Whatever the better wage was for sheepherders, that's what Oshley was paid. Nobody had very much money so we all did a lot of trading." In the early days, when he was working for "Four Fingers" (Hanson Bayles), Oshley received $22.50 a month; later, with the Nielsons, his pay climbed to $50; and by the time he retired, the amount was around $100 per month.[12]

Money was also necessary for entertainment. One thing that Oshley still loved to do—both as a young man and in his later years—was play

---

12.   Stan Byrd, "Navajo Oshley, A Walking History," *San Juan Record*, December 31, 1984, p.13; Norman Nielson interview.

cards. He often went to White Mesa to visit his friend, Sam. Together they would roll out a saddle blanket near a campfire, entice friends and relatives to put their stakes down, then play for hours. Nielson recalls,

> Oshley loved to play cards, and I mean he really loved to play cards. He must have had a pretty fair hand quite often because he would come and tell me how much he won. That was his sheer delight—to be able to sit down with the Utes and beat them. I just have the feeling that he was a little bit better than the average card player because he wasn't afraid to sit down to a card game with anybody.

One thing he was afraid of, however, was a car that went too fast when he was in it. As riding the range on horseback gave way more and more to using trucks and automobiles to move men and supplies to the pastures, Oshley had occasion to travel with a number of drivers. He never owned his own vehicle, but he was not afraid to tell the driver that he was speeding. Nielson remembers, "If I happened to be going a little too fast or take a turn too quickly, he would start hollering in Navajo and make quite a fuss about it. Sometimes when he rode with me, he would have a grip on the door handle, ready to jump."

This last image is a good place to end describing Oshley's livestock years. As he grew older, more feeble, and less able to handle the rigors of herding, he started to spend more and more time in town with his family. Indeed, his first few children rarely saw their father for an extended period of time because he had to be out on the range, away from school and the amenities of civilization. It hurt him deeply because he loved his children, but the job came first. With approaching retirement, he left the sheep for a different kind of pasture, one that he was not as comfortable in. Yet, as with the livestock industry, he maintained his reputation for hard work and honesty as he began the last phase of his life in Blanding.

The house on the left is the place where the Hurst oral interview of Navajo Oshley occurred, the one on the right is the "half house," showing its "normal" side. These houses were located in the center of Blanding; only the one on the left now stands. (Photo courtesy of the Oshley family)

Daily Life in Town

OSHLEY'S CHANGING WORLD

WHEN NAVAJO OSHLEY RETIRED FROM THE LIVESTOCK INDUSTRY and took up residence on the outskirts of Blanding, he began a new lifestyle. The Westwater community remained a haven for poorer Navajos, who depended on work in a town that was slow to accept them. The Utes, on the other hand, who had enjoyed some of the better campsites near wood and water in the same area, moved eleven miles to the south in 1953. Their recently constructed government housing enticed them to new horizons, opening up Navajo expansion into previously denied living areas along the western rim of Westwater.[1]

But Oshley desired many of the conveniences in the white community that were not present in Westwater. Family members recall that he wanted them to enjoy electricity and have some of the same possessions as the people he worked for. Undoubtedly, he recognized by the time of his retirement that the old means of survival were giving way to the complex world of Anglo America.

Other Navajos recognized it, too. In August 1950, the local newspaper ran an article declaring, "Navajos Near Starvation Waiting for Work."[2] The *San Juan Record* pointed out that fifty-five Navajos were camped on the outskirts of Monticello, hoping for employment. The people were suffering from that season's crop failure, coupled with the misrepresentations of wildcat recruiters, who enticed Navajos off the reservation with fictitious promises of guaranteed employment. The enrollees paid for their transportation and were taken to Monticello, where they were dropped off on the outskirts of town with no money, no job, and no way home. There they sat, waiting for something that never materialized. Literally, they had been "taken for a ride."

---

1. Winston Hurst, "A Brief History of Navajo Settlement at Blanding, Utah, to 1977," *Blue Mountain Shadows* 11 (winter 1992): 21–31.
2. "Navajos Near Starvation Waiting for Work," *San Juan Record*, August 10, 1950, p. 2.

Oshley, like most Navajos in the 1940s, lived only in hogans.
Beginning in the 1950s, that began to change. (Photo courtesy of the Oshley family)

A year later, the Federal Indian Service discontinued fieldwork on
the reservation, giving the responsibility of welfare assistance to the
states. In southeastern Utah, this meant that the programs that had
been administered from Moab were now headquartered in Monticello,
closer to the reservation, where a large population required help.[3]
Within a few years, most of the social service programs for Navajos were
being administered by the office in Blanding, a minimum wage of seventy-five cents an hour (six dollars a day) had been established, and
employment in mines, sawmills, and other businesses offered opportunities that could not be duplicated on the reservation.[4] The Navajo population continued to grow, with some people establishing residence in
the Westwater community while others had enough money to move
into town.

3. "Indian Problem Is Discussed at Welfare Meeting," *San Juan Record*, September 20,
   1951, p. 1.
4. Winston Hurst, "The Blanding Navajos: A Case Study of Off-Reservation Navajo
   Migration and Settlement" (master's thesis, Eastern New Mexico University, 1981),
   109–110.

A few statistics will clarify this image of change during this time. In 1960, approximately one-third (2,694 of 9,040) of the people in San Juan County were Native Americans, predominantly Navajos.[5] Of that number, 590 were living in what was called the Blanding Division, one of three areas which included the region north of the San Juan River in the western part of the county. While the report is imprecise, one can assume that the majority of those in this sector were grouped around Blanding, though this area could also include some Navajos living near Bluff. There were 771 households in the Blanding Division, with 122 belonging to nonwhites (Native Americans). The report went on to say that 20 percent of all families earned less than two thousand dollars annually, and that, although the census did not give income data by race, "it seems safe to assume that most of the low-income families are among the Indians."[6] Poverty continued to stalk the Navajos.

During the mid-1950s, mineral extraction brought newfound prosperity to southeastern Utah. The uranium boom went into full swing. Large trucks and earth-moving equipment traversed the canyons and hills where Oshley had herded his flocks. They tore at the land and transported the minerals to collecting points, then on to uranium mills that had been undreamed of five years before.[7] At the same time, the Aneth oil field erupted into a buzz of activity, becoming one of the largest petroleum producers in the United States. Oshley's ranges were again transformed, this time into whirring pumps and oil pads along the San Juan River.[8] Interest in uranium finally petered out by the early

5. The following statistical information is taken from "Population and Economic Base Study San Juan County, Utah," prepared by the Utah State Planning Coordinator from the Department of Housing and Urban Development, January, 1968, on file in the San Juan County Historical Commission, Monticello, Utah, pp. 22–29.

6. Ibid., 28.

7. Uranium and vanadium mining in San Juan County and the Four Corners region had been going on since the beginning of the twentieth century. World War II certainly gave a big impetus to mineral exploration and extraction, but it was the nuclear age that caused the industry to mushroom. The height of the boom occurred between 1953 and 1957, when production leaped from 700 to 17,800 tons per year. Monument Two, one of the two biggest mines on the Navajo Reservation, was in Cane/Monument Valley, fairly near where Gambler's home used to be. For further information concerning the uranium industry in this area, see Robert S. McPherson, *A History of San Juan County—In the Palm of Time* (Salt Lake City: Utah State Historical Society, 1995): 206–209; 255–262.

8. Oil companies began to explore and contract with the Navajo tribe in the Aneth area beginning in 1953. Humble and Shell Oil companies were the first of many to

Mary and Navajo Oshley outside their first non-hogan home, at the north
end of Blanding, 1950s. (Photo courtesy of the Oshley family)

1980s; oil production is still an important economic key in the Utah portion of the reservation.

The money generated by these activities created more and bigger
schools, paved roads where only a dusty track had once existed, provided
more sophisticated water-delivery systems, and prompted ever-increasing
control of the land through the growing tentacles of government
agencies—the Bureau of Land Management, the National Forest Service,
and the Utah State and National Park services. One wonders what Oshley
thought of all this. And what of the Pershing missiles being fired for ten
years within eight miles of his home, almost on top of old Navajo hogan
sites where he had stayed? One also wonders if he ever dreamed, as he
watched the shafts of moonlight play across his hogan's floor, that an
American was walking across this orb placed in the sky by the holy
beings. Dramatic changes indeed swept across the world during these last
thirty-plus years of Navajo Oshley's life.

---

sign agreements with the State of Utah and the Navajos. By 1956, the field was
yielding $34.5 million dollars a year in royalties to the tribe. Although the flow of
oil has greatly decreased, the area is still producing. See McPherson, 209–212; also
Robert S. McPherson and David Wolff, "Poverty, Politics, and Petroleum: The
Utah Navajo and the Aneth Oil Field," *American Indian Quarterly* (Summer 1997):
451–470.

How he felt about these events, both great and small, we don't know. For the most part, as he raised his family in a white community, Oshley's life remained private and unrecorded. During this time, he resided in three places, all within a three-mile radius. In a sense, where he lived indicated his attitude toward the growing acceptance of Native Americans by the white world in general, and the community of Blanding in particular.

Oshley mentions in his interviews that he lived in a hogan in the Navajo settlement across Westwater Canyon from Blanding. Eventually, he moved his family to the other side of the canyon on the edge of the white community. To do so was practical. The Oshleys were now close to the main ditch that brought water down from the mountain to the town, and there were plenty of trees for shade and firewood. He built a hogan not far from his friend, John Nakai, eventually had electricity to power lights, and settled into retirement.[9] This northern end of Blanding in those days was called "Jungle Town" because of the thickly growing juniper and piñon trees; most residents viewed it as the "other side of the tracks." Newcomers, looking for a place to settle, found one on this untamed edge of town.

In the mid-1960s, the Oshleys left their hogan and rented housing nearby for fifty dollars a month from Douglas Galbraith. They were the only Navajos there, with twelve white families as neighbors.[10] Their home was pink and boasted two bedrooms upstairs, two bedrooms down, a kitchen, and a bathroom. They remained there ten years until the family moved to the heart of Blanding and took up residence first in a home south of the post office, and finally in the half-house just east of the post office during the mid-1970s. By that time, the transition was complete—from hogan in Westwater to the center of town, surrounded by Mormons and twentieth-century development. Navajo Oshley had chosen the direction in which he wanted to move his family—figuratively and literally—though much of his own beliefs and behavior remained rooted in Navajo traditions and society.

It would be helpful at this point to explain how the townspeople viewed many of their Navajo neighbors in contrast to the Oshleys. During the 1940s, 1950s, and 1960s, most white residents of Blanding believed that Navajos were second-class citizens. These feelings were expressed in

9.   Norman Nielson, interview by author, tape recording, May 1, 1991, transcript in possession of author.

10. Ibid; also Bill Redd, interview by author, tape recording, August 26, 1995, tape in possession of author.

Joan Mosley's painting of the Oshley camp (1950s) in the section of Blanding known as "Jungle Town." (Painting courtesy of the Oshley family)

two ways. The first was to deny them education, keep the wage scale low, and restrict their employment to menial tasks. It should be noted that almost everyone in Blanding was poor by national standards, so poverty was a matter of degree. The second subtle form of discrimination was a loving, yet patronizing, attitude of helping the Lamanites or "red children." The Navajos might feel loved and even accepted, but not a lot was expected from them.

A few examples from oral histories and the newspaper will illustrate. In the 1940s, an article described the activities in Parley Redd's general mercantile store in Blanding.[11] The lead-in to the story told about a Navajo woman, "short and squattily built," whose "figure was drowned in folds of velveteen." She stuffed a cantaloupe down her blouse, though this "didn't change her outline at all." The store owners, who were the "only people in San Juan County who can look east with one eye and west with the other," had become "philosophical about the Indians' peccadillos." The

---

11. Tom Matthews, "General Store," n.p., n.d. Internal evidence in the article indicates it was probably written in the 1940s and published in a Salt Lake City newspaper.

owner approached the woman, who turned away quickly, accidentally knocking a roll of linoleum through the showcase window. She surrendered the cantaloupe and fled the store, leaving Parley Redd to "mutter over the peculiarities of trying to run a retail business in Blanding."

This article also depicts Navajos hiding potatoes in wool that they are purchasing, buying vanilla extract for its alcoholic content, and pawning their rifles ("He [Redd] generally has every Indian gun on the reservation in hock until deer season"). While readers today should not judge too harshly the attitudes of a half century ago—before the Civil Rights movements of the 1950s and 1960s, the enlightened consciousness of the 1970s and 1980s, and the cultural sensitivity and political correctness of the 1990s—one cannot miss the uneasiness and low-grade tension between the two cultures.

Grant Bayles and his wife, Josephine, had Navajos and Utes often as visitors to their home and employed them as workers.[12] The Bayleses mentioned some of these people were undependable because they drank and would show up on the doorstep for food, but generally, relationships were positive. Josephine said that she couldn't remember a time there were no Indians at her house. Sometimes Grant brought home a dozen-or-more guests, and those who could not eat at the large kitchen table sat out under the trees in the yard. Nez Hutchins, who worked for the family for many years, became particularly close, "adopting" Lloyd, the youngest of the Bayles boys, when he was born. Until Nez died, he and Lloyd called each other by the Navajo term of "my brother." Other families in Blanding enjoyed similar relationships, but in general, there was a large social chasm between the white and Navajo communities.

White Relations

This was the situation as Navajo Oshley moved further into the life of Blanding. Much of the information in the rest of this book comes from interviews with family members, unless otherwise specified.[13] The

---

12. Grant L. and Josephine Harris Bayles, interview by Mary Risher, July 7, 1971, pp. 31–32; Josephine Bayles, interview by Louise Lyne, July 12, 1972, pp. 2–4, 15, *Southeastern Utah Oral History Project*, (Salt Lake City: Utah State Historical Society and California State University at Fullerton).

13. Joanne Oshley Holiday, daughter, interview by author, tape recording, August 25, 1995 and May 8, 1996, tapes in possession of author; Marilyn Oshley, daughter, interview by author, tape recording, June 2, 1995, tapes in possession of author; Roselinda Oshley, granddaughter, interview by author, tape recording, February 16, 1984, tape in possession of author.

Oshley and his children learned to live in cramped quarters
and still have fun. (Photo courtesy of the Oshley family)

insider view provided by his daughters, Joanne Oshley Holiday and
Marilyn Oshley, composes a patchwork of thirty years of life, during
which Oshley adopted and adapted to a changing world. When one
recalls that Oshley walked this land before there ever was a Blanding, his
ability to change becomes even more poignant and profound. Yet
through it all, he found genuine happiness and general acceptance right
up to the time when he died.

There were, however, some activities in his daily life that never
changed. He arose early, while it was still dark, and began his day with
prayer. He would go outside with Mary and face the dawn, sprinkle his
pollen or white cornmeal, and invite the holy beings to be with his family.
Building a fire was next, followed by straightening up his bedding. Oshley
never liked sheets, so making a bed meant rolling his sleeping bag and
folding a blanket. Breakfast consisted of fry bread and some form of mutton, but as the years progressed and his teeth disappeared (he could never
get used to dentures), fried potatoes ("smooshed down"), scrambled eggs,
hot blue cornmeal or oatmeal cereal, and some type of bread replaced a
coarser diet. Always there was coffee.

The morning's activities included hoeing weeds, chopping wood
(almost up to the time he went into the nursing home), hauling water,

raking the yard, performing odd chores, and visiting with people in town or Westwater. His children remember him singing traditional songs as he went about these daily tasks. Navajo and Mary always worked, butchered a sheep, or traveled together, though Mary preferred staying home with the children.

Oshley, on the other hand, still enjoyed visiting as he had in the past. He never got a driver's license so he either walked or hitched a ride. He often attended chapter meetings in Oljato, over seventy-five miles away.[14] The people there respected his age and experience, asking him about the history of the area. In Blanding he helped bless the Blue Mountain Diné chapter building and shared his thoughts with other Navajos but shunned politics on a broader scale because he did not speak English.

Survival at this point in his life depended not upon his skill as a herder but upon his social security and welfare benefits. Norman Nielson emphasizes that, unlike some of the other Navajo people living on the outskirts of Blanding, who made a regular practice of importuning their white neighbors for some extra food or a little Christmas present, Oshley was too "proud." "He worked for what he got, and if he needed something, he would come and ask for it. . . . He was always appreciative and thanked you."

Joanne remembers when his check came in at the beginning of the month: "It was a big day for the Oshley family." He would go down to the post office while the children waited at home, so that if the check had not come in, there would be no public disappointment. If Oshley returned home empty-handed, that was the signal that he had not received his pay; a bag in his hand told otherwise. Often the children could not wait and would run to meet their dad halfway.

The family usually spent their money at Galbraith Mercantile, Parley Redd's Mercantile, or Blanding Market. The children often got a free pop as mom and dad shopped for staples—potatoes, flour, sugar, mutton, salt, baloney, and canned goods. Both Doug Galbraith and Bill Redd gave the family a ride home with their purchases, a common courtesy of the time

---

14. A chapter is a single unit of local government established for both on- and off-reservation Navajos. There are 110 chapters that can administer local lands or property, contract for program funds, appropriate and reallocate chapter funds from the tribal government, and establish mechanisms for resolving disputes. Chapter officials are elected by local members. The chapter system started in 1927 under John Hunt, superintendent of the Leupp Agency. For further information, see *Navajo Nation Government,* 4th ed. Office of Navajo Government Development (Window Rock, Ariz.: Navajo Nation, 1998).

Oshley in Parley Redd Mercantile. Both the store and the man represented much of the history of Blanding. (Photo courtesy of the Oshley family)

for those who did not have vehicles. Redd remembers that he helped bring the groceries to the door, and the family would take care of them from there. He also recalls one time when he was giving a ride to Oshley and a Ute man named Jim Mike. The truck was a two-seater, and because Mike was senior to Oshley, he very willingly climbed in the back, impressing Redd with his kindness.

Oshley's unobtrusive ways created a personal bridge of acceptance between the two cultures. His positive reputation remains to this day. The townspeople considered him scrupulously honest. Redd, a longtime merchant whose family had operated his store in Blanding for over fifty years, describes Oshley as "impeccably honest . . . keeping his name and his credit good." Redd feels that if Oshley had died owing the store money, it would not have mattered because he had "always been an honest, capable customer." In fact, Oshley was one of two people in town whom "you could set your watch by the payment of a bill"—usually about two hundred dollars per month for staples.[15]

---

15.   Bill Redd, interview by author.

Albert R. Lyman, a local historian and community leader, admired Oshley for his "great heart under his old canvas jacket." (Photo courtesy of the San Juan Historical Commission)

Another store owner, Riley Hurst, shared similar feelings. He saw Oshley as an "honorable man—he fulfilled his obligations . . . pawned a lot of stuff with me and picked it up when it was due. He was proud of his honor and his name."[16] Hurst did not feel that way about all of his customers. Ray Hunt held the same opinion of Oshley for over sixty years. He was the only Navajo from whom Hunt did not require credit in exchange for goods; they traded together until Oshley died.

One story, well known in the Mormon community, tells of the time Albert R. Lyman, a local historian and church official, gave an overcoat to

16. William Riley Hurst, interview by author, April 30, 1996, notes in possession of author.

Oshley. Lyman failed to check the pockets, one of which contained a jackknife. A few days later, Oshley appeared, knife in hand, to return the object. Lyman commented that although he had no formal education, Oshley knew enough about the world and ethics to get further in the afterlife than many Blanding citizens. As a Navajo, he won the hearts of many.[17] Indeed, it is difficult to find anyone—Native American or Anglo—who did not share these sentiments.

There were other characteristics that distinguished him. His features were rugged, dominated by a distinctive long, narrow nose. Lyman says that, before he met Oshley, people described him as homely. But after Lyman got to know him, he wrote, "I found that his face did me good; it somehow had in it the unclassified lines of cheer, honesty, good will, and human sympathy."[18]

Oshley loved to laugh, and although he never spoke much English, he was a master of pantomime. Lyman related an incident to illustrate this point. Late one evening, he and his wife were getting ready for bed. There was a knock on the door and Oshley entered. The first impression was that he needed help, but no, through gestures he made it clear that he had bedded down a flock of sheep he was tending on Mustang Mesa, about six miles away. He was just making a quick trip to see his family before returning to the herd in the morning. He had stopped at Lyman's place first, "to see us, to speak friendly words. . . . He cupped his fingers around his eyes as he looked at us, making it amusingly clear that it was a pleasure for him just to see us . . . his unusual face wreathed in hearty smiles . . . revealing the great heart under his old canvas jacket."[19]

Bill Redd remembers when Oshley came into the store and acted out the way mice had run over him the night before as he slept. Body language said it all—better, Redd thought, than many professional actors could have done.[20] Norman Nielson put it this way: "When he [Oshley] sat down to describe something to you, he used his fingers and whole body, if need be, to describe it, and you couldn't help but laugh because he was very descriptive; when he got through talking to you, there was no doubt in your mind about what he was trying to tell you."[21] People enjoyed how effortlessly he closed the communication gap and got them

17.   Nadine Bayles, interview by author, August 22, 1995, notes in possession of author.
18.   Albert R. Lyman, "Among the Indians," manuscript, 47.
19.   Ibid., 48.
20.   Bill Redd, interview by author.
21.   Norman Nielson, interview by author.

laughing, a universal language that endeared him to many in both cultures.

His black hat was another trademark. Riley Hurst was so impressed with it that he got one for himself. These hats—called by some whites "*naat'áanii*" (leader) hats but by the Navajos "*cheii*" (grandfather) hats—were a popular item among the Diné—almost stereotypically so; Oshley took extreme pride in his. He beaded his own band that wound just above the brim, allowed no crease in the crown, and never put the hat on the floor. As the brim became frayed from use, he carefully trimmed it, shrinking the shade toward his face. It was always clean.[22] The rest of his attire was pretty normal. He wore jewelry only for ceremonies, but a pair of leather work gloves always protruded from his back pocket—a habit acquired from earlier years on the range.

But Oshley was most famous for the care and concern he extended to his family. Many members of the white community expressed admiration for the love he showed for six girls—Jean, Joan, May, Donna, Joanne, and Marilyn—and two boys—Wesley and Dale. Albert R. Lyman remembers that when Jean went away to school in Springville, Utah, Oshley anxiously awaited her letters. When one arrived, he would "press it to his heart, saying, 'Jean, Jean,' before he asked to have it read and interpreted to him."[23] Bill Redd recalls that Oshley would come into the store and buy shoes for his children and grandchildren while he went without things that he needed. And Joanne recollects that, as a little girl, she and her father hitchhiked a ride to Allen Canyon to visit some friends, and Oshley ended up carrying her much of the way back to Blanding.

FORMAL AND TRADITIONAL EDUCATION

Besides kindness, Oshley was famous for the emphasis he placed on education for his children. This took two forms—formal white schools and the imparting of traditional Navajo teachings—illustrating his acceptance of two different worldviews. Family members agree that he wanted them to obtain a good education in the public schools so that they could progress economically. In 1968, when asked about school, Oshley said,

---

22. Bill Redd, interview by author; Riley Hurst, interview by author; Finley Bayles, telephone conversation with author, August 22, 1995; Joanne Oshley Holiday, interview by author, August 25, 1995.
23. Albert R. Lyman, "Among the Indians," 48.

Mary, Navajo, and daughter Marilyn Oshley play with the grandchildren in the "half-a-house." (Photo courtesy of the Oshley family)

"They came and told us that our children should go to school. I liked it. If they get an education, there's the possibility that they will add on to what we know, build on what we have."[24]

From the beginning, education for Navajo people in Blanding was a difficult process. In 1946, Albert R. Lyman, as a combined missionary effort for the Church of Jesus Christ of Latter-day Saints and an educational endeavor, decided to open a small school for the Navajos, an estimated three hundred of whom were living in Westwater at the time.[25] Lyman hauled a small, twenty-by-forty-foot wooden Civilian Conservation Corp one-room barracks across the canyon and for two years taught school there. Initially, he planned to teach only the Navajo children living nearby, but they were soon joined by Ute and Paiute children. The daily hot lunch, donated clothing, lessons, and discipline fostered an ever-increasing desire for education. Lyman recalls, "The

---

24. Navajo Oshley interview by Gary Shumway and Clyde Benally, August 13, 1968, Doris Duke #526, Special Collections, University of Utah, Salt Lake City, p. 2.
25. Albert R. Lyman. *A History of Blanding, 1905-1955* (self-published, 1955), 78.

children delighted us with their eagerness and ability to learn. As a teacher of many years' experience, I was astonished at their grasp of things about which they had known nothing. . . . They needed only teaching and opportunity. It was a startling revelation—a nation of choice people just waiting to be awakened from a long sleep."[26]

He hoped the school could eventually be moved back into town so that the children could have electricity and other conveniences. Unfortunately, not everyone in Blanding shared the same sentiments. Lyman, filled with missionary zeal, was "surprised and disgusted that there were people in Blanding who figured that the Navajos were a nuisance and already trespassing on us unduly."[27] When he tried to move the school into town, suddenly land was either not for sale or cost too much. After a lengthy battle that embroiled elements of local government, various levels of the LDS church leadership, and a small core of persistent citizens who wanted to help the Indians, a perceptible shift in attitude occurred. In 1948, the county school system assumed the responsibility of educating Navajos; by the 1950s, they were entering the high school, and by the 1960s, there was a significant flow of students, some of whom began to graduate.[28]

Oshley pursued education for his family just as vigorously as Lyman did for the general Indian community. He encouraged all of his children to go to school, and he set a determined example. A very familiar sight in town was Oshley walking his children and grandchildren to classes. Not only did he take them there, but he also picked them up after school in every season of the year. On the way, he taught his own lessons. He held their hands and encouraged them to do their best, explaining that he had never had an opportunity to go, that he did not understand English or the prices in the store, and that the child must master these things to do well. He would not be there forever; they needed to learn for their own good.

Joanne knew that her father was right, but she was scared. When she entered the first-grade classroom, she burst into tears and wanted comforting. Oshley received permission from Mrs. Adams, the teacher, and sat in the classroom for the entire day, the only parent there. The following day, Joanne was still unsettled; Oshley stayed that day, too, and the next, until she felt more at ease. Even though he understood little of what

26. Albert R. Lyman, *The Edge of the Cedars: The Story of Walter C. Lyman and the San Juan Mission* (New York: Carlton Press, 1966), 147–148.
27. Albert R. Lyman, "From Wagons to Rockets," manuscript, in possession of author, n.d., n.p., 226.
28. Cleal Bradford, conversation with author, March 12, 1999.

Oshley and his grandson on their way to school. (Photo courtesy of the Oshley family)

was being said, he communicated a powerful message to his child and all of the white children in that classroom. Joanne today holds a bachelor's degree and is a teacher.

Mary Oshley assumed a more traditional role. Her world included cooking, cleaning, weaving, and household chores that were made lighter by the help of many hands. She encouraged the girls to stay home and learn how to be mothers and providers. At one point, a school bus came up from Aneth (over forty miles away) to bring Joanne and Dale to the boarding school. Their mother hid them, telling them to go behind a nearby hill until the bus was gone. The following year, Oshley said both children must go to school, and they did. Mary said nothing.

On the other hand, there is no doubt that Oshley was aware of the consequences of this decision. Joanne and Marilyn, the two youngest daughters, grew up without understanding many aspects of traditional culture. Neither girl was interested in weaving, though Mary, who wove until her eyesight was totally gone in the 1980s, tried on numerous occasions to teach them. Joanne read books constantly so she never learned to butcher a sheep or make mutton stew. Unlike her older sisters, she never had a *kinaaldá* (puberty ceremony); if she became sick, she went to the health clinic and did not have a ceremony. And when Navajo brought her and Marilyn to an Enemy Way ceremony (squaw dance) near Mexican Hat, the girls did not like it. To them it was the "boonies," and the dirt, sleeping on the ground, lack of running water, and unfamiliar ceremony were all unappealing. To Navajo, it was home.

The next generation—the grandchildren—also felt the impact. Roselinda, one of Wesley's daughters, says,

> The Oshley family is known for its education. We have good schooling and do well. When other Navajo people look at us, they become jealous and say that we are not being taught the traditional ways. It should be the other way around; we should be jealous of them. Schooling is important but we should also know the traditional side. Navajo people in Blanding are mean to the Oshley family because they don't want us to get ahead. They put rumors and lies upon us, and that frustrates and upsets us. . . . Sometimes I don't want to go home and face it.[29]

At one point, she said that Oshley had told her that the Navajo people were assimilating into white society, and so he saw no reason to share traditional teachings because they would all be gone anyway. His ideal of having a person accept both ways of life was fraught with danger.

Yet time pushed him inexorably into the white world of the twentieth century. This was no more apparent than in his encounter with technology. His children enjoyed watching him accept things they took for granted. When Oshley went to the clinic, he had a hard time understanding why, if he had a headache, the doctor checked his legs and lungs and gave him a physical, while medicine men dealt with the specific place of sickness. What good is a urine sample if your stomach hurts? There certainly was a place for modern medicine, but ceremonies and visits to a sweat lodge in Westwater remained central in his life until his death.

Modesty was an important consideration that Oshley wrestled with when dealing with doctors and nurses. Bill Redd describes him as a "private man" and tells of the time he accompanied Oshley in an ambulance to Salt Lake City after he fell out of the back of a pickup truck. He remained unconscious for the entire trip, which included being placed on a gurney and transported to the fifth floor of the hospital. Not until a nurse started to unbutton his shirt to get him into his bedclothes did Oshley revive. He spared no language, even if she could not understand it,

---

29. Roselinda Oshley, interview by author.

Oshley never gave up the important part of his life rooted in Navajo tradition. This sweat lodge in Westwater symbolizes why he returned there often. (Photo courtesy of Winston Hurst)

in letting her know he wanted out and that he would put up with no foolishness. Redd, observing all of this from the sidelines, commented, "We had better get out of here because we will have to take Oshley's side, and I know what the nurse is doing is right."

Compare this scene to one related by Joanne, where Oshley stood out in front of his house in the middle of town in broad daylight and, for a half hour, washed off the blacking soot from an Evil Way ceremony. The children, inside the house, were mortified to have their father exposed to public gaze, but to him, this was part of the ceremonial cleansing and was nothing to be embarrassed about. Modesty depended upon context.

TECHNOLOGY AND ENTERTAINMENT

There were many things that Oshley encountered, either on his three trips to Salt Lake City or during his daily life in Blanding, that amazed him. Joanne especially delights in sharing some of Oshley's perceptions concerning the modern world. For instance, he did not understand how a television worked but told his children, "Those white men are very smart," and added that the next step would be when the image of coffee appeared on the screen and its aroma permeated the room. The traffic

Mary Oshley provided a stable home for the children and, like her husband, lived traditional Navajo culture. Her ankle-length satin skirts and velveteen blouses reflected these values. (Photo courtesy of the Oshley family)

lights in Salt Lake City raised the question about how so many people knew when to stop and go without a mass of confusion. He thought he would, however, enjoy driving some of the large trucks he saw there. Electric eyes at department stores mystified him. He wanted to know where the man sat who opened the door. He and Joanne had to laugh when he encountered a door he thought would open automatically, but it didn't. His face took a little beating.

Oshley also had trouble grasping the size of certain things. One time he talked to Joanne about buying a larger house, which would cost thirty-three thousand dollars. He could not imagine that amount of money, and so she went to the store and bought matchsticks, separated them into piles of one hundred, then proceeded to explain how much money it would take. Oshley was flabbergasted. A similar problem arose when he had a radio announcement translated that two commercial planes had collided in midair, killing many people. When he stepped out on the streets of Salt Lake City and saw all the traffic, he was convinced that the radio had lied.

Mary took the opportunity to do some traveling and encounter new technology, too. When she spoke on the telephone, she imagined the listener was seeing the same things she was. When she took a trip to Brigham Young University where Joanne was attending college, she was amazed by the Xerox machines, the size of the university library, the waterfall fountain, and the elevators and escalators in the department stores. When she encountered a buffet of desserts or had the opportunity to select a purse from a myriad of choices, her response was that the vendors should only make two so that the choice would be easier.

But even as husband and wife acquired growing sophistication about the world around them, there was still time for fun. Oshley enjoyed watching television. His favorite programs featured P. P. Longstockings, who flew an airplane with her feet and fought pirates, because she was "tough," and John Wayne cowboy and Indian movies. When the Indians started to lose in some of the films, Oshley laughed, said not to worry because it was only a movie, and continued to root for John Wayne. He even took his turn at being a star, playing the role of a medicine man in the movie, *The Returning*, filmed in Moab.

Sometimes family members would sit around and hold a contest to see who could make the ugliest faces—Oshley won every time. He enjoyed a distinct advantage. Because he did not have dentures, he was able to touch his nose to his chin without even raising a hand. He was the only one who could do it so everyone conceded defeat, but it was worth the laugh. He would also act like a weight-lifting muscle man he saw on television, taking off his shirt and flexing what was not there. Little children were amazed when he put a stone in his ear, then produced one from his mouth. For the older, more sophisticated youth around the house, he pretended to sing, in Spanish, the high falsetto of Plains Indian song, followed by opera, proving his boast that he could "sing in many languages."

His humor and ingenuity surfaced elsewhere. He would get down on his knees and shoot marbles with the children and played string games, an old Navajo custom, during the winter months. He illustrated making a string arrowhead, lightning, and rock formations. Oshley was also accomplished in making shadow pictures. With the light projected

Oshley stands next to his ever-present woodpile. Even into his eighties, he could be seen chopping wood in the cool of the morning.
(Photo courtesy of the Oshley family)

on his hands behind a screen, he created a sheep, horse, dog, and a rabbit
eating grass. These were some of the quiet ways he spent winter evenings.

In the spring and fall, however, Oshley had other ways of passing
time. The high school cross-country team used to run by the pink house
during afternoon practice. As soon as Oshley spied them coming, he
would race onto the road and pretend he had run all the way with them
and was still far in the lead. He ran hard, making Mary nervous. She
dreaded seeing the runners approach as she yelled to Oshley (who was
now in his eighties) to come back. "Don't let him run, don't let him run,"

she would call to the team as the laughing members disappeared into the distance with her husband maintaining his lead.

He frightened Mary at other times, such as during the neighborhood baseball games. She was basically very supportive of them. For instance, she often made a pot of beans as well as potatoes and fry bread for her children and others in the neighborhood to enjoy during the all-day Saturday and Sunday games. It was sandlot ball at its best, with frequent breaks for food and water. Even when one of her sons angered her by making the baselines out of commodity powdered milk, she still wholeheartedly encouraged the activity. But when Oshley got involved, swinging the bat, hitting the ball, and running bases, that was the last straw. Mary started screaming that he would get injured and that he was far too old for this ridiculousness. Usually her opinion prevailed.

Another time Oshley turned a serious situation into a lighthearted matter. Shortly before he entered the nursing home, he had some problems with medication. The doctor mistakenly prescribed the wrong kind, which caused him to hallucinate. The two youngest daughters, now adults, became very concerned as they watched their father sit on his bed with a blanket over him, picking off imaginary ants. All day long he pulled off these nonexistent insects while telling Mary that she should be cooking large quantities of food for the many people arriving for a ceremony that no one else knew about. He also tried to use an imaginary needle to sew a tear that did not exist in the blanket. When real people came into the house, he saw them sitting on other people he imagined.

After a couple of days of shattered nerves and no one understanding what was going on, the family brought him back to the doctor to see what could be done. The physician discovered the mistake, rectified the situation, and Oshley returned to his sane self. After he learned what he had been doing for the past few days, he decided to milk it for what it was worth. Whenever a new person entered the house, he "relapsed" into the previous pattern for about ten minutes, just to drive them crazy. The poor person had to face sitting on imaginary people, picking off ants, and mending nonexistent tears. Oshley loved it.

But of all the pastimes, the one he loved most was gambling. This was not the heavy winnings/losings of his youth but a friendly sharing in a game of chance. When the town held a local rodeo, Oshley took the children, fortified them with a watermelon and loaf of bread, then joined a group of Navajo and Ute gamblers under a juniper tree. There he would win enough money to pay for the children's entrance fee. When his eyesight became so poor that he had trouble reading the cards, he recruited one of his children to help him see them.

One time poor eyesight led to quite a fracas. An acquaintance from Montezuma Creek arrived at the half-house looking for a game of chance. Oshley obliged him, although Mary was not in favor of it, believing the man would take advantage of his bad vision. She was right. Mary had one of her daughters watch the game and report any problems. Soon she detected irregularities and reported them to her mother. Mary told Oshley, who ended the game, then watched the man grab all his money and head for the door. Oshley, in his nineties at this point, went after him while his daughters went after their dad. One daughter restrained her father and moved him toward the house, while the rest of the children and Mary descended on the thief like a host of Valkyries. The smallest child threw pebbles at his new truck; Mary, with full skirt flowing, wreaked havoc with a broom, while a niece pummeled the man in the head and chest and grabbed the money back as his car moved down the road. Concerned neighbors came charging out of their houses wanting to know what was happening to "Grandma and Grandpa" Oshley (terms of endearment used by the white neighbors). As for Oshley, when he learned what had happened, he could only laugh. That was, no doubt, one of the last gambling games he enjoyed in this life.

While gambling was an accepted pleasure, alcohol was a forbidden curse. He had seen the effects of "water" (whiskey) on the people around him and wanted nothing to do with it. He said,

> I don't like it [alcohol]. This generation is not going in the right direction. They [parents] are neglecting the children and drinking over them. Their eating utensils, their food—they are just walking on them, and the little children are crying. The children are thrown around roughly, and even to each other [the parents], they grab each other's hair and fight each other. It leads people off the cliff.[30]

Sometimes when he walked about with his children and spied a bottle, he would kick it and say the "glass" [alcohol] bothered a person's mind. He believed that because it was outside Navajo tradition, drinking, once it started, was hard to give up because there was no ceremony within the culture to cure it.

Oshley's children remember how he taught this and other lessons. He never used physical force; if a spanking was necessary, Mary would

---

30. Navajo Oshley, interview by Shumway and Benally, pp. 3–4.

Within the symbols of the Navajo wedding basket are teachings that speak of a journey through life. Oshley, by this time, had made that journey. (Photo courtesy of the Oshley family)

take care of it, but he would not. Oshley did not yell or hit but instead explained why something should not be done. He reasoned, "People are looking at you. You shouldn't do that; you are my daughter—respect me. Next time, don't do it."

At other times, he explained that if a child did a certain thing, there would be a consequence. For example, he would say, "Tears are dropping from your mother's eyes. Is this how you want to behave?" or "You are not from this family if you are doing this. I want my family to be respected. I don't want somebody to look at you and think it is me."

These were powerful teachings, and there were others. "The sheep are in chaos; when the mother is lost, the lamb is lost. If you are misbehaving, you are like a lost sheep trying to find its mother and father." Joanne also mentioned that apparently corn became a symbol, too. Oshley would speak of how it is sacred, just as a child is, and when the corn gets worms (the child misbehaves), the situation should be corrected. Perhaps the one saying that summed up all these important teachings—mother, corn, and sheep—was the one he used most often: "This is not the Navajo way." For Oshley, that said it all.

Religion and Death

MORMONISM, HAND TREMBLING, AND WITCHCRAFT

THE CORE OF ANY PERSON'S EXISTENCE lies in the values that are carried through life. Good or bad, the sum total of an individual's identity is dependent upon the way those values come into play during times of stress and ease. This was particularly true during the last years of Navajo Oshley's life. His religious values, formed by his experiences as a young boy and built upon through maturity, laid the foundation for his final days in Blanding. He continued to believe in the existence of the gods and their involvement in his daily activities, the power of witchcraft as a force to reckon with, and the central importance of his family. To the end, he remained faithful to many of the beliefs of traditional Navajo culture.

Never did he stop saying prayers early in the morning. His daughters remember how they were awakened at sunrise, especially when an important event was approaching. Outside they joined the family, faced the dawn, and sprinkled either pollen or white cornmeal, as Oshley sang about corn, the sun, and the sacred mountains—all part of the Blessing Way.

Another part of this traditional lifestyle revolved around herbs of healing. Oshley did not know as much as some Navajos, who have an extensive understanding about plants' properties. What he did know, however, he shared with those in need. His daughters remember his providing herbs for a woman having trouble with childbirth. To alleviate discomfort from bee stings, he used crushed dandelions. Some plants cured nightmares, venereal disease, and diarrhea, while others were too sacred to discuss. As he got older, sometimes Oshley sent his daughter, Joanne, and her husband to Westwater to gather herbs, and when they could not locate them, he went himself. When speaking of this traditional knowledge of plants, ceremonies, and customs, Oshley said it was "my body, my life."

While no one can doubt his conviction about these beliefs, he was also baptized into the Church of Jesus Christ of Latter-day Saints while living in Blanding. As with education, accepting Mormon religious doctrine did not come without a struggle. Prior to 1946, missionaries held meetings in crowded hogans or around outdoor fires in the Westwater community. The president of the LDS Church, George Albert Smith, and two apostles came from Salt Lake City to Blanding and encouraged those building the school/meetinghouse in Westwater to continue with their efforts, in spite of feelings by some that the project should be abandoned. For over a year, the completed building served as a place of education and religion, "pleading its cause . . . radiating from it as waves of truth against the barrier [of prejudice]."[1] Eventually it was hauled into the northern end of town, then replaced in 1953 by a cinder-block chapel (seventy-five by twenty-five feet), equipped with modern heating, lighting, and plumbing. The barriers of prejudice were beginning to crumble.

The Oshley family lived very near the LDS Indian Branch Chapel on the north end of town. Close proximity, however, was not the deciding factor in this family's membership. Part of the reason for joining the church was because of what Oshley perceived as similarities between traditional Navajo teachings and Mormon doctrine. In his words, "it [the religion] really does tie in with the stories of the old folk. . . . I don't know how long they [Mormons] have been carrying it on, but it is really about the same."[2] Perhaps he became a member because of this perceived alignment in beliefs, perhaps it was one more way of having his family in a more acceptable position in the white community, perhaps it was the sociability of being in a predominantly all-Navajo religious and social setting; most likely it was a combination of these factors. Whatever the reason, on September 23, 1960, he was baptized into the LDS Church and four months later was ordained a deacon in the Aaronic (a preparatory) priesthood.[3] Little is known about his level of participation once he joined.

Oshley had been taught long before he encountered the teachings of Christianity what to expect. His maternal grandmother used to say that the white men have their deity somewhere "across the wide waters" but that the Navajos had a separate religion. She went on, "And they [whites] have one god, one that is true, one that is real. Some time later, we will flow into each other or mix with each other."[4] His grandmother said that some of these Christian sects would "hold their hands up, and these will not be true; and some will be crying and saying things that will happen

1. Albert R. Lyman, "History of Blanding, 1905-1955" (self-published, 1955), 22–23.
2. Navajo Oshley, interview by Gary Shumway and Clyde Benally, August 13, 1968, Doris Duke #526, Special Collections, University of Utah, Salt Lake City, pp. 7–8.
3. Records Division, Church of Jesus Christ of Latter-day Saints, telephone conversation with author, March 12, 1999.
4. Navajo Oshley, interview by Shumway and Benally, pp. 5–6.

later." When Navajo asked which one was true, she replied, "You'll find out, just wait—the one on this side [?] will be real."

Even though he joined the Mormon Church and said he "liked it," his children did not remember him attending very often. Oshley encouraged his wife and children to go to the meetings, but he never escorted them as he did to school. Mary, on the other hand, rarely missed a Sunday meeting at the Indian Branch, but even so, she struggled in bringing both sets of teachings together. In general her daily practice was more deeply rooted in traditional beliefs.

From a purely practical standpoint, it also made sense to be LDS in a predominantly Mormon community. Both husband and wife respected their white neighbors and agreed that when they needed assistance, it usually came from Anglos and not Navajos. Oshley said on a number of occasions, "Whenever we need help, the only relatives we have are the white people."[5] This is an interesting insight since so often Native American and white relations in town were painted in grimmer colors.

Even in the midst of the white community, Oshley continued his practice of hand trembling for Navajos and Utes in the area. People traveled from within a hundred-mile radius—Kayenta, Dennehotso, Aneth, and Montezuma Creek—for his help because he was known for his honesty and fairness. He usually charged between five and fifteen dollars for his services, although if money was in short supply, he at times accepted only a dime. When patients offered items instead of cash, he might receive a watch, Pendleton blanket, or turquoise necklace.

People came night and day for his diagnosing. His daughters estimated that in an average year, he might serve up to 240 people. Sometimes two or three individuals waited outside his home for him to finish with one petitioner and make room for the next. Each had a different problem—some were sick and needed to learn what kind of ceremony would produce a cure, while others had lost items and needed supernatural help to locate them. In some instances, Oshley just counseled them to go to a medical doctor.

Joanne describes a typical hand-trembling session. When a knock on the door announced a patient arriving, Oshley invited him or her in and sat the person down, feet to the east, on a blanket in the living room. When individuals could not attend, some of their clothes were placed on the blanket instead. He then told his children to be quiet, that the holy beings

---

5. Joanne Oshley Holiday, interview by author, tape recording, May 8, 1996, tape in possession of author.

Many people sought Navajo for his hand-trembling skills even in his later life. This picture, taken in 1985, shows dramatically the effects of his aging. (Photo courtesy of the Utah Navajo Development Council)

were coming to tell him what he needed to know and that he could sense them, even specifying where the supernaturals sat. Oshley next sang the prayers that petitioned them for help in diagnosing the illness. As he did so, he sprinkled corn pollen on his hand and on the seated patient, starting with the feet and moving to the head. Next his hand hovered above the person's body and moved up to where the problem was located. Within ten to fifteen minutes, he had received a mental image, determined what was wrong, and prescribed the ceremony necessary to correct it.

As Oshley grew older, it became more difficult for him to discern what the spirits were trying to tell him. To help correct this, he made his prayers longer and added more chants. Joanne believes he formed general impressions of what was needed before prescribing what should be done or who could perform a particular ceremony. He did not stop practicing hand trembling until he entered the nursing home, approximately a year before his death.

Oshley also had a strong intuition and received dreams for guidance. A dramatic example of this power occurred one summer morning in the 1960s. Two boys, around eight or nine years of age, passed by the Oshley home on the way to the reservoir to go swimming. This was nothing unusual. But by evening, they had not returned home. Their clothes had been found on the west side of the pond, yet there was no trace of them. When Navajo heard the commotion from the searchers near his house, he went to see what was wrong, learned of the problem, and watched. Efforts to locate the boys concentrated on the side of the reservoir where their clothes had been found, but to no avail. Then, some people began talking about draining the water off to locate the corpses. Oshley went to the police and told them that the bodies were lying at the north end of the pond; when the searchers looked, they found the drowned victims where he said they would be.

These spiritual gifts also played a part in avoiding witchcraft. Even in old age, Oshley was concerned about skinwalkers and their ill effects. He would tell his family, "They [witches] are working against us." Although he knew who these people were, he never told his relatives and rarely talked about the witches' actions because the skinwalkers were "listening." He defended his loved ones by singing prayers of protection to ward off the evil; by keeping a mountain soil bundle,[6] corn pollen, and

---

6. The mountain soil bundle, often referred to as a Blessing Way bundle, holds supernatural powers that help the lives of its owners. Charlotte Frisbie in *Navajo Medicine Bundles or Jish: Acquisition, Transmission, and Disposition in the Past and*

other sacred objects that attracted the blessings of the holy beings; by raking the yard to see if intruders had come to the house and deposited evil
materials; and by warning his children not to indulge in alcohol, because it
made them vulnerable to things put in their drinks, making them "crazy."
Usually, incidents concerning witchcraft occurred while he was away.

When his children asked why this type of thing was practiced
against the family, Navajo replied, "I don't know why they are doing
witchcraft on us. We are just like everybody else—we are struggling."[7]
When pressed for an answer, the general thinking was that family members were better educated than many Navajo people, had been helped by
whites, or had a home with electricity—all of which prompted jealousy.
The retaliation that followed ranged from sickness, discord, and stolen
objects, to actual visitations.

A few examples will suffice. One morning the children heard Navajo
and Mary speaking very seriously about a dream he had had the night
before. In it he had learned that a woman (unspecified) would visit the
house and bring the family some meat. Something had been put in it that
would make people sick, and so Oshley gave his wife instructions that if
someone did offer her food, she should take it, then throw it away. That
evening, when he was not there, a woman from Westwater, who had been
"quite neighborly," showed up at the door. Mary accepted the delicious-
looking meat but threw it away, even though she was out of food. Oshley
later heartily concurred with her actions. Interestingly, there were other
times when this woman brought things to the family, and they were
accepted and eaten.

Present (Albuquerque: University of New Mexico Press, 1987), 69–70, cites a medicine man as saying, "That [mountain soil bundle] includes everything standing for
the Holy People, holy places, the earth people, the air. It is our means of communicating with the Holy People in all four directions and other places. When we use it
to say our prayers, even our problems get answered." Another person said, "That
[mountain soil bundle] is the most sacred thing a Navajo family can have; it's our
life, everything that you care about yourself, your relatives, your flocks."

Usually this bundle is owned by a medicine man, but it may be passed down
after the singer's death and will continue to bless the family. How Oshley obtained
this bundle is unknown, but his daughters remember that there was one in their
home.

7. Clyde Kluckhohn in *Navaho Witchcraft* (Boston: Beacon Press, 1967) discusses at
length the operative functions of witchcraft in Navajo society. One of its most
prominent goals is to serve as a leveling mechanism, keeping everyone in the same
social strata. Oshley is referring to this principle, noting that his family, because of
education, was rising above other Navajos in the community.

On another occasion, this time around 1962, Mary was the one forewarned. It was just another day, with the children playing outside, when she announced that they needed to get three strands of barbed wire. When they asked why, she told them that rather than sleep in the shade house, as was customary, that night they would sleep in a small ten-foot by ten-foot shack nearby. The children thought this a little strange and saw no pressing need to get the wire, but eventually, after strong coaxing from Mary, they managed to find what she wanted. As evening approached, mother and the four children trooped into their cramped quarters with baseball bat and frying pan for protection, and wire and chains to secure the door.

Around midnight a light showed through the one small window and played across the children's faces, then upon Mary's. A slow jerking at the door, followed by a man working to remove the wires, woke everyone. They lay still, feigning sleep. After repeated attempts, he managed to undo all three strands of wire and get his leg inside the door, which was now secured only by the heavy chain. The girls lit the lamp, armed themselves with weapons, and waited. The man decided to give up and went away.

An investigation in the full light of day showed no tracks in the dirt outside the shack, indicating to Mary that the prowler might have been a skinwalker. The fact that she had seen the leg—that of a Navajo man—suggested otherwise. But whatever or whoever it was, his efforts were stymied thanks to Mary's premonition.

At one point in this struggle against perceived evil, Oshley had a crystal gazer, a practitioner of another form of divination, come in and find some objects that had been removed and "worked against" to harm the family. The diviner located the materials buried in the yard, dug them up, and burned them to reverse the spell by putting it back on the offending person. After that, things went better for the family. All of these incidents with the supernatural are in keeping with what Oshley encountered in his earlier years. They are also typical of the more general Navajo experience.

THE LAST DAYS

Like his life, Oshley's death had its mystical side. On October 31, 1987, he entered the Four Corners Regional Care Center for the last time. Old age and a hard life had taken their toll, and he did not want to burden his family, especially Mary, with the work associated with his deteriorating

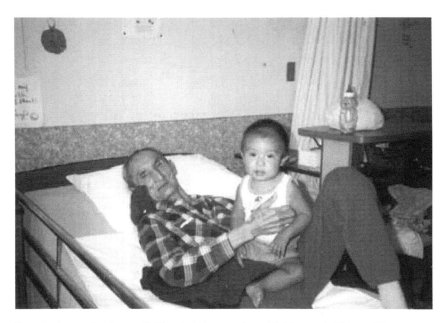

Even in the nursing home, Oshley had time to play with his grandchildren. (Photo courtesy of the Oshley family)

health. Once admitted, Oshley adapted to his new surroundings. It was a strange world for him—one of white sheets, stainless steel appliances, a wheelchair, and young nurses—in which to finish his life's journey.

Family members visited him, but by now his hearing was almost gone, so he did most of the talking. One thing that is absolutely certain is that he did not suffer from senility. His mind was crystal clear, a point important in understanding future events. His children, Navajo and Anglo nurses, and the director of the care facility all testify to his being mentally alert.

Starting about three months before he died, Navajo began to have an increasing number of dreams or visions. He said that a young Navajo girl, who knew him but whom he did not recognize, came to visit. She stood about four feet tall, wore a yellow dress, held a matching flower in her hand, and told him that he should prepare to go. Joanne believes this was her daughter, Shastee, who had died seven-and-a-half years before at the age of six months. The baby, when laid to rest in her coffin, was clothed in a yellow dress with a daffodil in her hand. A grandson, who had also died but whom Oshley did recognize, also came to visit. He, too, urged Oshley to go.

The most dramatic manifestation came in a vision. A spiritual world opened to Navajo's gaze in which he saw a beautiful land with trees and a lake. There were "people below," but he did not explain what he meant by that. In front of him, he saw deceased members of his family—his brother, daughters, his former wives (the person relating this conversation was surprised to learn that he had had two previous wives), a man he believed was his father (although he had never seen him before), and the girl in the yellow dress. A black horse that he had owned as a young man was also there, along with some other people he named but whom the listener did not recognize.

These individuals waited behind a line in front of which stood three men. Oshley did not recognize these three except to say that they were not Navajos. Their job seemed to be to block his way, saying that it was not time. When the vision ended, he told his family that there were people waiting for him and that he would be going to them soon. First, however, he wanted John Holiday, his relative and a medicine man, to hold a final ceremony. People doubted if John would be willing to conduct it in the foreign environment of the nursing home. The ceremony was never performed; Oshley lived only a few more weeks.

Oshley's greatest concern was not his death. In fact, Joanne says that he was tired of this world and wanted to see those people he now missed. He was, however, worried about who would take care of Mary. This rested heavily upon his mind, and on numerous occasions, he encouraged his children to look after their mother. By now Mary was legally blind, had only a social security check to live on, and was also feeling the effects of old age. All of the children were grown and independent, most had families of their own, and a number had moved far from southeastern Utah. Who would care for Mary?

Oshley decided to hold a family conference. He gathered his children around him and exacted a promise that they would look after their mother. During this meeting, everyone remarked about how clear and sharp his thinking was (though he recognized there were many people in the nursing facility who were, as he said, "out of their minds"). He showed his children his skin and told them that his mother had said that just before a person dies, his or her skin peels off. He poked his skin and peeled some off. He was ready to die.

A few days after this gathering, it happened. At eight o'clock on the morning of October 16, 1988, Oshley again received spiritual visitors. The nurse on duty recalls that Oshley talked in Navajo and gestured to those who had come to take him. Navajo nurse's aides refused to go into the room because of the supernaturals present. Oshley stood up for the last time, grasped his wheelchair for balance, spoke some final words, then slumped back onto the bed—dead.[8]

Five days later, the family held funeral services in the LDS Stake Center. A large number of people—both Anglos and Navajos from Blanding and surrounding towns—filled the seats. Friends of the family who had worked with Oshley in his younger years, such as Norman Nielson, Bill Redd, and Lloyd Bayles, participated in the service and "dedicated" or blessed the grave. His daughter, Joanne, as part of the eulogy, summarized his life history, while Navajo friends offered prayers and a speech before accompanying the body to the burial site.

Mary was pleased with the funeral but suffered a tremendous loss. Her part in the final arrangements was minimal, although she insisted, per his request, that Oshley be buried in a brown shirt with some of his favorite pieces of jewelry. But for the most part, she wanted to be left alone to grieve the traditional Navajo four days of mourning. Joanne handled the arrangements and accepted donations of help from the white community. Many of the older relatives and friends avoided the funeral service.

In two and a half years, Mary followed her husband in death. She died on April 4, 1991, released from a life restricted by arthritis and other ailments that plagued the eighty-five-year-old woman. Her daughters had taken care of her the best they could, but after Oshley's death, she said, "I lost the best part of myself—there is no use going on." Her enthusiasm for life dwindled while all of her children had their own family and responsibilities. All Mary had were memories. To Joanne it seemed as if "she gave up on everything." And so it was probably with a great deal of happiness that she departed this life.

With the passing of Navajo and Mary Oshley, a way of life, a bit of history also ended. This couple had cast familiar shadows on the land since the town of Blanding began. From the days of the early livestock industry, to the establishment of the Westwater community, to the labor pool formed by itinerant Navajo workers, Navajo Oshley witnessed it all. Advances in technology from wagons to cars and from bows and arrows to missiles were a part of his life.

But it was not the material things that made Oshley's life important—it was his values. At a time when prejudice built fences between two cultures, his example created a gate that swung both ways. Oshley's general

---

8. Angie Wilson, nurse, conversation with author, October 16, 1996.

Mary Oshley, blind and crippled with arthritis, joined Navajo two and a half years after his death. (Photo courtesy of the Oshley family)

acceptance in both communities illustrated possibilities in race relations that most people had not yet acknowledged. His example of honesty, fairness, and hard work spoke loudly for the inner man.

Today, as people drive through the town of Blanding, it is hard for them to imagine what it was like fifty years ago. The hogans that comprised the Navajo community on the outskirts of town have crumbled into a few telltale rings with some neighboring middens. Westwater is now mostly modern housing with cars and trucks parked out in front, while the northern edge of Blanding has expanded far beyond the Jungle Town of the early days. Even the half-house, a symbol of Oshley's life and

"A man's real life is that accorded to him in the thoughts of other men by reason of respect or natural love." —Joseph Conrad, *Under Western Eyes*

physical movement into the heart of the white community, has been leveled, leaving behind a weed-choked pile of rubble. Indeed, the only physical reminder of the man, beyond the lives of his children and grandchildren, is the headstone in the Blanding cemetery.

The real legacy, however, lies with the memories of the man left behind. His life is worthy of contemplation as an example of what it takes to be human and noble under trying circumstances. It was never a question of how much money he could amass, but rather how well he could do a job, how honest he could be. Many of the people who felt his impact, those he worked for and with, are gone now. But his example remains a testament to a good man leading a fulfilled life in an often-forgotten corner of southeastern Utah.

Index